ECONOMIES OF DESTRUCTION

Why do people destroy objects and materials that are important to them? This book aims to make sense of this fascinating, yet puzzling social practice by focusing on a period in history in which such destructive behaviour reached unseen heights and complexity: the Bronze Age and Early Iron Age in Europe (c. 2300–500 BC).

This period is often seen as the time in which a 'familiar' Europe took shape due to the rise of a metal-based economy. But it was also during the Bronze Age that massive amounts of scarce and recyclable metal were deliberately buried in the landscape and never taken out again. This systematic deposition of metalwork sits uneasily with our prevailing perception of the Bronze Age as the first 'rational-economic' period in history – and therewith – of ourselves. Taking the patterned archaeological evidence of these seemingly un-economic metalwork depositions at face value, it is shown that the 'un-economic' giving-up of metal valuables was an integral part of what a Bronze Age 'economy' was about. Based on case studies from Bronze Age Europe, this book attempts to reconcile the seemingly conflicting political and cultural approaches that are currently used to understand this pivotal period in Europe's deep history. It seems that to achieve something in society, something else must be given up.

Using theories from economic anthropology, this book argues that – paradoxically – giving up that which was valuable created value. It will be invaluable to scholars and archaeologists interested in the Bronze Age, ancient economies, and a new angle on metalwork depositions.

David Fontijn is Professor in the Archaeology of Early Europe at the Faculty of Archaeology, University of Leiden, and affiliated member of the German Archaeological Institute (DAI). His research focuses on ritual landscapes and on the social evolution of prehistoric farming societies in Europe and Eurasia. Previous books include the award-winning *Sacrificial Landscapes* (2003) and *Transformation through Destruction* (2013; co-written/edited with S. Van der Vaart and R. Jansen).

ECONOMIES OF DESTRUCTION

How the Systematic Destruction of Valuables Created Value in Bronze Age Europe, c. 2300–500 BC

David Fontijn

LONDON AND NEW YORK

First published 2020
by Routledge
2 Park Square, Milton Park, Abingdon, Oxon OX14 4RN

and by Routledge
52 Vanderbilt Avenue, New York, NY 10017

Routledge is an imprint of the Taylor & Francis Group, an informa business

© 2020 David Fontijn

The right of David Fontijn to be identified as author of this work has been asserted by him in accordance with sections 77 and 78 of the Copyright, Designs and Patents Act 1988.

All rights reserved. No part of this book may be reprinted or reproduced or utilized in any form or by any electronic, mechanical, or other means, now known or hereafter invented, including photocopying and recording, or in any information storage or retrieval system, without permission in writing from the publishers.

Trademark notice: Product or corporate names may be trademarks or registered trademarks, and are used only for identification and explanation without intent to infringe.

British Library Cataloguing-in-Publication Data
A catalogue record for this book is available from the British Library

Library of Congress Cataloging-in-Publication Data
Names: Fontijn, David R., author.
Title: Economies of destruction : how the systematic destruction of valuables created value in Bronze Age Europe, c. 2300-500 BC / David Fontijn.
Description: Abingdon, Oxon ; New York : Routledge, 2019. | Includes bibliographical references and index.
Identifiers: LCCN 2019003884 (print) | LCCN 2019012457 (ebook) | ISBN 9781315109879 (eBook) | ISBN 9781351614399 (Adobe Reader) | ISBN 9781351614375 (Mobipocket Unencrypted) | ISBN 9781351614382 (ePub3) | ISBN 9781138088412 (hardback : alk. paper) | ISBN 9781138088399 (pbk. : alk. paper) | ISBN 9781315109879 (ebk.)
Subjects: LCSH: Bronze age--Europe. | Metal wastes--Europe--History. | Economic anthropology.
Classification: LCC GN778.2.A1 (ebook) | LCC GN778.2.A1 .F66 2019 (print) | DDC 936--dc23
LC record available at https://lccn.loc.gov/2019003884

ISBN: 9781138088412 (hbk)
ISBN: 9781138088399 (pbk)
ISBN: 9781315109879 (ebk)

Typeset in Bembo
by Taylor & Francis Books

 Printed in the United Kingdom
by Henry Ling Limited

For Monique, Rivka and Channah

CONTENTS

List of figures viii
List of tables xiii
Acknowledgments xiv
Preface xvi

1 Systematic irrationalities? The Bronze Age 'destructive economy' 1

2 Selective deposition – what does it entail and how can it be studied? 22

3 The value conundrum: What common things and splendid items share and why their deposition is selective 44

4 Pre-Bronze Age selective deposition 63

5 Trade hoards: The un-economic nature of the Bronze Age metal economy 86

6 Gifts to familiar gods? 112

7 The receiving landscape 135

8 Economies of destruction: 'keeping-while-destroying'? 153

Index 177

FIGURES

1.0	Sites mentioned in this chapter: 1. Trundholm; 2. Ommerschans; 3. Maure-de-Bretagne; 4. Schkopau; 5. Gröbers-Bennewitz; 6. Stoboru.	2
1.1	The ceremonial sword or dirk from the Ommerschans hoard (l.68 cm)	4
1.2	The smaller items which accompanied the ceremonial sword of Ommerschans (the bronze spiral is not shown)	5
1.3	Map showing metalliferous and non-metalliferous zones in Europe (copper and tin)	8
1.4	Schematized view of short-term sphere of interaction, indicating main actors and qualification of things and transactions. Based on information in Bloch & Parry 1989 and Lambek 2008.	14
1.5	Schematized view of long-term sphere of exchange, organized like Figure 1.4. It represents the long-term sphere as the overarching realm of the short-term one. Information from Bloch & Parry 1989; Godelier 1999; Lambek 2008.	15
2.0	Sites mentioned in this chapter: 1. Staffordshire; 2. Oxborough; 3. Drouwen; 4. Ommerschans; 5. Wageningen; 6. Veldhoven; 7. Schkopau; 8. Pile; 9. Rørby.	23
2.1	The different ways in which things and places may relate in a deposition. Scenario A: a specific object could be deposited in a variety of places. Scenario B: a specific object was only to be deposited in one specific kind of location.	30

2.2	Scenario C: all kinds of objects were deposited but only in one specific place.	32
2.3	Scenario D: only after a specific treatment, any kind of object was allowed to be deposited in a variety of places. Scenario E: only after a specific treatment, any kind of object was allowed to be deposited, but only in one specific kind of location.	33
2.4	Single affiliation network depicting the frequency of associations between different objects in graves and hoards in the British Early Bronze Age, based on Needham 1989, table 2 (uncertain associations left out)	38
3.0	Sites mentioned in this chapter: 1. Ommerschans; 2. Grembergen; 3. Nebra; 4. München-Luitpoldpark; 5. Inowrocław.	45
3.1	The Nebra hoard	46
3.2	*Ösenringe* hoard of München-Luitpoldpark, Archäologische Staatssammlung, Munich	47
3.3	Schematized presentation of how things can be alienated from persons by conversion into other things, but within a more encompassing cultural framework where such things are always linked to higher ideals and values of society in question through reference with inalienable things and notions	53
3.4	Elongated bronze axe found in the river Scheldt, Grembergen (Belgium)	55
3.5	Detail of sword of Ommerschans, showing its high quality casting	56
3.6	Model showing how *Ösenringe* as common exchange items refer to neck ornaments as valuables of social status that are worn, and to rare versions with excessive weight	57
4.1	Area inhabited by early LBK farmers in northern Europe and area inhabited by foragers. Both had the same stone adzes and tools and deposited them in the landscape. Distribution area LBK: based on information in Louwe Kooijmans 2017, 410, shown in simplified form. Adzes symbol is a schematized picture of a generic stone adze.	67

4.2	Part of Europe where jade axes (west) prevail versus part of Europe where copper objects occur (east), simplified after information in Pétrequin et al. 2002, figure 12. Sites mentioned in the text are indicated. 1. Bygholm; 2. Mollerup; 3. Monte Viso; 4. Vendeuil; 5. Ostheim; 6. Durankulak; 7. Varna; 8. Vâlcele; 9. Moigrad; 10. Čoka; 11. Cărbuna. There is an overlap between jade and copper distributions in Denmark. Symbols: schematized drawings of generic objects that give an impression what a jade and copper axe may look like.	69
4.3	Model of selective deposition showing how from the Bell Beaker period onwards, particular objects were deposited in graves, whilst others were deposited in different locations in the landscape. Objects shown are simplified versions of real ones and only serve to give some impression of what they may look like.	79
5.1	Figures showing a generic *Ösenring* ('ring'; left) and *Rippenbar* ('rib'; right). Such a ring usually has a length of c. 12 cm.	90
5.2	Schematized figure showing approximate position of Zones I–III in Europe and sites mentioned in the text. 1. Aschering; 2. Pfedelbach; 3. Riedl; 4 Obereching; 5. Ragelsdorf; 6. Haag a.d. Amper; 7. Cap Hornu; 8. Dieskau; 9. Gröbers-Bennewitz; 10. Schkopau.	92
5.3	Zones I–III as different regimes of selective deposition for Early Bronze Age *Ösenringe* and axes	94
5.4	The Gatteville palstave hoard (Normandy, France) during its excavation	95
5.5	Schematized figure showing zone with many palstave hoards (encircled) and comparable finds outside the concentration mentioned in the text for Middle Bronze Age south England and northwest France and Late Bronze Age northwest Iberia. 1. Hoogeloon; 2. Voorhout; 3. Birchington; 4. La Chapelle; 5. Saint-Thois; 6. Gingleta; 7. Cobidalto; 8. Abelheira.	96
5.6	Zones I–III as different regimes of selective deposition for Middle Bronze Age palstave depositions in the south England–northwest French Channel zone. A situation similar to that of Zone I (token versus other axes) does not exist. There is patterned deposition of one-type *aes formatum* axes (Zone II), as well as deposition of single axes outside these areas (Zone III).	97
5.7	One of the two Agneaux token axe hoards during the excavation	99

5.8	Simplified picture of regions where clusters of Early Iron Age token axe hoards occur. Symbols of axes are simplified and only serve to give an impression of their appearance. A. Belgian-Dutch-German Meuse-Rhine region: Amelsbüren and Geistingen token axes; B. northwest France: Armorican token axes; C. southern England: Portland token axes; 1. Geistingen (Belgium); 2. Amelsbüren (Germany); 3. Maure-de-Bretagne; 4. Menez-Ru; 5. Guesman; 6. Agneaux; 7. Langton Matravers (UK).	100
5.9	Zones I–III as different regimes of selective deposition for Early Iron Age axes. There are areas where token axes and other axes are deposited in axe hoards, but separately (Zone I). The latter also occur outside of that zone (Zone II). Beyond, there is deposition of single (token) axes outside these areas (Zone III).	102
6.0	Sites mentioned in this chapter: 1. San Sosti; 2. Gela; 3. Bloody Pool hoard; 4. Staffordshire; 5. (East-)Rudham; 6. Ommerschans; 7. Nebra; 8. Egtved; 9. Rørby; 10. Grevensvaenge; 11. Viksø; 12. Trundholm; 13. Simris. 14. Olympia.	113
6.1	Model showing possible life-cycles of a fragmented object (in this case a bracelet)	120
6.2	Objects that may have been part of the presentation of one supernatural entity and how these were separated in deposition. Based on the Grevensvaenge figurine and hoards of paired helmets (Viksø) and cult axes (Kaul 1998; Kristiansen & Larsson 2005, see text).	123
6.3	Rock art figure depicted at Simris (Scania)	126
7.0	Sites mentioned in this chapter: 1. Cap Hornu; 2. Voorhout; 3. Hoogeloon; 4. Haelense Beek; 5. Roermond; 6. Ommerschans; 7. Bourtanger Moor (also Bargeroosterveld and Angelslo-Emmerhout); 8. Pile; 9. Mooschbruckschrofen (Piller); 10. Rabenwand (Kainischtal).	137
7.1	Metalwork depositions in the Meuse valley of the southern Netherlands/northern Belgium. Left: metalwork deposition sites dating to the Late Bronze Age (1100–800 BC); right: metalwork deposition dating to the Late Iron Age, showing a cluster around the confluence of the rivers Meuse and Roer near present-day Roermond. Information from Fontijn 2002, figure 14.1.	138

7.2	Artist's impression showing locations of Middle- and Late Bronze Age deposition sites projected on a transsect from Angelslo-Emmerhout settlement to Bourtanger Moor. Hoards are to be found both on dry land (probably heath with barrows) and at various locations in peat bogs (in which there were several trackways and a ceremonial building). One of the depositions is a human body. Based on more exact information in Butler 1961 and 1990; Casparie 1972; Fontijn 2012; Van der Sanden 1996.	140
7.3	Metalwork deposition zone in the Rabenwand area, along the river Traun. Indicated are locations of hoards in the valley which cuts through the mountains. Schematized and with simplified contour lines. After information in Windholz-Konrad 2012, figure 3.	142
8.0	Sites mentioned in this chapter: 1. Marchésieux; 2. Agneaux; 3. Voorhout; 4. Hoogeloon; 5. Ommerschans.	154
8.1	Zones in Europe where there are many Bronze Age/Early Iron Age metalwork hoards (hatched). Information after Reinhold 2005 and Hänsel & Hänsel 1997 but shown here in simplified form.	156
8.2	Political versus moral economies as spatial model, displaying zones where value is produced and where it is realized, after information in Bloch & Parry 1989; Graeber 2005; and Platenkamp 2016.	159
8.3	Model showing how material acquired in short-term transactions may have been transformed and transferred to the long-term sphere through deposition. A large part of deposited material, then, was taken out after some time to be inserted in short-term transactions. Based on a theory in Needham 2001.	162
8.4	Model illustrating differences between 'archival' and 'sacrificial' economies, based on a theory discussed in Wengrow 2011 and further points raised in the text of this chapter. Objects in the temple deviate from what was really offered and only serve for comparison of practices.	166
8.5	The three-zone model discussed in Chapter 5, now extended with the hypothetical 'Zone 0' (Wengrow's (2011) 'archival economies') in which the value of metal was managed by circulation and hardly any selective deposition took place.	167

TABLE

1.1 Contrast between transactions in the short- and long-term sphere, based on information in Bloch & Parry 1989, Graeber 2005 and Lambek 2008   13

ACKNOWLEDGMENTS

This book was written as part of my VICI-research project 'Economies of Destruction' (file no. 277-60-001) funded by NWO, the Netherlands Organisation for Scientific Research. Thanks to Matthew Gibbons of Routledge for the invitation to write it and to Katie Wakelin for her editorial support.

I would like to thank the team members of the 'Economies of Destruction' project for their enthusiasm and the inspiring discussions: Sabrina Autenrieth, Leah Powell, Marieke Visser, Erik Kroon, Dr Catalin Popa, Dr Maikel Kuijpers, Dr Marieke Doorenbosch and Dr Krijn Boom. Special thanks are due to Maikel, for his never-ending support.

The book was written parallel to the production of a children's book on the same topic (*BRONS- over glimmende schatten in mistige moerassen* by Fontaine Publishers). Translating archaeological ideas to a young public helped enormously to resolve its complexities. I wish to thank the author, Linda Dielemans, for many memorable discussions!

The thriving Faculty of Archaeology of Leiden University was surely the best place to situate this project. Thanks are due to many colleagues and friends for their interest and moral support: Prof. Corrie Bakels, Dr Quentin Bourgeois, Dr Bleda Düring, Prof. Harry Fokkens, Prof. Corinne Hofman, Richard Jansen, Dr Jorrit Kelder, Prof. Jan Kolen, Prof. Leendert Louwe Kooijmans, Arjan Louwen, Louise Olerud, Prof. Marie Soressi, Dr Tesse Stek, Prof. Frans Theuws, Femke Tomas, and Prof. Miguel-John Versluys.

Thanks are also to my Leiden colleagues of Indoeuropean Studies: Prof. Sasha Lubotsky, Dr Guus Kroonen and Dr Tijmen Pronk.

I am much indebted to Prof. Hans-Peter Hahn (Frankfurt), Prof. Pieter ter Keurs (Leiden) and Prof. Jos Bazelmans for much-appreciated comments from social anthropology. A special word of thanks is due to Prof. Raymond Corbey, who has been discussing the work of Mauss with me for so long – Raymond really has been a great source of inspiration for what I have been doing in this book. Thank you, Raymond!

When the writing was at a crucial stage, I stayed at the Archaeological Department of Aarhus University. Thanks are due to Dr Lise Frost, Dr Mette Løvschal, Prof. Helle Vandkilde and many students and staff members for a fantastic time and stimulating discussions – it was almost like Leiden! A special word of thanks to Lise for making me feel at home and taking care of everything.

Many colleagues were helpful in providing me with information, pdfs or figures. Dr Katharina Becker (Cork), Dr Sebastian Becker (Vienna), Dr Sylvie Boulud-Gazo (Nantes), Dr Fleming Kaul (Copenhagen), Dr B. O'Connor (Edinburgh), Dr M. Gabillot (Dijon), Dr Cyril Marcigny (Rennes), Prof. Marc Pearce (Nottingham), Dr Regina Maraszek (Halle), Dr Daniel Neumann (Hanover), Dr Tim Pestell (Norwich), Jan Roymans (Weert), Dr Martin Rundkvist (Umea), Dr Tudor Soroceanu (Berlin), Claudia Späth-Schier (Munich), Bettina Stoll-Tucker (Halle), Dr Tilmann Vachta (Berlin), Leon Van Hoof (Berlin), Dr Benjamin Roberts (Durham), Dr Vladimir Slavchev (Varna), Dr Heiner Schwarzberg (Munich), Prof. Timothy Taylor (Vienna), and Prof. Eugène Warmenbol. I am much obliged for permission to use photos taken in or by the following museums: Archäologische Staatssamlung München, Landesamt für Denkmalpflege und Archäologie Sachsen-Anhalt, and the National Museum for Antiquities Leiden (RMO): thank you all!

Over the years I have been so fortunate to be able to discuss Bronze Age issues with colleagues, and I think some of its results are in this book. Thank you Prof. Anthony Harding (Exeter), Prof. Kristian Kristiansen (Gothenberg), Prof. Marc Pollard (Oxford), Prof. Chris Gosden (Oxford), Dr Chris Evans (Cambridge), Prof. Johannes Müller (Kiel), Dr Neil Wilkin (London), and Dr Matthew Knight (Edinburgh)!

Special thanks are due to five scholars who have inspired and influenced my research on depositions more than anyone else: thank you Prof. Richard Bradley (Reading/Oxford), Prof. Svend Hansen (Berlin), Dr Stuart Needham, Prof. Marie-Louise Sørensen (Cambridge/Leiden) and Prof. Helle Vandkilde (Aarhus).

Joanna Porck (GeoDesigns) created most of the figures in this book – working with you was absolutely great!

Erik Kroon and Luc Amkreutz (both Leiden) provided meticulous comments on drafts of some chapters, from which I greatly benefitted. Dr Sasja Van der Vaart-Verschoof corrected the English, provided much needed editorial help, and gave useful comments on its content. Thanks! Prof. Joanne Brück (Bristol) and Dr Mette Løvschal (Aarhus) commented on the entire manuscript and I cannot thank them enough. All remaining errors are my own.

My life-long friend Ruurd Kok stimulated me to finally write this book. Thank you for this and for all the other things Ruurd! Thanks to my parents for their love and support.

This book is about what is valuable in life. That is why I dedicate it to Monique, Rivka and Channah.

PREFACE

This book is about a question that has been occupying my mind for a long time. Why do people give up things that are valuable to them? Why do we consider 'giving things up' as human behaviour that needs to be explained in the first place? Both come together when we study our deep past. In this book, I revisit the evidence of Bronze Age and Early Iron Age Europe, when small-scale communities in large parts of Europe buried valuable things and resources – bronze in particular – in the ground on a massive scale for a period of more than 1,500 years. This large-scale deposition of metalwork is one of the most enigmatic practices of our past, and the question why prehistoric people did this has been a topic of heated debate for more than 150 years now.

I do not claim to solve this problem in this book – far from it. What this book intends to do is to reflect on why it has been a problem for so long. Understanding this, I think, already means taking one step forward towards finding an answer. In a way, the problem seems to be of our own making. It may be impossible to get into the minds of prehistoric people, but I do think much is to be learnt from what they were doing when they deposited metalwork in the landscape. Taking patterns in deposition practices as a starting point – a particular kind of 'selective deposition' – much is to be learnt about what prehistoric people were trying to accomplish when they did this.

This book is not a synthesis of depositional practices carried out in Europe thousands of years ago, nor does it give insight in the themes addressed in depositions (like for example warfare and martiality), or how it changed through the centuries. Although I am aware that prehistoric people deposited much more than just metal, my focus will be on their deposition of bronze, and to some extent also of copper, gold and silver objects. This is not only because it is with the emergence of bronze metallurgy that its systematic deposition increases tremendously, but particularly because it is this metalwork deposition that has of old posed the biggest interpretive challenge. I will concentrate on two main issues – depositions that are conventionally seen as either 'economic' or 'religious'. Studying empirical examples of supposed 'economic' or 'religious' depositions will help to better understand what implicit assumptions come with *our* use of such terminology. The deposition of so much metalwork in the landscape seems to be un-economic from our perspective, but appears to have been systematic, coherent and crucial social behaviour in the Bronze Age. Taking the evidence at face value – as tangible results of patterned human behaviour from the past – may help us to re-think what *our* concepts of 'economy' or 'religion' actually could have been to *them*.

My strategy will be to use a limited number of examples, like so-called 'trade hoards' or splendid ceremonial objects like the sword of Ommerschans. These will keep returning in a text that I first and foremost consider to be one extended essay, where each chapter builds on what came before. Although I think the examples chosen are helpful to illustrate the main issues of metalwork deposition, there is no claim to be representative of all the depositional trends of the European Bronze Age and Early Iron Age. I will concentrate on the Bronze Age and Early Iron Age, though I do pay some attention to Neolithic and Copper Age deposition as well. The later part of the Iron Age is left out. This is not because it is less interesting for a study of deposition, but rather because it marks a decisive change in the way things and landscape shaped people. I slightly hint at these changes in Chapter 7, but the later Iron Age deserves a book of its own.

Some practical points: discussions on chronology and typology are kept to an absolute minimum. This book is about the system behind depositional practices, not so much on its exact content and chronological setting. Datings given are based on calibrated ^{14}C-datings. When no material is indicated in case studies, it is always bronze items that are referred to.

I have been developing ideas voiced in this book over the last fifteen years or so, and readers familiar with my previous work will recognize that it builds on points I made before. However, the overwhelming evidence on the significance of short-term, political economic actions sat uneasily with my previous emphasis on cultural processes. I now see that this is because I lacked an adequate theory of value to make sense of the crucial fact that it is *both 'ordinary' commodities and highly singular things* that were being selectively deposited in the landscape. The seminal works of the anthropologists Graeber and Lambek have provided me with such a theory of value, and I am heavily indebted to both.

Although this is first and foremost a book of ideas, it finds its inspiration in archaeological evidence. I very much hope that the ideas voiced here will be tested by empirical evidence again, finally leading to further adjustment or corrections. The essence of the book is that Bronze Age metalwork deposition may have many unfamiliar or even irrational aspects to us; yet it was also systematic, selective and strictly patterned. This I see as the most crucial clue for getting to grips with what once motivated people to place such valuable things in the land and leave them there forever.

1

SYSTEMATIC IRRATIONALITIES? THE BRONZE AGE 'DESTRUCTIVE ECONOMY'

People have a tendency to destroy what is important to them. The massive removal of recyclable and often precious metalwork that took place in Bronze Age Europe is an extraordinary example thereof. Why people did this has been a key question for archaeology since the 19th century. This chapter argues that this is because the massive destruction of 'wealth' signals an economically 'irrational' and 'unfamiliar' attitude in the very period in which the outline of the first 'familiar' Europe is thought to have taken shape. The discovery that deposition was selective and followed certain conventions indicates deposition was anything but irrational. Two theories have been formulated to make sense of this. One focuses on political economies and sees metalwork as prestigious valuables, the access to which was key to power. The alternative sees metal primarily as cultural valuables that were crucial in upholding an encompassing social, cultural and moral whole. This chapter argues that these competing theories are not necessarily contradictory and should even be taken into account simultaneously if we wish to understand the destruction of metalwork. It will offer a perspective that makes this phenomenon researchable, by focusing on its selective nature and on how value is constituted and transformed in the very process by which valuable things are destroyed.

At the end of the nineteenth century, a forester made a spectacular discovery while digging on an estate near Ommerschans, in the northeastern Netherlands. To his great surprise, he found an extraordinary bronze sword on a platform of wooden stakes that had been buried in a former peat bog. The gold-glimmering sword was accompanied by a range of smaller, more unremarkable bronze artefacts, such as small woodworking tools, a razor, pieces of what seemed to be scrap metal (a spiral) and a few flint chisels (Figures 1.1 and 1.2). Although this bizarre discovery caused quite a stir locally, it would take more than sixty years before its true significance became apparent. In the 1950s, the archaeologists Butler and Bakker (1961) found out that this 'sword' was actually an absurdly 'aggrandised'[1] ceremonial dirk, which was made some 3,500 years ago. Even by modern standards, the

2 The Bronze Age 'destructive economy'

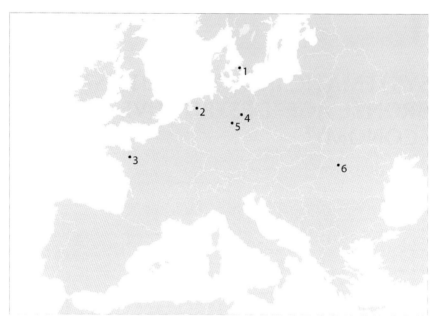

FIGURE 1.0 Sites mentioned in this chapter: 1. Trundholm; 2. Ommerschans; 3. Maure-de-Bretagne; 4. Schkopau; 5. Gröbers-Bennewitz; 6. Stoboru.
Source: J. Porck, Faculty of Archaeology, University of Leiden.

sword represents an extraordinary level of crafting. Their research showed that it must have been a special object to the prehistoric communities who once possessed it. The Ommerschans sword appears to be one out of a group of six (Fontijn & Amkreutz 2018). These ceremonial blades are not only well crafted, but they are extremely similar. This is why it is generally thought that they all were made by the same master smith who performed her/his craft in a place that was probably very far from Ommerschans.[2] But the very realization that this ceremonial object must have been of great value to Bronze Age people, reveals the problem that this find represents. If the sword was so special to them, why did prehistoric people decide to remove this outstanding object from their society forever, by letting it sink down in a bog? And why was this 'extravagant' ceremonial item accompanied with a range of – in our eyes – inconspicuous, small and mundane items?

What happened in Ommerschans is not a one-off. During the Bronze Age and Early Iron Age (c. 2300–500 BC), tens, perhaps even hundreds, of thousands of metal objects underwent a comparable fate all over in Europe, from Ireland to the Caucasus (Reinhold 2005). For an important part these are objects of copper alloys, particularly classic bronze (90 per cent copper, 10 per cent tin), but also items made of gold and incidentally silver and tin (Eogan 1994; Hansen 2011; Vandkilde 2016). For example, some 297 axes (weighing 68.8 kg!) were placed in a ceramic vessel and buried around 2000–1750 BC in Gröbers-Bennewitz in eastern Germany (Von Brunn

1959, 57–58). Around the sixth century BC, in the earlier Iron Age, a staggering 4,000 bronze axes were buried in Maure-de-Bretagne (northwestern France; Briard 1965, 242). Like at Ommerschans, there are many cases where things were consigned to the ground in a special manner. The bronze swords found in Stoboru (Romania) were placed in vertical position with their points facing the sky (Soroceanu 1995, 74). The 124 Early Bronze Age axes (c. 2000–1750 BC) found in a river bed at Schkopau (eastern Germany) are reported to have been lying in a circle with their cutting edges pointed inward (Von Brunn 1959, 66). There are cases where bronzes were bent, broken, wrapped or hit, apparently with the intention to render them un-useable or even to destroy them.[3] This seems all the more puzzling if we realize that such destructive behaviour preceded their permanent burial in the landscape – an act that already may be seen as a termination of its use-life.

In many parts of Europe where bronze was used, the main constituents of bronze – copper and tin – were not regionally available. Bronze therefore must have been recycled on a massive scale. There are studies that argue that the effects of recycling are indeed recognizable in the composition of the metalwork found there (Bray & Pollard 2012). This recycling possibility makes the massive presence of bronze in the archaeological record intriguing, especially in non-metalliferous regions (Coles & Harding 1979, 517). Detailed regional studies of metalwork finds demonstrate that the presence of such massive amounts of metalwork in the ground in general does not reflect casual loss or the non-retrieval of what were originally intended to be temporary stores of material. Rather, such finds should be interpreted as attempts by prehistoric people *to place things in the landscape and leave them there*. The main argument for this is that the presence and absence of metal in certain contexts shows a patterning that cannot be explained by post-depositional decay and research factors.[4] In the southern Netherlands, for example, important and widely used tools like axes are rarely found on Middle Bronze Age settlements, even though bronze could potentially be preserved there. A good and representative record of settlement excavations (usually including systematic metal detection) ensures this *is* evidence of absence. Axes are found, however, in large numbers at some distance from settlements, like in stream valleys or peat bogs (Fontijn 2002, 144–146). Very large quantities of metalwork in Europe come from watery zones like peat bogs or rivers (Bradley 1990). This includes top items like the Ommerschans sword or the sun wagon of Trundholm (Denmark; Kaul 1998, 31–34). It is unlikely they all ended there by accident. This is particularly so as it appears that what is found in such watery places often does not figure at all in graves or other parts of the landscape (e.g. Hansen 1994; Needham 1989).

Selective deposition: recognizing a logic in un-economic behaviour

Why did Bronze Age people consign to the landscape so many things that were valuable to them? What happens to a society that systematically gives up the very things that are important? These questions represent one of archaeology's most

4 The Bronze Age 'destructive economy'

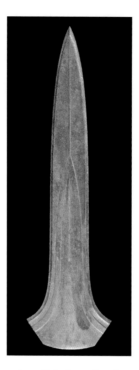

FIGURE 1.1 The ceremonial sword or dirk from the Ommerschans hoard (l.68 cm)
Source: Copyright National Museum of Antiquities, Leiden (RMO).

contentious problems since its inception as a profession in the nineteenth century. Many scholars consider such finds as material stored in the ground for further trade or re-melting that for some reason was never recovered (e.g. Evans 1881; Thomsen 1845). This implies that these objects were never supposed to stay in the ground for such a long time. However, in a paper published in 1867, the Danish archaeologist Worsaae suggested a quite different interpretation. He argued that such metalwork was left in the ground for ritual reasons. According to him, they were meant to stay in the landscape forever and represented votive offerings, gifts to gods. Seminal papers like the one by Worsaae set in motion a debate on the interpretation of Bronze Age metalwork hoards that continues until today and has been the subject of hundreds of books and papers.[5] Instead of reviewing the debate in detail (for this, see e.g. Verlaeckt 1995, chapter 3), I wish to reflect on why *metalwork deposition has posed such an interpretive challenge to archaeology*.

A closer look at the arguments brought forward in the last 150 years or so reveals that the debate actually revolves around a deceptively simple question: do these metalwork finds represent profane 'economic' or ritual/'religious' actions (Fontijn 2002, chapter 2; Geisslinger 1984)? This question is in itself problematic for two reasons.

First, because it risks confusing the categorization of human behaviour with discovering what motivates that behaviour. When we qualify what happened in Ommerschans as a 'ritual' act, this does not bring us any closer to understanding

FIGURE 1.2 The smaller items which accompanied the ceremonial sword of Ommerschans (the bronze spiral is not shown)
Source: Copyright National Museum of Antiquities, Leiden (RMO).

why the Bronze Age people did it. It is particularly problematic that 'ritual' as opposite of 'profane' implies this deposition is disconnected from mundane concerns (cf. Brück 1999). The Ommerschans hoard indeed contains a practically unusuable, 'out of the ordinary' sword for which a ceremonial religious function is likely (Butler & Bakker 1961). However, it also contains 'mundane', intensively used woodworking tools – how do these fit the 'ritual-religious' picture?

Second, an analysis of interpretation of metalwork depositions has made clear that usually practical, mundane, behaviour is assumed and taken for granted. Religious/ritual action, however, is something that needs to be proven (Fontijn 2002, 17–18). This reflects a view in which human behaviour is steered by a specific rationalist logic where individuals strive to get maximal results out of least sacrifice (Chang 2014, 19–21). Such an assumption is rooted in rational choice theory and post-Enlightenment philosophy (Brück 1999) and characteristic of a modern market economy (Graeber 2005, 443). The very fact that metalwork depositions have posed such a challenge to archaeological interpretations for so long is perhaps the best illustration thinkable. They are a problem to *us* precisely *because they seem to defy rationalist-economic thinking* (Brück 1999).

As Dumont (1977) once argued, the problems we have in making sense of 'anomalous' economic behaviour, in our case the massive deposition of metalwork in the Bronze Age, indicate that our modern market economy is not just a field of practice. Economy has reified and become an ideology in itself, bringing with it fundamental assumptions of what defines rational action (see also Graeber 2005, 443). Economic rationality is so deeply rooted in modern thought it cannot but cause epistemological problems when considering the behaviour of 'other', 'non-modern' economies (Lemaire 1985, 78). If action that qualifies as 'minimizing-loss-maximizing-gain' is considered rational, this makes behaviour that fails to meet such standards implicitly irrational (cf. Brück 1999). There is no doubt, however, that depositional behaviour made perfect sense to the people who left all this material in the landscape, or they would not have done so on such a massive scale. Worsaae (1867) already recognized evidence for this. Depositional practices appear to have followed certain conventions – specific items appear in specific contexts only and were excluded from other contexts.

To give some examples:

- *Copper shafthole* axes occur widely in Eastern Europe and Eurasia between c. 3500–3000 BC. In the Caucasus and the zone to the north, they are known exclusively from graves. In the Carpathian Basin, however, they seem to have been deposited mainly as hoards in settlements or in the surrounding landscape and seem to avoid graves (Hansen 2011, 145–146).
- *Lunulae* are gold neck ornaments which were worn during the Early Bronze Age in Northwest Europe (c. 2300–1700 BC). Unlike contemporary ornaments, however, they were only rarely associated with the dead in graves. They rather seem to have been deposited singly or in pairs in dry land, often close to prominent landscape markers like standing stones (Eogan 1994, 34–36).
- As an aggrandized version of a regular *sword*, the one from Ommerschans was placed in a wet place. This was the fate of hundreds of other swords in Western Europe which also seem to have been kept out of graves and settlements during the Bronze Age (Fontijn 2002; Needham & Burgess 1980; Verlaeckt 1996).
- Early Iron Age *token axes* in the Lower Rhine-Meuse zone are predominantly known from dry locations where they occur in large numbers in hoards with similar axes. They hardly occur in contemporary depositions (cf. Chapter 5).

Such a selective treatment hints there was logic or 'rationale' behind such – to us – 'irrational' acts. Such conventions are known as 'selective deposition' (Fontijn 2002; Needham 1989). This phenomenon forms the point of departure for this book, which tries to make sense of what prehistoric people tried to achieve when they systematically 'destroyed' valuable things and materials. Recognized as something that defies modern notions of economy, I will use this puzzling Bronze Age behaviour to reflect upon the very notion of economy that created the problem in the first place. What *is* economic behaviour?[6]

In order to study this 'destructive' Bronze Age behaviour, it is important to first elucidate why it is the case of Bronze Age deposition that is so challenging. After all, comparable behaviour is found in many other periods and cultures as well. It is, for example, known from pre-Bronze Age cultures in Europe. In the fifth millennium BC, skilfully crafted and extremely rare jadeite axes were deliberately deposited in the European landscape, sometimes at places 2,000 km away from the location where they were once produced (Pétrequin et al. 2012). Deposition is also not unique to Europe. Presumably in the second half of the second millennium BC, large collections of copper artefacts were deposited in the landscape of India and never recovered (Yule 1985). There are also many cases from non-Western societies of more recent periods. Decorated copper shields, for example, were highly valuable to the Kwakiutl, the native population of the nineteenth-century AD American Northwest coast. However, Kwakiutl society occasionally also threw such coppers into the sea during ceremonies (Wolf 1999, 121).

The notion of Bronze Age 'destructive economies' is so problematic not because it is a unique phenomenon. It rather has to do with how modern archaeology conceptualizes the significance of the Bronze Age as an epoch in Europe's deep history.

Bronze Age economies and the rise of the first 'familiar' Europe

The Bronze Age is often seen as the period in which the foundations of Europe were laid (Demakopoulou et al. 1998; Niklasson 2014, 61). Large-scale farming landscapes emerged all over Europe (Brück & Fokkens 2013). Recent aDNA research indicates that there was a profound genetic transformation in the third millennium BC due to massive migrations from the Steppe, and that the DNA of modern inhabitants of Europe has many more similarities with that of people who inhabited Europe from the Bronze Age onwards than with their Neolithic predecessors (Haak et al. 2015). It was during the Bronze Age that the proto-Indo-European languages, from which the majority of modern European languages evolved, spread through Europe and almost completely erased older Neolithic languages (cf. Iversen & Kroonen 2017). Specific social and ritual institutions that are known from early historical sources are also thought to be rooted in this proto-Indo-European Bronze Age legacy, like the warrior ideal (as celebrated in Homeric epics) or representations of gods as 'divine twins' (Kristiansen & Larsson 2005). The emergence of institutions of warriorhood is thought by some to herald the rise of a system of gender with masculine dominance that has characterized societies in Europe ever since (Harris et al. 2013, 74–78; Treherne 1995).

Above all, the reason the Bronze Age is often seen as heralding the rise of the 'first familiar Europe' is the widespread adoption of the material that lends the period its name: bronze. The Bronze Age is thought to have been decisive for the course of Europe's early history because it saw the emergence of an unprecedented trade network in bronze which for the first time structurally linked remote parts of Europe. It is therefore seen as the very period *in which a 'concept of Europe' originated* (Childe 1925, xiii–xiv; Rowlands 1984, 149). This metal trade has been interpreted as the first example of globalization. To emphasize the crucial role of bronze in it, Vandkilde (2016) recently even called it 'bronzization'. It is thought to have had profound social

8 The Bronze Age 'destructive economy'

consequences, setting in train a process of unprecedented competition over access to these metal exchange networks. Following Earle and others (Earle 2002; Earle et al. 2015), an entirely new, 'political' economy took shape, leading to more hierarchical power relations and the rise of elites controlling metal circulation networks. The reason for the emergence of these new economies, typically called 'Bronze Age economies' (Earle 2002), lies in the fact that the copper alloy tin-bronze came to be widely desired as crucial for manufacturing an unprecedented broad range of things, from essential mundane tools to ceremonial items. However, the downside is that its sources, copper and tin, are highly unevenly spread across the continent, with tin even being excessively rare (Childe 1930, 8; Figure 1.3).

The widespread adoption of bronze – a recyclable resource – not only heralded what may be called the first truly circular economy in history. Recycling and re-casting also had a profound impact on the perception of materials and things. *A bronze axe was no longer merely an artefact; it was now simultaneously a material resource*, potentially being transformable into any other shape, ranging from a mundane tool to insignia of high social status (Hansen 2011, 138).

Thus, the vital material bronze was effectively scarce, and access to bronze a source of social influence and power. The control of mines and trade in commodities like copper and salt is nowadays even regarded as having 'the same

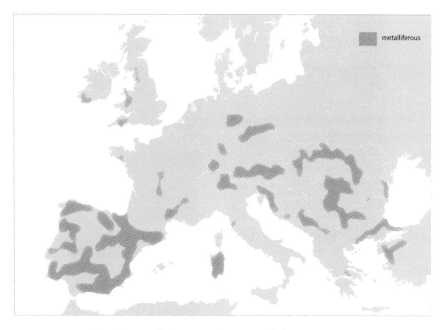

FIGURE 1.3 Map showing metalliferous and non-metalliferous zones in Europe (copper and tin)
Source: Schematized after information in Bradley 1990, figure 15; and Hänsel 2009, 108. Drawing by J. Porck, Faculty of Archaeology, University of Leiden.

economic significance as the control of and trade in oil and gas resources have today' (Kristiansen 2016, 158).

In the above, we may recognize elements of the previously mentioned economic rationality that is so strongly present in modern, post-Enlightenment thinking and capitalism (cf. Brück & Fontijn 2013, 202; Shennan 1999, 362). Theories of political economies speak of bronze as 'wealth' that people seek to accumulate and consume (Earle et al. 2015). They speak of institutions of rule that are 'financed' (Earle 2002, 1). In explanatory models, there is a focus on (male) individual entrepreneurship and competition in bronze exchange networks (Brück & Fontijn 2013, 202). In this way, the Bronze Age is not only conceived of as a disruptive period in European history, but also as the very beginning of a new era in which foundations were laid for the first Europe that is familiar to us (cf. Goody 2012b).

Or should we say: a conceptualization which pays lip service to *a particular view on Europe*? A perception that historians and archaeologists have fostered in order to align Europe's dominant role in recent history with characteristics thought to have taken shape in its deep past? Through time, historians have been trying to find out how such a small continent came to play such a dominant role in recent world history (Davies 1998). Ferguson (2011), for example, has located this in 'a special brand of winning tools' like emerging competition, capitalism, and scientific innovation. Although he sees this taking shape only in the post-Renaissance, it is intriguing to see that some of his so-called 'killer apps' (like competition and innovation) also figure in the discourse described above in which the Bronze Age has been defined as a key period of change ever since the work of Childe (1930; cf. Rowlands 1984, 149).

Destructive economies and the 'unfamiliar' face of the European Bronze Age

Against this background, the massive metalwork depositions of the Bronze Age are problematic. The large-scale 'giving up' of metal brings a profound 'economically irrational' and 'unfamiliar' element to the very period in which the outlines of the first 'familiar' Europe are thought to have taken shape. If metal is the 'oil and gas' (Kristiansen 2016, 158) of the Bronze Age, then the permanent deposition of so much recyclable bronze would equal the systematic destruction of oil and gas without using it.

As remarked above, when economic/profane explanations did not suffice, scholars tended to interpret such destructive behaviour as ritual. However, seeing such destructive economies as primarily ritually or religiously motivated would merely be to replace the economicity of the Bronze Age with its opposite. It would amount to seeing one's supposed ancestors as motivated by a profound religiosity, making way for a conceptualization of Europe's deep past that is profoundly unfamiliar to modern eyes.

How the European Bronze Age is conceptualized is not simply about 'matters of fact'. Following Latour's (2004) famous dictum, it is particularly about 'matters of concern'.[7] After all, emphasizing the merits of economic rationality, competition and entrepreneurship in European prehistory is to single out key elements of later capitalism and see them rooted in Europe's deep past. This may just as well be used as an argument to legitimize the same dominance of capitalist thinking (and all the social implications it had in terms of a profoundly unequal distribution of wealth across the world) as something that was preordained by things that happened in the deep past (cf. Chakrabarty 2008). There is a serious risk of self-congratulation and Euro-centrist thinking. It is, for example, questionable whether the entrepreneurship and competition that are thought to emerge in Europe are really so particular to this continent (cf. Goody 2012a; Morris 2011; Wengrow 2010). The conclusion is unavoidable that what happened in Europe's Bronze Age matters because conceptualizing the Bronze Age *is closely linked to how we see Europe (and the west) today*. The new, pan-European circulation of bronze is an important argument to conceive the Bronze Age as a familiar 'economic' *us*. The large-scale deposition of metalwork, however, gives reason to perceive the Bronze Age as an unfamiliar, un-economic *them*.

Such a contrasting of extremes is unhelpful and unrealistic. In contemporary archaeology, there are basically two approaches that systematically include ubiquitous large-scale metalwork deposition and claim to acknowledge the cultural 'otherness' of the Bronze Age. The first sees the circulation of bronze as a specific form of political economy. The second focuses more on cultural values and meanings. They are usually seen as competing theories that are hard to reconcile. After introducing and assessing both, it will be discussed whether they really are so irreconcilable as widely believed.

Political economy models: a Bronze Age 'other' as economic 'same'?

Understanding the circulation of bronze as a specific example of a political economy is by far the most widely accepted model today. The concept of political economy is rooted in Marxist theory and has been presented in different versions (Robotham 2005). In archaeology, it has particularly become influential since the seminal work of Friedman and Rowlands (1977); for Bronze Age archaeology, it finds its most elaborate version in the models presented by Kristiansen, Earle and others (e.g. Earle 2002; Earle et al. 2015; Kristiansen 1998).

Earle (2002, 1) defines a political economy as 'the material flows of goods and labour through a society, channelled to create wealth and to finance institutions of rule'. He recognizes such – as he terms it – 'Bronze Age economies' in different forms all over the world. For the present discussion, I particularly focus on how he (and others) interprets the system for the northern parts of Europe, as these models are the most explicit on the phenomenon of metalwork deposition.

A fundamental starting point is that this model sees bronze as crucial to the social system, and takes into account its binary potential as object that carries social/ritual meaning *and* material resource. Bronze is valuable in both fields, because it is a desired but scarce material the components of which were unavailable in large parts of Europe. As such, possession of bronze was key to power and bronzes were primarily significant because they were valued as 'prestige goods' (Earle 2002,

294–295 with further references). Having access to the flow of prestigious bronze – so-called 'networked strategies' (Earle 2002, 17) – is assumed to have been an important source of power, and the emergence of new elites during the Bronze Age is thought to have been primarily linked to this (Kristiansen 1998). Control of the supply of bronze through such networks must by definition have been problematic, giving rise to elite positions that must have been unstable and fluid since they tend to be based on the contingencies of alliance-making and partnerships stemming from individual or small-group agency (Earle 2002, 17; Friedman & Rowlands 1977, 228). Bronze Age societies are usually conceptualized as chiefdoms with warrior elites at the top (Kristiansen & Larsson 2005). In line with the supposed significance of networks in political strategies, several of such ranked social formations developed in regions that were in supposedly strategic intermediate positions in Europe bronze circulation networks, like the so-called Early Bronze Age Wessex elites in southern England (Cunliffe 2012, 220) or those of the Únětice groups of central Germany (Jockenhövel 2013, 726).

Political economy models of the Bronze Age claim to take the 'otherness' of Bronze Age society into account (Kristiansen & Larsson 2005, 376–378). The massive deposition of 'prestigious' bronze is primarily interpreted in a ritual sphere. Depositions are then made sense of as a specific form of 'ritual consumption' (Kristiansen 1998, 76) that is ultimately linked to the maintenance and creation of power by controlling access to bronze. First, the deliberate giving up of prestigious things may have been a prestigious act in itself (Bradley 1990, 139–142). Second, an important practical effect of such rituals would be that they remove prestigious goods from society – hence keeping the amount of prestige goods in check and therewith supposedly preventing 'inflation' (Kristiansen 1998, 79). Such rituals also might have a levelling effect, as they have the effect of limiting the scope for competition through such rituals (cf. Levy 1982, 102).

Whether metal is deposited in graves or elsewhere in the landscape, all such depositional practices are seen as 'variations on a common theme, the ritualised formation and enforcement of power' (Kristiansen 1998, 76). We may thus recognize emphasis on ends over means, and an implicit notion of value as power that can be accumulated and quantified – aspects that bring to mind the economic thinking described above.

Thus, we see that political economy models situate the logic behind depositional practices in the maximization of individual power; they are one particular way to control the prestigious nature of bronze. *A seemingly un-economic act becomes economic in the end* (Fontijn 2002, 20). The Bronze Age 'other' thus appears to have features of an economic 'same'.

Metalwork deposition as 'moral' acts: Bronze Age as cultural 'other'

The same finds, however, also allow a different interpretation. As Worsaae (1867) already remarked, bronze deposition was selective. It seems to have followed specific conventions. Certain items were consistently excluded from certain contexts. This means the value of bronze lay in more than just the fact that it was a scarce, prestigious material. For example, in the Late Bronze Age of the Low Countries, thousands of urnfield burials are known. These rarely contain weapons or lavish ornaments of the supra-regional Plainseau style (Fontijn 2002, 110–112, 149, 188–189; cf. Roymans & Kortlang 1999, 56). Weapons are predominantly known from watery places like rivers, whereas ornaments occur in large hoards in dry or semi-wet locations (Fontijn 2002). We can be sure these bronze weapons and ornaments were in use by the same people who buried their dead in these urnfields. Yet, time and again, they did not adorn their dead with either weapons or ornaments in Plainseau style (although other things were included; cf. Louwen forthcoming). But when, for some reason, the time had come to deposit metalwork in the landscape, weapons and such ornaments seem to have been kept separate and were surrendered at different kinds of locations (watery sites like rivers vs. inland zones; Fontijn 2002, figures 8.21 and 8.22).

This phenomenon, emergent from depositional acts conducted hundreds of times all over the Low Countries, implies that weaponry and Plainseau ornaments were not considered comparable or commensurable, but as different, even though they were all made of the same scarce material bronze. This is an example of the remarkable 'selective deposition' discussed above.[8] That deposition was selective, reveals that the things figuring in it were valuables in a cultural sense; things that were somehow – inalienably – linked to people and ideas that ought to maintain a specific identity – that were to be 'kept' (Godelier 1999; Weiner 1992). This 'keeping' was accomplished by treating things in a particular way, including selection and separation – tantamount to imbuing them with some kind of human contemplation (Lambek 2008, 137). This may remind us of situations in which only particular practices are thought to fit the circumstances – not so much as 'rules' but rather as conventions on what was culturally considered 'the right way of acting' (ibid.). Such practices were probably situated more in a sense of morality than in conscious decisions or rules (Durkheim 2014). With regard to Late Bronze Age weapons, there may, for example, have been a shared cultural notion that items of violence, conflict and aggression were not meant to accompany the remains of an individual deceased in an urnfield (cf. Fontijn 2002, 231–232; Roymans & Kortlang 1999, 56).

So in this moral or cultural sphere of thinking, and in marked contrast to political economy, the 'means' (the practices) were much more important than the 'ends'. This is where actions like the physical transformation of things, their arrangement in a specific order (cf. the Schkopau axes placed in a circle mentioned above; Von Brunn 1959, 66) or the selection of a particular place in the landscape (like for the ceremonial sword of Ommerschans) may have been quintessential to its value (cf. Graeber 2001, 45).

Short-term and long-term logic: breaking the political–moral deadlock?

Thus, we seem to end with a confusing deadlock: the study of same phenomenon, the deposition of metalwork, gives rise to two very different views on the Bronze

Age: political economy theory emphasizing the period as an 'economic same', moral or cultural economy theory as a 'cultural other'. The former focuses on individual-based acquisitive behaviour (trade), competition and political process; the latter on collective-based practices in the long-term sphere of cultural values and morals where competition is not an issue (Table 1.1). Put differently: a contrast between quantifiable value in political economies, versus value*s* as cultural or moral qualities in moral/cultural 'economies' (cf. Lambek 2008). It is no coincidence that the same word *value* is used to describe two different things. Following the work of the anthropologist Graeber (2001; 2005), this book uses this double-edged concept of 'value' to break the deadlock between the political and the moral and to formulate an approach to make sense of 'un-economic' metalwork depositions.[9] In order to do that, it is necessary to first sketch the fundamentals of the two transactional spheres of economic action: short-term and long-term transactional orders (Bloch & Parry 1989).

Activities aimed at the maximization of individual needs that are central in a market economy are situated in the so-called 'short-term' transactional sphere or cycle of exchange (Bloch & Parry 1989, 23–28). In this sphere, alienation and acquisition of things, individual competition and therewith least-sacrifice-maximum-gain principles are primary (Figure 1.4). Value is quantifiable, commensurable and can be expressed 'as price' (Graeber 2005, 443). It is this kind of value that is meant when we express amazement at the fact that Bronze Age people permanently surrendered objects made of a scarce material resource which could have been recycled (i.e. converted into something else). It is in this sphere that the focus is on 'ends', not so much on 'means' (Lambek 2008, 136–137). Archaeologists' search for what could be the 'gain' in the deliberate 'loss' of such an outstanding object like the Ommerschans sword is a characteristic example of the kind of questions one asks from a short-term sphere perspective. It is short-term

TABLE 1.1 Contrast between transactions in the short- and long-term sphere, based on information in Bloch & Parry 1989, Graeber 2005 and Lambek 2008

Political economies	*Moral economies*
Emphasize	*Emphasize*
Value as quantifiable	Value as qualities
Value as price	Cultural values
Ends	Means
Action	The 'right'/appropriate action
Individual competition	Collectivity
Maximization of individual gain (power)	(Maintenance of) cultural/religious values, morality
Interaction between individuals	Society at large (including ancestors, supernatural entities)
Supra-regional scale	Regional/local scale

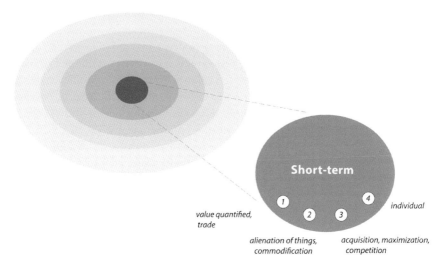

FIGURE 1.4 Schematized view of short-term sphere of interaction, indicating main actors and qualification of things and transactions. Based on information in Bloch & Parry 1989 and Lambek 2008.
Source: Drawing by J. Porck, Faculty of Archaeology, University of Leiden.

sphere-thinking that makes us perceive Bronze Age depositional actions as practices in which things and materials are *given up*.

In contrast, the 'long-term' sphere of exchange (Figure 1.5; Bloch & Parry 1989, 23–28) is not profit-based, individual or competitive. Rather, it is aimed at sustaining the overarching human order of sociality, culture, ideals and morality (ibid.). This means that something of these people and their broader ideals ends up in the things considered here. As humanity is 'in doing, creating and contemplating' (Lambek 2008, 137), the means this time are more important than the ends; the way Bronze Age people shaped objects, how these intertwined with their lives, how they were put into the landscape, is therefore more important than the fact that they were made of the material bronze. Things and cultural notions cannot be disconnected or alienated from people and their ideals and values here (Lambek 2008, 135–136). To say that the Ommerschans sword was valuable to Bronze Age people in this sphere means it was seen as inextricably bound up with a particular cultural notion. As we are dealing with an aggrandizement of a particular weapon, it has been argued that this object was meant to reify an ideal of martiality (Fontijn 2001). Thus, it is no longer three kilograms of bronze, but it is now a cultural valuable and owes its role to how it was crafted, used and publicly recognized as such (cf. Graeber 2005, 452). Its value cannot be quantified (it is priceless, cf. Hart 2005, 164–165) and is incommensurable. The rigid keeping separate of certain objects seen in their selective deposition may result from such incommensurability.

Sphere of exchange

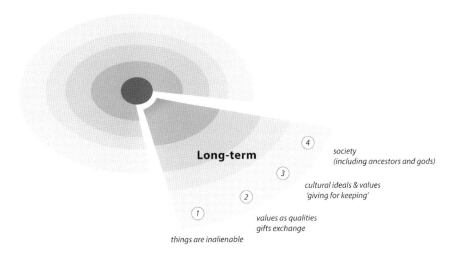

FIGURE 1.5 Schematized view of long-term sphere of exchange, organized like Figure 1.4. It represents the long-term sphere as the overarching realm of the short-term one. Information from Bloch & Parry 1989; Godelier 1999; Lambek 2008.
Source: Drawing by J. Porck, Faculty of Archaeology, University of Leiden.

The long-term sphere is an order that need to be preserved and shielded and therefore it is concerned with 'keeping' things. When things are exchanged (as gifts) they therefore never become the full property of the receiver; they are inalienable (Figure 1.5; Mauss 1993). 'Giving' is tantamount to 'keeping' (Weiner 1992). A short-term notion of a thing being 'destroyed' or 'given up' then (as in the phrase 'destructive economy'), seems out of place. It is more apt to speak of 'singularization' of things (Kopytoff 1986, 65).

Returning to the juxtaposition of political versus moral or cultural approaches to the Bronze Age, we may recognize traits of short-term-sphere thinking in the former interpretations, and something of long-term thinking in the latter. Political economies provide the most coherent answer to the question why it was particularly *bronze* that was deposited on such a massive scale in the Bronze Age. This is because this approach takes into account both the role of bronze as a scarce material resource and its general social desirability. Moral or cultural approaches, however, are best equipped to deal with the question why bronzes *were deposited in these particular, selective, ways*. Whilst political economies work best at supra-regional scales, cultural approaches are better suited to make sense of the particular depositional conventions at smaller spatial scales.

The key point is that short- and long-term exchanges must co-exist in any society. In a world in which everything is alienable and 'for sale' or part of a power play, nothing can last and there can be no culture (Kopytoff 1986, 70). This is why there always has to be an overarching, long-term order in which things and ideas are inalienable, kept and shielded from change (Kopytoff 1986, 70; Sandel 2012; Weiner 1992, 7–8). However, a world in which everything is inalienable is inconceivable. In order to survive in and adapt to a world that is continuously changing, it is essential that humans also have 'ideological space' (Bloch & Parry 1989, 26) where they can appropriate things, and convert certain things into other things. Therefore, there also need to be a realm in which things can be alienated, and thus are not connected to people, or higher-order ideals (ibid.). This is the short-term sphere of exchange mentioned previously, where individual acquisition is the aim, and where maximization and commercial behaviour reside (ibid.). The Ommerschans sword may have been a key cultural valuable, the deposition of which in a peat bog required a special treatment and care. The metal from which the ceremonial sword of Ommerschans was made, however, once started its life as normal material which must have been produced and exchanged in short-term transactions. As Lambek (2008, 149) puts it, *the value of commensurable 'economic' things is implemental in the creation of the incommensurable 'cultural' value of acts.*

Outline of this book

This book aims to make sense of the massive deposition of metalwork that took place during the European Bronze Age by approaching such acts as practices in which value as price is transformed into cultural values. Focusing on the selective, patterned nature of metalwork deposition, it will attempt to recognize a system behind a seemingly un-economic, unfamiliar phenomenon.

Chapter 2 first explores how depositional practices can be selective and how a 'system' behind practices that are so variable across Europe can be explored. Chapter 3 goes on to link such selectivity to a concept of value. How can value refer to both short- and long-term logic and why do both fields lead to a selective treatment of things? To get a better grasp on what Bronze Age selective deposition is, a comparison with older practices is necessary. In Chapter 4, the question is asked whether, and if so in which way, Bronze Age selective deposition is fundamentally different from depositional practices of pre-Bronze Age cultures. In Chapters 5 and 6, the two poles in the interpretation of metalwork deposition, 'economy' and 'religion', will be discussed on the basis of empirical evidence. Chapter 5 addresses the paradox that so many of these 'un-economic' depositions actually contain material that immediately refers to short-term transactions like massive trade. What can be learned from this about the nature of Bronze Age 'economy'? Following on this, Chapter 6 does the same by focusing on depositions consisting of 'religious' items. Often seen as the opposite of rational, profane trade hoards, such 'religious' or 'ritual' hoards were pivotal in the construction of the Bronze Age as an 'irrational other'. How do such depositions actually inform us on Bronze Age 'religiosity'? Whereas Chapters 5 and 6 are mainly about patterns in associations and dissociations between objects, Chapter 7 deals with how things were selectively deposited in the landscape. As receiver of countless metal objects, the landscape is a key player in any consideration of deposition, next to the people and the objects. What is this landscape of deposition, and how does selective deposition construct landscape? Finally, Chapter 8, brings the results of all these discussions together to address the question what this 'economy of destruction' is, what it brought about and how the Bronze Age may provide food for thought on the question of how we perceive ourselves through conceptualizations of economy.

Notes

1 This term is from Needham 1990 and will be used throughout this book.
2 Presumably in Northwest France or Southern England: Butler & Bakker 1961; Needham 1990.
3 Fontijn et al. 2012; Knight 2018; Nebelsick 2000.
4 Becker 2013; Fontijn 2002; Hansen 1991; 1994; Needham 1989; Soroceanu 1995; Vandkilde 1996; Verlaeckt 1996; Von Brunn 1959; Worsaae 1867.
5 For overviews, see e.g. Bradley 1990, chapter 1; Fontijn 2002, chapter 2; Geisslinger 1984; Hansen 1991, 161–164; Verlaeckt 1995, chapter 3.
6 Graeber (2005, 443) argues that it seems to have become anthropology's task to make sense of 'irrational' (i.e. non-market) economic behaviour in non-Western societies. In a similar vein, one could say it has become archaeology's task to do the same for 'un-economic' behaviour in the past.
7 I am grateful to M.L Sørensen (Cambridge & Leiden) who suggested Latour's work to me.
8 This term was coined by Needham 1989.
9 In a paper that did not get the attention it deserved, Stjernquist (1965/1966) was one of the first to try to systematically link 'trade' and 'ritual' deposition.

Bibliography

Becker, K., 2013. Transforming identities: new approaches to Bronze Age deposition in Ireland, *Proceedings of the Prehistoric Society* 79, 225–263.
Bloch, M. and J. Parry, 1989. Introduction: money and the morality of exchange, in: *Money and the morality of exchange*, eds J. Parry and M. Bloch. Cambridge: Cambridge University Press, 1–31.
Bradley, R., 1990. *The passage of arms. An archaeological analysis of prehistoric hoards and votive deposits*. Cambridge: Cambridge University Press.
Bray, P.J. and A.M. Pollard, 2012. A new interpretative approach to the chemistry of copper-alloy objects: source, recycling and technology, *Antiquity* 86(333), 853–867.
Briard, J., 1965. *Les dépôts Bretons et l'age du bronze atlantique* (Travaux du Laboratoire d'Anthropologie Préhistorique). Rennes: Faculté des Sciences de Rennes.
Brück, J., 1999. Ritual and rationality: some problems of interpretation in European archaeology, *European Journal of Archaeology* 2, 313–344.
Brück, J. and H. Fokkens, 2013. Bronze Age settlements, in: *The Oxford handbook of the European Bronze Age*, eds A. Harding and H. Fokkens. Oxford: Oxford University Press, 82–101.
Brück, J. and D.R. Fontijn, 2013. The myth of the chief: prestige goods, power and personhood in the European Bronze Age, in: *The Oxford handbook of the European Bronze Age*, eds A. Harding and H. Fokkens. Oxford: Oxford University Press, 197–211.
Butler, J.J. and J.A. Bakker, 1961. A forgotten Middle Bronze Age hoard with a Sicilian razor from Ommerschans (Overijssel), *Helinium* I, 193–210.

Chakrabarty, D., 2008. *Provincializing Europe. Postcolonial thought and historical difference.* Princeton NJ and Oxford: Princeton University Press.
Chang, H.-J., 2014. *Economics: the user's guide.* New York: Penguin Books.
Childe, V.G., 1925. *The dawn of European civilization.* London: Routledge & Kegan Paul.
Childe, V.G., 1930. *The Bronze Age.* Cambridge: Cambridge University Press.
Coles, J.M. and A.F. Harding, 1979. *The Bronze Age in Europe. An introduction to the prehistory of Europe c. 2000–700 BC.* London: Methuen.
Cunliffe, B., 2012. *Britain begins.* Oxford: Oxford University Press.
Davies, N., 1998. *Europe. A history. A panorama of Europe, East and West, from the Ice Age to the Cold War, from the Urals to Gibraltar.* New York: HarperCollins.
Demakopoulou, K., C. Eluère, J. Jensen, A. Jockenhövel and J.P. Mohen (eds), 1998. *Gods and heroes of the Bronze Age. Europe at the time of Ulysses.* New York: Thames & Hudson.
Dumont, L., 1977. *From Mandeville to Marx. The genesis and triumph of economic ideology.* Chicago: University of Chicago Press.
Durkheim, E., 2014 [1906]. *Over moraliteit.* Amsterdam: Boom.
Earle, T., 2002. *Bronze Age economies. The beginnings of political economies.* Boulder CO: Westview Press.
Earle, T., J. Ling, C. Uhnér, Z. Stos-Gale and L. Melheim, 2015. The political economy and metal trade in Bronze Age Europe: understanding regional variability in terms of comparative advantages and articulations, *European Journal of Archaeology* 18(4), 633–657.
Eogan, G., 1994. *The accomplished art. Gold and gold-working in Britain and Ireland during the Bronze Age.* Oxford: Oxbow Books.
Evans, J., 1881. *The ancient bronze implements, weapons and ornaments of Great Britain and Ireland.* London: Longman, Green and Co.
Ferguson, N., 2011. *Civilization. The six killer apps of western power.* London: Penguin Books.
Fontijn, D.R., 2001. Rethinking ceremonial dirks of the Plougrescant-Ommerschans type. Some thoughts on the structure of metalwork exchange, in: *Patina. Essays presented to Jay Jordan Butler on the occasion of his 80th birthday*, eds W.H. Metz, B.L. van Beek and H. Steegstra. Groningen and Amsterdam: Privately published by Metz, Van Beek & Steegstra, 263–280.
Fontijn, D.R., 2002. Sacrificial landscapes: cultural biographies of persons, objects and 'natural' places in the Bronze Age of the southern Netherlands, c. 2300–2600 BC, *Analecta Praehistorica Leidensia* 33/34, 1–392.
Fontijn, D.R. and L. Amkreutz, 2018. Het verzonken zwaard van Ommerschans, in: *Wereldgeschiedenis van Nederland*, eds L. Heerma van Voss, M. 't Hart, K. Davids, K. Fatah-Black, L. Lucassen and J. Touwen. Amsterdam: Ambo/Anthos, 39–43.
Fontijn, D.R., L. Theunissen, B. van Os and L. Amkreutz, 2012. Decorated and 'killed'? The bronze sword of Werkhoven, *Analecta Praehistorica Leidensia* 43–44, 203–211.
Friedman, J. and M. Rowlands, 1977. Notes towards an epigenetic model of the evolution of 'civilisation', in: *The evolution of social systems*, eds J. Friedman and M. Rowlands. London: Duckworth, 201–278.
Geissinger, H., 1984. Depotfund. Hortfund, in: *Reallexicon der Germanischen Altertumskunde V*, ed. J. Hoops. Berlin and New York: De Gruyter, 320–338.
Godelier, M., 1999. *The enigma of the gift.* Cambridge and Oxford: Polity Press.
Goody, J., 2012a. *The theft of history.* Cambridge: Cambridge University Press.
Goody, J., 2012b. *Metals, culture and capitalism. An essay on the origins of the modern world.* Cambridge: Cambridge University Press.
Graeber, D., 2001. *Toward an anthropological theory of value: the false coin of our own dreams.* New York: Palgrave.

Graeber, D., 2005. Value: anthropological theory of value, in: *A handbook of economic anthropology*, ed. J.G. Carrier. Cheltenham and Northampton MA: Edward Elgar, 439–454.

Gregory, C.A., 2015 [1982]. *Gifts and commodities*. Chicago: Hau Books.

Haak, W., I. Lazaridis, N. Patterson, N. Rohland, S. Mallick, B. Llamas, G. Brandt, S. Nordenfelt, E. Harney, K. Stewardson, Q. Fu, A. Mittnik, E. Banffy, Ch. Economou, M. Francken, S. Friederich, R. Garrido Pena, F. Hallgren, V. Khartanovich, A. Khokhlov, M. Kunst, P. Kuznetsov, H. Meller, O. Mochalov, V. Moiseyev, N. Nicklisch, S.L. Pichler, R. Risch, M.A. Rojo Guerra, Ch. Roth, A. Szecsenyi-Nagy, J. Wahl, M. Meyer, J. Krause, D. Brown, D. Anthony, A. Cooper, K. Werner Alt and D. Reich, 2015. Massive migration from the Steppe was a source for Indo-European languages in Europe, *Nature* 522, 207–211.

Hänsel, A., 2009. Die Bronzezeit, in: *Atlas der Vorgeschichte. Europa von den ersten Menschen bis Christi Geburt*, ed. S. Von Schnurbein. Stuttgart: Konrad Theiss Verlag, 108–149.

Hänsel, A. and B. Hänsel (eds), 1997. *Gaben an die Götter. Seminar zur Ur- und Frühgeschichte der Freien Universität*. Berlin: Museum für Vor- und Frühgeschichte.

Hansen, S., 1991. *Studien zu den Metalldeponierungen während der Urnenfelderzeit im Rhein-Main-Gebiet* (Universitätsforschungen zur prähistorischen Archäologie 5). Bonn: Habelt Verlag.

Hansen, S., 1994. *Studien zu den Metalldeponierungen während der älteren Urnenfelderzeit zwischen Rhônetal und Karpatenbecken* (Universitätsforschungen zur prähistorischen Archäologie 21). Bonn: Habelt Verlag.

Hansen, S., 2011. Metal in South-Eastern and Central Europe between 4500 and 2900 BCE, in: *Anatolian Metal V. Veröffentlichungen aus dem Deutschen Bergbau-Museum Bochum, Nr 180*, ed. Ü. Yalçin. Bochum, Germany: Bergbau-Museum, 137–149.

Hansen, S., 2013. Innovative metals: copper, gold and silver in the Black Sea region and the Carpathian basin during the 5th and 4th millennium BC, in: *Metal matters. Innovative technologies and social change in prehistory and antiquity* (Menschen-Kulturen-Traditionen; Forschungskluster 2, Bd 12), eds S. Burmeister, S. Hansen, M. Kunst and N. Müller-Scheessel. Rahden: Marie Leidorf Verlag, 137–167.

Harris, O.J.T., K. Rebay-Salisbury, J. Robb and M.L.S. Sørensen, 2013. The body in its social context, in: *The body in history. Europe from the Palaeolithic to the future*, eds J. Robb and O.J.T. Harris. Cambridge: Cambridge University Press, 64–97.

Hart, K., 2005. Money: one anthropologist's view, in: *A handbook of economic anthropology*, ed. J.G. Carrier. Cheltenham and Northampton MA: Edward Elgar, 160–175.

Iversen, R. and G. Kroonen, 2017. Talking Neolithic: linguistic and archaeological perspectives on how Indo-European was implemented in southern Scandinavia, *American Journal of Archaeology* 121(4), 511–525.

Jockenhövel, A., 2013. Germany in the Bronze Age, in: *The Oxford handbook of the European Bronze Age*, eds A. Harding and H. Fokkens. Oxford: Oxford University Press, 723–745.

Kaul, F., 1998. *Ships on Bronzes. A study in Bronze Age religion and iconography* (Studies in Archaeology and History Vol. 3). Copenhagen: Publications from the National Museum.

Knight, M., 2018. The intentional destruction and deposition of Bronze Age metalwork in South West England. Unpublished Ph.D. thesis, Exeter University.

Kopytoff, I., 1986. The cultural biography of things: commoditisation as process, in: *The social life of things*, ed. A. Appadurai. Cambridge: Cambridge University Press, 64–91.

Kristiansen, K., 1998. *Europe before history* (New Studies in Archaeology). Cambridge: Cambridge University Press.

Kristiansen, K., 2016. Interpreting Bronze Age trade and migration, in: *Human mobility and technological transfer in the prehistoric Mediterranean*, eds E. Kiriatzi and C. Knappett. Cambridge: Cambridge University Press, 154–181.

Kristiansen, K. and T.B. Larsson, 2005. *The rise of Bronze Age society. Travels, transmissions and transformations*. Cambridge: Cambridge University Press.

Lambek, M., 2008. Value and virtue, *Anthropological Theory* 8(2), 133–157.

Latour, B., 2004. Why has critique run out of steam? From matters of fact to matters of concern, *Critical Inquiry* 30(2), 225–248.

Lemaire, T., 1985. De 'homo economicus' tussen ruil en uitwisseling. Enkele beschouwingen rond de economische antropologie, *Antropologische verkenningen* 5, 77–106.

Levy, J.E., 1982. *Social and religious organization in Bronze Age Denmark* (British Archaeological Reports International Series 124), Oxford: Archaeopress.

Louwen, A.J., forthcoming. *Making and breaking the ancestors*. Leiden: Sidestone Press.

Mauss, M., 1993 [1923/1924]. *The gift. The form and reason for exchange in archaic societies*. London: Routledge.

Morris, I., 2011. *Why the West rules – for now. The patterns of history and what they reveal about the future*. London: Profile Books.

Nebelsick, L., 2000. Rent asunder: ritual violence in Late Bronze Age hoards, in: *Metals make the world go round. The supply and circulation of metals in Bronze Age Europe. Proceedings of a conference held at the University of Birmingham in June 1997*, ed. C.F.E. Pare. Oxford: Oxbow Books, 160–175.

Needham, S., 1989. Selective deposition in the British Early Bronze Age, *World Archaeology* 20, 229–248.

Needham, S., 1990. Middle Bronze Age ceremonial weapons: new finds from Oxborough, Norfolk and Essex/Kent (with a contribution from D. Hook), *The Antiquaries Journal* LXX–LXXII, 239–252.

Needham, S. and C. Burgess, 1980. The Later Bronze Age in the Lower Thames Valley: the metalwork evidence, in: *Settlement and society in the British Later Bronze Age* (British Archaeological Reports Series 83), eds J. Barrett and R. Bradley. Oxford: Archaeopress, 437–469.

Niklasson, E., 2014. Shutting the stable door after the horse has bolted. Critical thinking and the third science revolution, *Current Swedish Archaeology* 22, 57–63.

Nongbi, B., 2013. *Before religion. A history of a modern concept*. New Haven CT: Yale University Press.

Pétrequin, P., S. Cassen, E. Errera, L. Klassen, A. Sheridan and A.-M. Pétrequin, 2012. *Jade. Grands haches alpines du Néolithique européen*. Besançon: Presses Universitaires de France-Comté.

Reinhold, S., 2005. Vom Ende Europas? Zu den Depotfunden im Kaukasus, in: *Interpretationsraum Bronzezeit. Bernhard Hänsel von seinen Schülern gewidmet* (Universitätsforschungen zur prähistorischen Archäologie 121), eds B. Horejs, R. Junge, E. Kaiser and B. Teržan. Bonn: Habelt Verlag, 345–373.

Robotham, D., 2005. Political economies, in: *A handbook of economic anthropology*, ed. J.G. Carrier. Cheltenham: Edward Elgar, 41–58.

Rowlands, M.J., 1984. Conceptualising the European Bronze and Early Iron ages, in: *European social evolution. Archaeological perspectives*, ed. J. Bintliff. Bradford: University of Bradford, 147–156.

Roymans, N. and F. Kortlang, 1999. Urnfield symbolism, ancestors, and the land in the Lower Rhine region, in: *Land and ancestors. Cultural dynamics in the urnfield period and the middle ages in the southern Netherlands* (Amsterdam Archaeological Studies 4), eds F. Theuws and N. Roymans. Amsterdam: Amsterdam University Press, 33–61.

Sandel, M.J., 2012. *What money can't buy. The moral limits of markets*. New York: Farrar, Straus and Giroux.

Shennan, S., 1999. Cost, benefit and value in the organization of early European Copper production, *Antiquity* 73(280), 352–363.

Sørensen, M.L.S., 1987. Material order and cultural classification: the role of bronze objects in the transition from Bronze Age to Iron Age in Scandinavia, in: *The archaeology of contextual meanings* (New Directions in Archaeology), ed. I. Hodder. Cambridge: Cambridge University Press, 90–101.

Soroceanu, T., 1995. Die Fundumstände bronzezeitlicher Deponierungen. Ein Beitrag zur Hortdeutung beiderseits der Karpaten, in: *Bronzefunde aus Rumänien* (Prähistorische Archäologie in Südosteuropa 10), ed. T. Soroceanu. Berlin: Spiess Verlag, 15–80.

Stjernquist, B., 1965 / 1966. Models of commercial diffusion in prehistoric times, *Scripta Minora regiae societatis humaniorum litterarum lundensis* 2. Lund: C.W.K. Gleerup.

Thomsen, C.J., 1845. Om den nordiske oldtids broncearbeider, *Antiquariske Tidsskrift* 1, 171–175.

Treherne, P., 1995. The warrior's beauty: the masculine body and self-identity in Bronze-Age Europe, *Journal of European Archaeology* 3(1), 105–144.

Vandkilde, H., 1996. *From stone to bronze: the metalwork of the Late Neolithic and Earliest Bronze Age in Denmark* (Jutland Archaeological Society Publications XXXII). Aarhus, Denmark: Aarhus University Press.

Vandkilde, H., 2016. Bronzization: the Bronze Age as pre-modern globalization, *Prähistorische Zeitschrift* 91(1), 103–123.

Verlaeckt, K., 1995. Sociale evolutie tijdens de metaaltijden in Denemarken. Analyse en interpretatie van 'depotvondsten' als basis voor een modelvorming van de samenleving in de late bronstijd en de vroege ijzertijd (ca. 1000 BC–0). Unpublished Ph.D. thesis, University of Ghent.

Verlaeckt, K. 1996. *Between river and barrow. A reappraisal of Bronze Age metalwork found in the province of East-Flanders (Belgium)* (British Archaeological Reports International Series 632). Oxford: Archaeopress.

Von Brunn, W.A., 1959. *Die Hortfunde der frühen Bronzezeit aus Sachsen-Anhalt, Sachsen und Thüringen*. Berlin: Akademie Verlag.

Weiner, A.B., 1992. *Inalienable possessions: the paradox of keeping-while-giving*, Berkeley CA, Los Angeles CA and Oxford: University of California Press.

Wengrow, D. , 2010. *What makes civilization? The ancient Near East and the future of the West*. Oxford: Oxford University Press.

Wolf, E.R., 1999. *Envisioning power. Ideologies of dominance and crisis*. Berkeley CA, Los Angeles CA and London: University of California Press.

Worsaae, J.J.A., 1867. *Sur quelques trouvailles de l'âge du bronze faites dans des tourbières, mémoire lu dans une réunion de la Société des Antiquaires du Nord chez sa majesté le roi, au palais d'Armalienborg, le 2. Mai 1866*. Copenhagen: Köngelige Nordiske Oldskriftselskab.

Yule, P., 1985. *Metalwork of the Bronze Age in India* (Prähistorische Bronzefunde XX-8). Munich: C.H. Beck.

2

SELECTIVE DEPOSITION – WHAT DOES IT ENTAIL AND HOW CAN IT BE STUDIED?

What makes a depositional practice selective? As a necessary step for what follows, this chapter offers a closer look at what selectivity entails, and discusses what we can and cannot study archaeologically. It is argued that selective deposition of metalwork reflects 'average behaviour'. There were conventions on 'the right way to act' when prehistoric people considered it necessary to bury things in the ground. Selective deposition is argued to reflect an emergent social phenomenon the meaning of which cannot be reduced to a single motivation. As it is based on association and dissociation between things and places, selective deposition can work in similar ways for different cultures. Evidence-based examples of the relational logic behind Bronze Age depositional practices are identified, such as conventions and convention-breaking, the contrast between local and foreign, and small-world effects.

How important were things people deposited?

This book studies prehistoric society through the lens of their depositional practices. However, models that estimate what percentage of the metalwork actually ended up in the archaeological record show this is a surprisingly low number. Wiseman (2017) recently suggested no more than 5–15 per cent ended up in the archaeological record of Late Bronze Age South England. A comparable figure has been suggested for the Southern Netherlands, based on a different way of modelling (Fontijn 2002, 215).

It is essential to realize *that an act of destruction of materials or objects and subsequent deposition of it are two different practices.* If we think about the breaking of a glass during a Jewish wedding, the act of breaking is integral to the wedding ceremony. The burial of the splinters of the glass, however, is not. The deliberate glass-breaking during the wedding stands out, yet the disposal of its fragments follows generic patterns of waste disposal. Archaeologically, this ceremonial act would therefore be impossible to recognize. The same holds true for the majority of Bronze Age metal. Objects the life of which was considered over, usually ended up in the melting pot for recycling (Bray & Pollard 2012; Wiseman 2017). The bronzes that ended up in the archaeological record therefore represent exceptions to the recycling rule (cf. Becker 2013, 230; Needham 2001). Thus, there is a risk of a confirmation bias: we tend to overstate what we observe and not fully realize what we might miss. The majority of metal was not deposited, but remained in circulation. Depositions of metal therefore represent events that must have had an exceptional character in social life.

Sometimes, there are indirect clues as to what was *not* deposited. *Ösenringe* are exchange items that probably were made in the North Alpine region during the Early Bronze Age (2000–1750 BC; cf. Chapters 3 and 5), and must have circulated across large parts of Europe. They were made of a distinctive type of metal (Junk et al. 2001) that is unknown from contemporary axes in the same region. Butler (1995/1996, 166) argues that a bronze axe found in the Netherlands was made of this metal, implying *Ösenringe* reached this area as well. However, they are unknown among the Early Bronze Age finds from the Low Countries (ibid.). This could imply that they were recycled but not deposited.

Thus, when dealing with metalwork deposition, it is important to realize that archaeology only allows us to make statements on those things whose life-paths ended in deposition (cf. Needham 2001).

FIGURE 2.0 Sites mentioned in this chapter: 1. Staffordshire; 2. Oxborough; 3. Drouwen; 4. Ommerschans; 5. Wageningen; 6. Veldhoven; 7. Schkopau; 8. Pile; 9. Rørby.

Source: J. Porck, Faculty of Archaeology, University of Leiden.

Seeing depositions as part of a bigger, relational whole

Through time, studies of deposited metalwork have focused on particular aspects only. Metalwork from hoards, graves and settlements tends to be studied in isolation. Single finds are not always included in studies of hoards and vice versa. This is problematic, as it is through comparison of objects in different contexts that patterns of selective deposition can be revealed. The need for an integrated approach can sometimes even be grasped from one find. For example, there are cases where a whetstone was inserted without a tool to sharpen (Van Wijk et al. 2009, secondary grave in mound 2). For the Early Iron Age in Europe, there are many burials where pieces of horse-drawn wagons were deposited with crucial parts missing (Pare 1991, 194; Van der Vaart-Verschoof 2017, 149–150). However, what may look like a part from the perspective of a single deposition, can be a whole when individual depositions are considered together. Bradley and Ford (2004) give the example of Staffordshire (UK), where the lower part of a sword was found on one hill, and its upper part on an adjacent one. At Oss (NL), three Early Iron Age elite burials were found. Considered separately, each appears to have an incomplete set of Hallstatt elite paraphernalia. However, taken together, the three burials can be seen as complementary (Fontijn et al. 2013, 309–312). This suggests that for each new burial, the mourners referred to what was inserted into previous ones. In such a way, deposition may have worked to forge links between people and places (Brück 2004; forthcoming; Brück & Fontijn 2013). Chapman (2000) calls this 'enchainment'.

This is why it is essential for depositional studies to not focus on one aspect, like for example 'hoards' or 'graves', as was common practice in the past, *but to include evidence from all available contemporary depositional contexts, ranging from settlements to single finds in the landscape* (Fontijn 2002). Only in this way can we grasp something of this bigger, relational whole.

Selective deposition as 'average behaviour'

What kind of behaviour are we actually studying when focusing on this phenomenon of selective deposition? Suppose a bronze spearhead is found during an excavation of a Middle Bronze Age settlement. It is in the nature of archaeologists and public alike to ask questions such as: How did it end up there? What happened? Attempts to reconstruct a historical event that explains how the spear ended its life here are primary. Yet, by its very nature, the archaeological record does not allow much in the way of event-reconstruction, let alone the minds of the prehistoric people involved in depositing a particular spearhead. Several scenarios may be suggested, ranging from this spearhead simply being discarded among debris, to a scenario where it gets lost during replacement of the wooden shaft or even the spear being sacrificed to gods at this location. Judging by its find circumstances alone, there is no basis for deciding between these motivations.

Suppose now that we have large numbers of spearheads recorded from Middle Bronze Age sites in the same region. The majority of them are found in and along streams, and they are absent on settlements which have been systematically surveyed with metal detectors. This still does not answer the question why people left that one specific spearhead at that settlement. It does inform us, however, that Bronze Age people usually did not leave bronze spearheads at settlements – it was not part of the discarding or depositional habits of people living in this region. So whilst we cannot fully explain the individual act of depositing this spearhead at this settlement (nor of any other individual spearhead found in the region), we are able to say something about 'average behaviour' (Ball 2004, 48–49), which 'smoothes out individual unpredictability' (ibid., 8). In this case, whatever the background, motivations and intentions that led to each individual spearhead ending up in the ground in this region (and they may have differed!), the end result is a tendency to leave spearheads in streams.

Further research can qualify such a tendency. When ample burials from the Middle Bronze Age are known in the region and spears are clearly under-represented there as well, such evidence of absence shows that there was a tendency to leave spearheads in streams *to the exclusion of other contexts*. This is the selective deposition that is known from the Bronze Age and is the focus of this book. It is an emergent property (Buchmann 2001) of depositional behaviour in its broadest sense, which can only be recognized as such when average depositional behaviour in all kinds of contexts is systematically compared.

If it is possible to recognize a certain behavioural tendency in depositional patterns, this does not imply each constituent individual act was done with the same idea in mind. It only means that when people left spearheads in the ground, this was rarely done on settlements or in graves, but usually in streams. Average patterning also does not mean each individual act went with outspoken symbolical or ritual connotations (cf. Garrow 2012). Not leaving spearheads on settlements or in graves may also have felt like a non-discursive 'proper way of acting' (Bloch 1995; Bourdieu 1977, 78).

As 'average behaviour', selective deposition is an emergent social and historical phenomenon (the pattern represents individual acts conducted over hundreds of years). Durkheim's classic example of such a social phenomenon may be referred to here: his study of suicide (1951). Ending one's own life seems like the most individual decision one can make, and reasons will have differed from individual to individual. Yet, Durkheim showed that even these profoundly individual decisions show trends through time, indicating that suicide is an emergent social phenomenon.

The individual act of depositing one spearhead, however, is not entirely separate from another such act. Selective deposition is the 'aggregate result' (Ball 2004, 150) of individual actions that relate to each other. People depositing a spearhead in a stream near Veldhoven in the Netherlands, for example, were probably not aware that people living in what is now London also deposited spears in streams and rivers (Fontijn 2002, app. 6.2; Needham & Burgess 1980). However, the community at Veldhoven must have seen or heard of previous acts of spearhead deposition in their region (and there must have been many: Fontijn 2002, figure 7.10). Deposition was learnt behaviour on what is 'the right way of acting', in which, as Bourdieu (1977) argues, people may reproduce behaviour without fully realizing how it amounts to the sustaining of a broader order. Behaviour is by definition relational, as it is based on local perception of the world (cf. Ball 2004, 15). If spears – or bronze in general – rarely was left at settlements, the one case where this happened will have been recognized *socially* as an exception from what was normative behaviour (cf. Kopytoff 1986, 67).[1]

Selective deposition as 'the right way to act'

Thus, a distinction must be made between the individual 'itinerary' (Hahn & Weiss 2013) of an object and the general trajectory that is socially considered as desirable in a culture. Kopytoff (1986) famously calls this an object's 'cultural biography'. One could also describe it as what feels as 'the right way to act'. This involves the notion of conventions, not necessarily of 'rules'. It is about judgment rather than choice (Lambek 2008). When it touches upon cultural values that are important, there may be a moral side to 'the right way of acting'. The Late Bronze Age avoidance of weaponry in Dutch and Belgian burials, for example, may express that items of violence and power had no place in the urnfield cemeteries where social values such as collectivity and egalitarianism were emphasized (Chapter 1; Fontijn 2002, 278; Roymans & Kortlang 1999, 56).

The adjective 'cultural' indicates that perceptions of what is considered an appropriate 'itinerary' for an object are based on shared views and may differ from culture to culture (Kopytoff 1986, 67). For the Bronze Age, the most common 'cultural biography' of bronze would have been the one that ends in the melting pot. For the evidence that is the topic of this book, we are dealing with a more exceptional kind of cultural biography: biographies where metalwork ended up in the ground (Fontijn 2002, 33; Needham 2007). The term 'cultural biography' has recently been criticized (Fontijn 2013; Hahn & Weiss 2013; Hahn 2015). Using the metaphor of life brings implicit notions with it that are better avoided. If an object's circulation is seen as its 'life', should its deposition then be considered as its 'death'? From a long-term perspective (Chapter 1), this is not something that should immediately be assumed. For example, landscape zones where objects were deposited usually lack humanly-made, lasting markers. Yet, many are known to have very long depositional histories, implying people returned to such zones time and again to bury valuable objects (Chapter 7). This suggests that the deposited objects still played a role in people's life and need not have been considered 'dead'. It is also unclear where the notion of an object biography relates to (Hahn 2015, 27–28). If a sword is broken and only a fragment of it deposited (as in the case of the Staffordshire sword mentioned above; Bradley & Ford 2004) are we then still talking about the biography of a *sword*? This should be taken into account because in deposition, it is often fragments of things that are deposited ('scrap' or 'founder hoards'; cf. Knight 2018; Wiseman 2017). For these reasons, the notion of a biography will be avoided in what follows.

Selective deposition reflects what Bronze Age people considered the socially and culturally appropriate way to deposit things in the ground. Their preferences and conventions may be alien to our culture. However, as reflections of behavioural patterns that can be observed from the archaeological record, selective deposition at least offers us the possibility to start our inquiry from the relations Bronze Age society itself considered relevant and meaningful (Fontijn 2002, 21). Taking depositional patterns themselves as a starting point at least helps us to avoid *a priori* assumptions about meaningful behaviour. As set out in Chapter 1, the biggest problem with the interpretation of metalwork depositions has been that scholars have tried to fit them in an interpretive straitjacket of our own making: 'profane' vs. 'ritual'. This may not only be anachronistic (cf. Brück 1999), but also unhelpful as it brings the risk of blinding researchers to depositional patterns that cross the 'profane–ritual boundary'.[2]

In what follows, we will simply take for granted what Bronze Age people were actually doing when they left metalwork in the ground, whether it happened in a settlement, grave or somewhere else in the landscape. It is a search for 'average' Bronze Age behaviour as it emerges from many recorded cases of depositions and involves picking out *only those patterns that* cannot *be explained by research factors or post-depositional decay*.

Our focus will be on average depositional practices that usually existed for a long time and were shared by many people. As an emergent phenomenon, they cannot be reduced to explicit, single-symbolic-concept motivations. To a great extent, meaning lies in the careful execution of the practice itself and in what it finally achieves (for example: reification, separation, association or transformation of valuables and value, see Chapters 3 and 8 and references cited there).

It is important to be aware that what Bronze Age society considered to be the 'right' way of acting may involve actions that do not necessarily make sense to us. Categorizations we traditionally use ('trade stock', 'tool', etc.) need not necessarily have mattered to Bronze Age people. This calls for research strategies where scholars go beyond traditional classifications of metalwork. For empirical research, I argue at least the following aspects as worthy to be taken into account.

The 'right' appearance

One reason why metal has fundamentally upset perceptions of materiality is that it is material resource and valuable item at the same time (see Chapter 1). Unlike stone, bare metal lacks visual properties that potentially inform people on where it came from (cf. Sørensen 1987). This means that its appearance is everything. Appearance matters – things can have many shapes, but in order to fulfil certain roles, objects apparently needed to have the 'right shape'. *Ösenringe*, Early Bronze Age exchange items (Chapters 3 and 5) mimic neck rings. The Ommerschans sword is an aggrandized, other-worldly version of a regular sword. Such examples show that 'object citation' (Sørensen 2015) is an important material strategy. In the Bronze Age this is probably even more so than in the Neolithic, as bronze casting facilitates straightforward copying (ibid.).

The 'right' selection

The observation that certain things are rarely associated in deposition is the basis for the entire phenomenon this book studies. The selective associations of things and other things, and things and places in the landscape are a case in point for the notion that 'things' are not just materials but come with expectations on their nature, agency and capacity – in short with the shared cognitive order imposed on the world (Kopytoff 1986, 70). It discriminates between things that are perceived as having something in common and can easily be joined, as opposed to things where it is vital to recognize heterogeneity and set them apart and separate (ibid.). It is important for archaeology to not just think of things in terms of our own object categorizations like 'axe' or 'halberd', but also to be open to the fact that what linked things in the eyes of Bronze Age people may also have been aspects less obvious to us. For example: a comparable use life (several things were deposited in streams, what they share is they were all used; cf. Fontijn 2002, 212), or a common origin irrespective of function or appearance.

The 'right' treatment

There is much evidence that physical transformation of items, be it bending, breaking or wrapping them up, was a decisive step in the process of singularization that depositional practice tried to achieve (Knight 2018). In Ireland, bronze ornaments are only known as fragments in hoards. Becker (2013, 231) argues this may imply it was only after having been broken that they were allowed to be placed in hoards. She notes that this is in marked contrast to gold ornaments, which tend to be deposited in a complete state. Most items in the lavish Early Iron Age 'chieftains' graves' of the Low Countries were deliberately transformed or wrapped in textiles, indicating these acts themselves itself might have been decisive in achieving their transformation from one state to another (Van der Vaart-Verschoof 2017).

The 'right' ordering

The same may have been achieved by specific orderings. As demonstrated in the work of Soroceanu (1995), things frequently were placed in the ground or grave following highly specific orderings. One may think of the careful ordering of the Dutch Ommerschans sword and other items on a platform (Chapter 1; Butler & Bakker 1961), the swords that were placed in upright position at Stoboru in Romania (Soroceanu 1995, 74), or the German Schkopau find, where axes were placed in a circle in a stream bed (Von Brunn 1959, 66).

The 'right' location

One of the most decisive actions then is to locate things in the landscape. Certain objects tend only to have been buried in certain kinds of location, which implies there was a balanced evaluation of which cultural notions were thought to reside where in the local landscape (Chapter 7). The tendency to deposit weaponry in major rivers of Western Europe, for example, indicates rivers had martial connotations or were the locations where notions of violence were to be pacified (Fontijn 2002, 259–260).

Average behaviour with a logic that tends to be exclusive

If depositional patterns were patterned and evidence of emergent notions on 'the right way to deposit things', this does not mean that they are always easily recognizable to us. Rather, there are several kinds of selective depositions that may be difficult to identify. We will now pay some more attention to which kind of selective deposition has the best potential to be recognizable archaeologically.

For the sake of the argument, let us suppose that the uncultivated zones that lie beyond settlements held a special significance to people who lived in Northwest Europe in late prehistory. In order to express the special relationship they entertained with these peripheral lands, people brought things and raw materials that mattered in daily life to it, and buried them there. Suppose people were convinced the things deposited there should have been involved in everyday life, and suppose that what they offered there varied at each event. On one occasion it could be a pot with a piece of meat, on another, it might be spindle whorls. Chances are that such deliberate offerings would not differ that much from what one would find on a contemporary settlement. Now imagine twenty-first-century archaeologists find remnants of these offerings in the land – it would not be that easy to make out what these things represent. There *is* a system, a logic behind such offerings, but it results from a broad variety of actions that do not strongly distinguish what happened in this part of the land from what happened in settlements in terms of depositional patterns. Though this is a result in itself, it is not one that is easy to make sense of for archaeology. There is considerable overlap between depositional patterns in different contexts (cf. Brück 1999). The offerings may have served to express the special significance of the uncultivated off-settlement zone, but by its content the depositions themselves do not distinguish between settlement and off-settlement. For that reason, such an 'offering' may easily go unnoticed to archaeologists and interpreted as 'discard' like we have it in a settlement (cf. the discussion in Garrow 2012).

The example used here is not made up. If we replace 'uncultivated zone' with 'peat bog' we have a phenomenon that is like the Iron Age 'mixed bog deposits' (Kok 2008). It is an example of one way in which the deposition of things may be the expression of the special significance a specific zone of the landscape had. Like in our hypothetical example, some depositional patterns allow several interpretations. In what follows, I will explore the different ways or scenarios in which depositions may be selective. We will see that most result in depositional patterns that are multi-interpretable.

In the first scenario, selection applies solely to the object. There is a preference for a specific kind of thing – say a sword – for a particular social practice like a funeral. A sword is seen as the object that is indispensable for the event, and as such it is not on a par with any other kind of object. Suppose it is relevant to the ceremony that the sword ends up buried in the ground, but that where this happens is related to personal events in the deceased's life. This would mean that for every sword buried, the location would be different. A heterogeneous distribution of swords in the landscape would be the result (Figure 2.1: A).

In the second scenario, there was not only a preference for a particular object, but also for a particular kind of place to plant it in. A sword, for example, ought to be placed in a river and not anywhere else. This is what people perceived as the 'right' location for the sword to rest (Figure 2.1: B).

In the European Bronze Age, there is convincing evidence for this second case of selective deposition. In large parts of Europe, swords tend to be left in rivers and not in other places (e.g. Torbrügge 1970/1971). There is preference for a certain

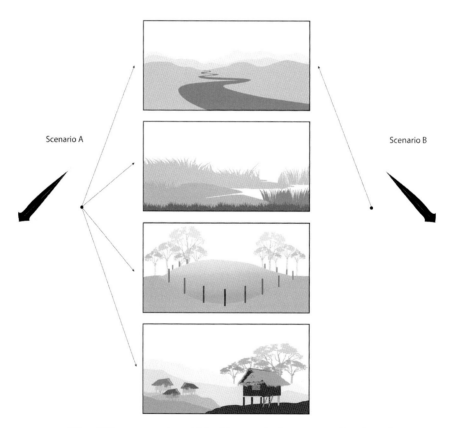

FIGURE 2.1 The different ways in which things and places may relate in a deposition. Scenario A: a specific object could be deposited in a variety of places. Scenario B: a specific object was only to be deposited in one specific kind of location.

Source: Drawing by J. Porck, Faculty of Archaeology, University of Leiden.

kind of context and avoidance of others. For some Bronze Age items, we may lack good information on what constituted 'the right place' for an object, but we can observe from depositional patterns which kind of places were avoided. For example, Early Bronze Age halberds and gold *lunulae* were both rarely deposited in burials. Apparently, graves usually were not considered an appropriate depositional location for such objects (Eogan 1994, 36, 39; Needham 1989; Von Brunn 1959, 26–8). Such statements can only be made when there are ubiquitous empirical patterns that are taphonomically not explainable in other ways.

Third, there are also cases where the selection only seems to involve a preference for a particular place in the landscape, like one spot in the river, but where there was no strict selection of objects. A broad range of things may have been deposited (Figure 2.2). This seems to apply to some Late Iron Age 'cult places', where we find almost anything ranging from prestigious metal to mundane pottery and animal bones (e.g. Kok 2008, 163–176). Many of the Early Neolithic depositions in Northwest Europe (especially in Denmark and the Netherlands, see Chapter 4) also fall under this heading, as it seems to have been peat bogs that were selected for the deposition of all kinds of things (Louwe Kooijmans & Nokkert 2001). Needless to say, it is more difficult to interpret such sites because the variety of material allows multiple explanations (particularly when similar finds are also discovered in settlements; ibid.).

A fourth scenario is that it is also possible that the selection does neither apply to objects nor places, but only to how the object is treated. In order to become suitable to be deposited, items would only need to have followed a special treatment, like fragmentation, physical transformation or a specific ordering (Figure 2.3: D). Such cases are more difficult to recognize. After all, there may be many reasons why one would break objects (like for re-melting purposes; Wiseman 2017). The same applies to ordering things (stored material is usually also ordered).

However, when a special treatment goes hand in hand with a repeated preference for a specific context (Figure 2.3: E), patterns allow fewer different interpretations. Many of the items in the most lavish Early Iron Age elite graves in Northwest Europe were bent, folded, broken or otherwise physically transformed (Van der Vaart-Verschoof 2017), in contrast to material found in contemporary hoards (like those of Armorican and Geistingen axes; Chapter 5). Following Van der Vaart-Verschoof (2017), the fact that most items in such graves were physically transformed and fragmented suggests this treatment was quintessential to allowing the objects in such burials.

An exclusive logic may thus pertain to different aspects of the act: to judge which thing(s), place(s) and treatment(s) are appropriate to it (Figure 2.1; Lambek 2008, 145). For patterns to be discernable archaeologically, there have to be enough data available (statistically speaking). Also, there must be sufficient evidence of absence of these things in other contexts (which means a thorough assessment of research and taphonomical processes; Fontijn 2002, chapter 4). If all of this applies, it is at least those practices with a *double exclusive logic of association* (Figure 2.1: B and Figure 2.3: E) where we can be confident a link between specific things and

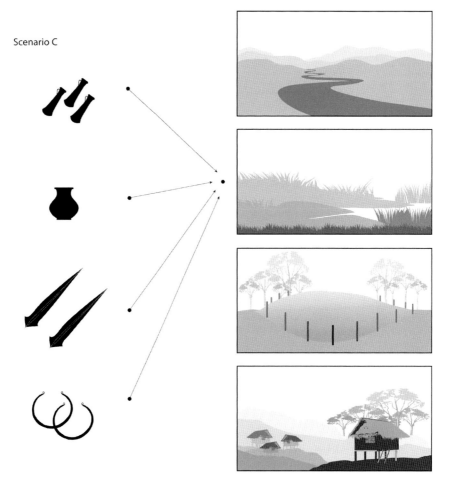

FIGURE 2.2 Scenario C: all kinds of objects were deposited but only in one specific place.
Source: Drawing by J. Porck, Faculty of Archaeology, University of Leiden.

specific places mattered to prehistoric people. These are cases where there is both a clear preference for a specific kind of thing (and therewith an avoidance of others) and for a specific depositional context (avoiding others). Alternatively, there may be a clear preference for a particular treatment and a specific depositional context.

This is an approach that takes the actions of Bronze Age communities themselves as a starting point. It tries to avoid *a priori* assumptions on the meaning of things and places that have occupied archaeology for so long.[3] An example of the latter is the assumption that depositions on 'dry' locations were potentially retrievable and therefore unlikely to represent material that was deposited there with the intention to leave it there forever. In Chapter 5, however, a series of dry hoards is represented for which it is unlikely that they were just temporary stores that people forgot to empty.

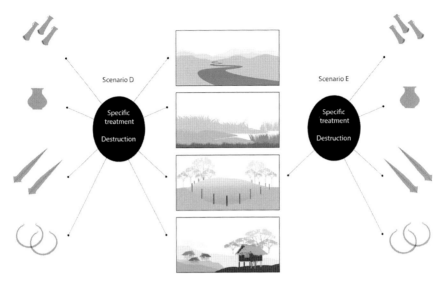

FIGURE 2.3 Scenario D: only after a specific treatment, any kind of object was allowed to be deposited in a variety of places. Scenario E: only after a specific treatment, any kind of object was allowed to be deposited, but only in one specific kind of location.
Source: Drawing by J. Porck, Faculty of Archaeology, University of Leiden.

As Figure 2.1-3 implies, there may have been many more depositional practices that may be more difficult to recognize.[4] It should be realized that this book focuses on *one specific practice among others*, but as will hopefully become clear reading it, this limitation is worthwhile: selective deposition of metalwork in the European Bronze Age represents a phenomenon of extraordinary nature and profound societal impact.

'Think locally, act globally'[5]

The double-exclusive logic of selective deposition was not an *a priori* given informing individual behaviour. Rather, it was something that emerged as a social phenomenon, as average behaviour, out of many individual depositional actions. All the examples of selective deposition mentioned so far are supra-regional or even 'transcultural' in nature (*sensu* Vandkilde 2014). Think of the example mentioned in Chapter 1 on the deposition of *lunulae* in the Early Bronze Age. When people considered it necessary to deposit such items in the ground, there are interesting similarities in how this was done between distant regions like Britain and Denmark. In both, *lunula*e were deposited in different kinds of places in the landscape but only rarely occur in graves (Eogan 1994, 34–36). In both regions, *lunulae* apparently were usually not considered appropriate for burial with the dead.

In making sense of such similarities, we should be careful to disentangle cause and effect. Let us, for the sake of argument, suppose that such depositional actions had to do with beliefs people held about spirits and gods dwelling in the land, to whom offerings ought to be made (cf. Chapter 6). Observing such similarities, sometimes even at a pan-European scale, makes it easy to suppose there was something like a shared religion across Bronze Age Europe resulting from mobility and globalization processes (as argued by Hänsel & Hänsel 1997). We may even stretch this to the extent that as answer to the question why people in distant regions deposited things in the same way is something like 'religion made them do it' (cf. Ball 2004, 92). This view of religion, however, is derived from hundreds of individual depositional actions. When it came to the selection of thing and location, together all these individual actions had the average result that *lunulae* apparently preferably were not to be associated with remains of the deceased. Although there is no doubt Bronze Age communities shared information, it is unlikely that each individual act that contributed to these conventions is directly explainable from such contacts.

The people who left the large ceremonial sword in the Ommerschans peat bog (Chapter 1; Figure 1.1) probably did not know that people living at the other end the North Sea, near present-day Oxborough in England (Needham 1990) had an almost identical sword which they also buried in the peat. The Ommerschans community, however, in all likelihood did know how their neighbours and immediate forebears deposited swords. Even if they did not know in detail what others in their vicinity did with a ceremonial version of it (which is possible as these were rare items), they are likely to have acted out of a general understanding of how to act when it came to placing swords in the land. It is well possible that a self-organized system[6] of deposition, based on principles of association and dissociation of things, and things and places, could end up with the same 'solution' for treating a rare ceremonial weapon in both England and the Netherlands. The point that the 'rare item' in both regions was the same, may even have been trivial to the outcome.

Citing Ball (2004, 36), in a reversal of a well-known environmentalist phrase, people primarily thought locally, but this finally amounted to acting globally.

Many different practices, one relational logic?

Selective deposition is about associating and dissociating things and places. Both in Oxborough and Ommerschans, local communities had a number of conventions (emergent from individual actions) when it came to depositing metalwork in general and swords in particular. Having a special ceremonial sword, they either may have judged it right to follow such conventions or not. As such, depositional practices had a *relational logic*.

By its very nature, selective deposition implies there is a relational logic behind depositional practices *beyond* cultural idiosyncrasies. It relates to existing depositional conventions, and there may be different ways in which it does so. This is an important point, as it allows us to discuss the broad variety of depositional practices across Europe as a whole in generic terms, separate from local idiosyncrasies. In what follows, I will describe a number of ways in which depositional practices can be selective, derived from empirical studies. In one case, an affiliation network will be used to visualize selectivity and associations. Network science can be an efficient tool for coming to terms with relational data (Brandes et al. 2013; Brughmans 2010).

Conventions and convention-breakers

Around 2000 BC, in Pile, southwest Sweden, a large hoard was deposited in a wetland. It consisted of a heterogeneous assemblage of regionally produced axes of Værsleve type and things imported from the east German Únětice region, including numerous axes and daggers (Vandkilde 2017). Over 700 km away, in the centre of what is now the Netherlands, probably a few generations earlier, local communities also deposited a lavish hoard containing a halberd, axe, dagger, rings and what probably was scrap metal in Wageningen. This time it happened in a dry landscape, close to a barrow group (Butler 1990, 68–71; Fontijn 2002, 72–73; Visser forthcoming). Do the events in Pile and Wageningen have anything in common? At first sight, they do not. The contents of both are different, they were carried out in different kinds of landscapes and by people who did not have structural trade or exchange connections with each other. They are not even contemporaneous. However, Visser (forthcoming) recently made an interesting observation. In both cases, things which normally were kept separate in depositions were deposited together. In the Netherlands, flat axes, daggers and halberds are known. Yet, they are usually found as single depositions (cf. Fontijn 2002, 73). The same is true for Únětice imports on the one hand, and regional axes of Værsleve type in the region around Pile. In both regions, there appear to be conventions in depositional practices which had the effect of keeping certain things separate. But where there are conventions, there can sometimes also be special occasions where conventions were broken. The Pile and Wageningen cases are the exceptions where different valuables were deposited together. If we visualize the associations of such things in depositions in a region as an affiliation network, such exceptions stand out as connectors between separate systems (which is why Visser (forthcoming) speaks of 'connector hoards'). Even though they differ completely in content, nature and date, Pile and Wageningen both represent comparable sorts of actions in relation to dominant depositional behaviour.

Identifying such events can be the start of interpretation of depositional activities as social events. For example, were such 'convention-breaking' events special moments in the history of communities? Once identified, were such exceptional cases also breaking the conventions when it comes to burial in the landscape? Were they buried at places that had a special significance? Pile, for one, was deposited in a wetland as seems to be conventional in southwest Sweden. However, Vandkilde (2017, 52) points out that there is reason to suppose it was a special wetland in the social landscape which stood in relation to settlements, the sea and important ritual sites. For Wageningen, it is worth noting that it was located close to, but not in barrows (Fontijn 2002, 73). Here, also the rare addition of a stone axe (an heirloom?) to the assemblage adds to its special and unconventional character.

Contrasting foreign and local in depositions

There are indications that emphasizing boundaries between what were considered local and foreign items gained an added significance in the Bronze Age (Sørensen 1987). This may have become more important once Pan-European exchange networks became more and more crucial for the supply of vital metals from the beginning of the second millennium BC onwards (Vandkilde 2016). As copper alloys themselves do not reveal their origin by material properties such as colour to the human eye without scientific research, it is their shape by which their local or foreign origin became evident. In a seminal paper, Sørensen (1987, 94) argued for Late Bronze Age and Early Iron Age hoards from Denmark that there are indications that this tension between (what was perceived as) foreign and local appearances mattered and was played out in depositional practices (ibid.). The 'right way' to deposit bronzes often involved emphasizing contrasts between both.

More recent studies show how ahead of her time Sørensen's study was and found indications from other regions that the foreign–local contrast was a critical factor behind the organization of metalwork deposition. It may apply to any kind of object and could take many forms. For southwest England, for example, Knight (2018, 433) recently argued that in the Late Bronze Age Stogursey hoard it was items with supra-regional or foreign appearance which were deposited intact, whereas regional ones were physically transformed. The same contrast was played out in the northeast Netherlands, but reversed. When deposited together in hoards, imported axes were broken and regional ones kept intact (ibid.; Arnoldussen 2015). Another way to negotiate the foreign–local contrast may have been to keep them separate in depositions. During the Middle Bronze Age in the southern Netherlands, bronze axes were rarely deposited in burials. Yet, the few exceptions to that convention are imported axes from Central Europe. Apparently, a foreign origin could lead to a convention-breaking deposition (Fontijn 2002, 93–95).

These examples all demonstrate that the foreign and local contrast may have been an important axis in organizing selective deposition, but the way in which it was played out in depositional conventions may have differed from region to region.

Small-world effect

Another instance of the foreign–local contrast may come to the fore if we consider depositional acts from different spatial perspectives. An act that seems to break all the conventions regionally may be perfectly normal when seen from a wider, supra-regional perspective. The Middle Bronze Age warrior grave from Drouwen (northeastern Netherlands), containing among others a decorated Sögel sword, razor, a nick-flanged axe and golden rings, is at odds with contemporary depositional practices in barrows and hoards in the region where it was found (Butler

1990, 71–73). Nevertheless, if we zoom out and consider this region together with northern Germany and Jutland, we find many more graves with such equipment (e.g. Vandkilde 1996, 238–241). As a matter of fact, the Drouwen one is actually the most lavish of all in terms of content.

Thus, what is a regional anomaly can be part of a supra-regional pattern of depositional practices. In network science terms, this is known as the 'small-world effect' (e.g. Coward 2010; Newman 2010, 241–243). Many depositional actions that took place in the Bronze Age that seem enigmatic and odd to us from a regional perspective, become easier to understand when studied from a supra-regional perspective (cf. Chapter 5).

Mappa Mundi depositions

The above discusses actions that seem to be one-offs on a small spatial level, but appear to be part of patterned behaviour at a higher spatial scale of analysis. Sometimes, we find assemblages for which the latter does not apply. They display a deliberate concern with 'foreigness' but to the effect that links with many distant places are emphasized, often including ones that are outside regular trade connections of the region in question. Following Needham (2000), the presence of imported British material in Early Bronze Age northwest French graves is an example thereof. He links such assemblages to a theory by Helms (1993, 99), who presented ethnographic examples of long-distance interactions where the aim was not so much to 'engage in exchange *per se*' (Needham 2000, 188), but rather for a community to extend its reach to a 'mythical' world beyond the horizon (ibid.; Helms 1993, 99). Helms (1993, 91–100) terms this 'cosmological acquisition'. If we realize that knowledge of the world in non-modern societies often travels with the things circulating, the deposition of such things is like showing a map of the world – an indication of the wide reach a local community is capable of. Such assemblages have a '*Mappa Mundi*'[7] nature about them: very local things need to be there as well – to emphasize how the local is entwined with the exotic. The unique composition of the Dutch Ommerschans hoard that this book opened with seems a case in point. Next to an exceptional ceremonial sword of outstanding quality that was not and could not be practically used, it consists of very small tools that were extensively used. However, it also contains a razor of rare Pantalica type – a type known from the Mediterranean (Butler & Bakker 1961, 206–208).

Such actions are a special version of the foreign–local relation that is at stake in depositional action. By definition, they are rare, if not truly one-offs, the only constant being their cosmopolitan content and an emphasis on displaying access to sources within and beyond the horizon of the known world.

Things with high associative potential …

The associative potential of certain things can be much broader than others. In Western Europe, this appears to be the case for axes. In her study of Irish metalwork finds, Becker (2013) observed that in Ireland, axes are the objects that occur

38 Selective deposition

in the largest variety of contexts (though not in burials). Something similar can be seen in Needham's data for deposited metalwork from the British Early Bronze Age (Needham 1989, esp. table 2). Visualized as an affiliation network, his point becomes even more clear (Figure 2.4). Axes allow for several combinations with other things. The range of objects that are associated with halberds, however, is much more limited; they appear peripheral to the network even though 45 of them are known (compared to 997 axes; Needham 1989, table 1).

A class of their own …

Conversely, there may also be things that are viewed as standing out to such an extent that they may preclude associations with other kinds of things. This is the case for Early Bronze Age golden *lunulae*, which in most Northwest European regions are usually only known as single finds. By exception, they are associated with other *lunulae* (Eogan 1994, app.). Whilst *lunulae* are rare, but still transcultural objects, this is not true for items like the Danish scimitars (Vandkilde 1996, 231–232). In shape, appearance and decoration these lack visual links to other metalwork items and may be called 'unique'. In deposition, they are only

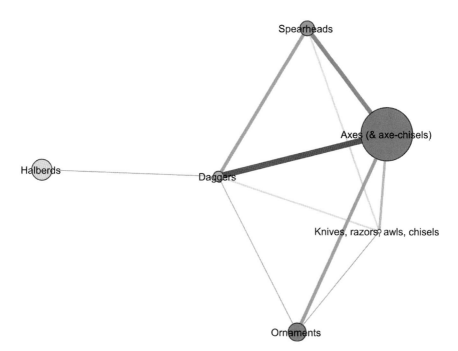

FIGURE 2.4 Single affiliation network depicting the frequency of associations between different objects in graves and hoards in the British Early Bronze Age, based on Needham 1989, table 2 (uncertain associations left out)

Source: Drawing by Erik Kroon, Faculty of Archaeology, University of Leiden.

associated with each other (they appear as twins in the Rørby hoard), not with any other kind of object. Sørensen (1987) recognized that 'unique' things had a clear effect on depositional actions in Late Bronze Age and Early Iron Age Denmark. As such things need not literally be unique, I prefer to speak of things that are considered 'a class of their own'. There may be several reasons why things are understood as such – the things in question could be considered as at odds with conventional appearances or styles to such an extent that it was thought inappropriate to associate them with other, more regular items. Ceremonial items of the highest order, for example, could fall into such categories. Helms (1993, 46–51) argues that skilled crafting in itself results in creating distance from more worldly things, and depositing such things separately may be another instance of expressing such a distance. The same, however, may also hold true for things that are ambiguous in meaning. Whatever the reasons (and there may be many), the effect is similar: the objects remain isolated in depositional practices.

Conclusion

This chapter narrowed down the archaeological scope for a study of selective deposition. Practices in which people buried things in the earth may involve many selections. Not all of them, however, will be easily identifiable in the archaeological record. The focus in this book is on those practices with a double exclusivity (an association between a particular kind of thing and a particular place). These are studied from depositional patterns that are not the result of taphonomical processes or substantial research biases. This comes down to open-minded research that includes all depositional contexts that are usually studied in isolation (graves, hoards, settlements, single finds, etc.), avoiding as much as possible *a priori* assumptions on the significance of certain contexts.[8] It was argued that what we study is 'average' behaviour. This is an emergent property of many individual actions and therefore cannot be reduced to one single motivation. Rather, selective deposition reflects preferences on what is called here 'the right way to act'. As it goes back to a relational logic, it is argued that behind the bewildering variety of depositional practices in the European Bronze Age, there may be similar principles. There are indications that in different cultures, the same issues were played out during depositional acts (such as emphasizing local and foreign items in terms of difference or similarity). This leaves us with the question: what does it tell us about prehistoric social behaviour when deposition practices had such selective traits? This will be the topic of the next chapter.

Notes

1 The spearhead case is a real one. At Rhenen-Remmerden (NL) one was found in the fill of the post of a Middle Bronze Age longhouse (Van Hoof & Meurkens 2005, 66–68).
2 It should be mentioned that Stjernquist (1965/1966) may have been one of the first who tried to focus on the study of practices over categorizations.
3 This is a plea for an open-minded evidence-based approach to what Bronze Age communities themselves considered relevant. This is not an easy task and there is no claim the

present book reached such a goal. Problems may also arise in other categorizations we use. In the example mentioned here, I refer to 'a river' as being a relevant landscape zone for Bronze Age people. Chapter 7, however, will argue that it is not that easy to make out what it was in a 'river' that made people select it for depositional practices. See for further elaborations on this Autenrieth forthcoming; Powell forthcoming.
4 See Brück forthcoming for convincing examples of more heterogeneous ones which also include other materials than metal from the British and Irish Bronze Age.
5 Ball 2004, 36.
6 For the concept of self-organized phenomena see e.g. Centola & Baronchelli 2015; Løvschal & Holst 2018; Sugden 1989.
7 This term is adopted with kind permission from Brück forthcoming, though it is given a slightly different meaning here.
8 For a similar point: Becker 2013; Brück 1999.

Bibliography

Arnoldussen, S., 2015. Something near, something far: the referencing of local and supra-regional origins in Middle- and Late Bronze Age hoards from the northern Netherlands, in: *Forging identities. The mobility of culture in Bronze Age Europe. Volume 2* (British Archaeological Reports International Series 2771), eds P. Suchowska-Ducke, S.S. Reiter and H. Vandkilde. Oxford: Archaeopress, 17–27.

Autenrieth, S., forthcoming. *The emergence of metalwork deposition in the German-French-Dutch Rhine area, c. 2300–1500 BC.* Leiden: Sidestone Press.

Ball, Ph., 2004. *Critical mass. How one thing leads to another.* London: Arrow Books.

Becker, K., 2013. Transforming identities: new approaches to Bronze Age deposition in Ireland, *Proceedings of the Prehistoric Society* 79, 225–263.

Bloch, M., 1995. Questions not to ask of Malagasy carvings, in: *Interpreting archaeology. Finding meaning in the past*, eds I. Hodder, M. Shanks, A. Alexandri, V. Buchli, J. Carman, J. Last and G. Lucas. London: Routledge, 212–215.

Bourdieu, P. 1977. *Outline of a theory of practice.* Cambridge: Cambridge University Press.

Bradley, R. and D. Ford, 2004. A long distance connection in the Bronze Age: joining fragments from a Ewart Park sword from two sites in England, in: *From megaliths to metal: essays in honour of George Eogan*, eds H. Roche, E. Grogan, J. Bradley, J. Coles and B. Raftery. Oxford: Oxbow Books, 174–177.

Brandes, U., G. Robins, A. McCranie and S. Wasserman, 2013. What is network science? *Network Science* 1, 1–15.

Bray, P.J. and A.M. Pollard, 2012. A new interpretative approach to the chemistry of copper-alloy objects: source, recycling and technology, *Antiquity* 86(333), 853–867.

Brück, J., 1999. Ritual and rationality: some problems of interpretation in European archaeology, *European journal of Archaeology* 2, 313–344.

Brück, J., 2004. Material metaphors: the relational construction of identity in Early Bronze Age burials in Ireland and Britain, *Journal of Social Archaeology* 4, 7–33.

Brück, J., forthcoming. *Personifying prehistory. Relational ontologies in Bronze Age Britain and Ireland.* Oxford: Oxford University Press.

Brück, J. and D.R. Fontijn, 2013. The myth of the Chief: prestige goods, power and personhood in the European Bronze Age, in: *The Oxford handbook of the European Bronze Age*, eds A. Harding and H. Fokkens. Oxford: Oxford University Press, 193–211.

Brughmans, T., 2010. Connecting the dots: towards archaeological network analysis, *Oxford Journal of Archaeology* 29(3), 277–303.

Buchmann, M., 2001. Emergent properties, in: *International encyclopedia of the social and behavioral sciences*, eds N.J. Smelser and P.B. Baltes. Amsterdam: Elsevier Science, 4424–4428.

Butler, J.J., 1990. Bronze Age metal and amber in the Netherlands (I), *Palaeohistoria* 32, 47–110.

Butler, J.J., 1995/1996. Bronze Age metal and amber in the Netherlands (II:1). Catalogue of the flat axes, flanged axes and stopridge axes, *Palaeohistoria* 37/38, 159–243.

Butler, J.J. and J.A. Bakker, 1961. A forgotten Middle Bronze Age hoard with a Sicilian razor from Ommerschans (Overijssel), *Helinium* I, 193–210.

Centola, D. and A. Baronchelli, 2015. The spontaneous emergence of conventions: an experimental study of cultural evolution, *PNAS* 112(17), 1989–1994.

Chapman, J., 2000. *Fragmentation in archaeology. People, places and broken objects in the prehistory of South Eastern Europe*. New York: Routledge.

Coward, F., 2010. Small worlds, material culture and ancient Near Eastern social networks, *Proceedings of the British Academy* 158, 453–484.

Durkheim, E., 1951 [1897]. *The suicide: a study in sociology*. New York: Free Press.

Eogan, G., 1994. *The accomplished art. Gold and gold-working in Britain and Ireland during the Bronze Age*. Oxford: Oxbow Books.

Fontijn, D.R., 2002. Sacrificial landscapes. Cultural biographies of persons, objects and 'natural' places in the Bronze Age of the southern Netherlands, c. 2300–2600 BC, *Analecta Praehistorica Leidensia* 33/34, 1–392.

Fontijn, D.R., 2013. Cultural biographies and itineraries of things – second thoughts, in: *Mobility, meaning and transformation of things: shifting contexts of material culture through time and space*, eds H.P. Hahn and H. Weiss. Oxford: Oxbow Books, 183–195.

Fontijn, D.R., R. Jansen, S. Van der Vaart, H. Fokkens and I.M. Van Wijk, 2013. Conclusion: the seventh mound of seven mounds – long-term history of the Zevenbergen barrow, in: *Transformation through destruction. A monumental and extraordinary Early Iron Age Hallstatt C barrow from the ritual landscape of Oss-Zevenbergen*, eds D.R. Fontijn, S.van der Vaart and R.Jansen. Leiden: Sidestone Press, 281–316.

Garrow, D., 2012. Odd deposits and average practice: a critical history of the concept of structured deposition, *Archaeological Dialogues* 19(2), 85–115.

Hahn, H.P., 2015. Dinge sind Fragmente und Assemblagen, in: *Biography of objects. Aspekte eines kulturhistorischen Konzept* (Morphomata 31), eds D. Bosschung, P.-A. Kreuz and T. Kienlin. Paderborn: W. Fink Verlag, 11–33.

Hahn, H.P. and H. Weiss, 2013. Introduction: biographies, travels and itineraries of things, in: *Mobility, meaning and transformation of things: shifting contexts of material culture through time and space*, eds H.P. Hahn and H. Weiss. Oxford: Oxbow books, 1–14.

Hänsel, A. and B. Hänsel (eds), 1997. *Gaben an die Götter* (Seminar zur Ur- und Frühgeschichte der Freien Universität). Berlin: Museum für Vor- und Frühgeschichte.

Helms, M.W., 1993. *Craft and the kingly ideal: art, trade, and power*. Austin: University of Texas Press.

Junk, M., R. Krause and E. Pernicka, 2001. Ösenringbarren and the classical Ösenring copper, in: *Patina. Essays presented to J.J. Butler on the occasion of his 80th birthday*, eds W.H. Metz, B.L. van Beek and H. Steegstra. Groningen and Amsterdam: privately published by Metz, Van Beek & Steegstra, 353–366.

Knight, M., 2018. The intentional destruction and deposition of Bronze Age metalwork in South West England. Unpublished Ph.D. thesis, Exeter University.

Kok, M.S.M., 2008. The homecoming of religious practice. An analysis of offering sites in the wet low-lying parts of the landscape in the Oer-IJ area (2500 BC–AD 450). Unpublished Ph.D. thesis, University of Amsterdam.

Kopytoff, I., 1986. The cultural biography of things: commoditisation as process, in: *The social life of things*, ed. A. Appadurai. Cambridge: Cambridge University Press, 64–91.

Lambek, M., 2008. Value and virtue, *Anthropological Theory* 8(2), 133–157.

Louwe Kooijmans, L.P. and M. Nokkert, 2001. Sporen en structuren, in: *Een kampplaats uit het Laat-Mesolithicum en het begin van de Swifterbant-cultuur (5500–4450 v. Chr.)* (Rapportage Archeologische Monumentenzorg 88), ed. L.P. Louwe Kooijmans. Amersfoort: Rijksdienst voor Cultureel Erfgoed, 75–115.

Løvschal, M. and M.K. Holst, 2018. Governing martial traditions: post-conflict ritual sites in Iron Age Northern Europe (200 BC–AD 200), *Journal of Anthropological Archaeology* 50, 27–39.

Needham, S., 1989. Selective deposition in the British Early Bronze Age, *World Archaeology* 20, 229–248.

Needham, S., 1990. Middle Bronze Age ceremonial weapons: new finds from Oxborough, Norfolk and Essex/Kent (with a contribution from D. Hook), *The Antiquaries Journal* LXX-II, 239–252.

Needham, S., 2000. Power pulses across a cultural divide: cosmologically driven acquisition between Armorica and Wessex, *Proceedings of the Prehistoric Society* 66, 151–207.

Needham, S., 2001. When expediency broaches ritual intention: the flow of metal between systemic and buried domains, *Journal of the Royal Anthropological Institute incorporating Man* 7, 275–298.

Needham, S., 2007. Bronze makes a Bronze Age? Considering the systemics of Bronze Age metal use and the implications of the selective depositions, in: *Beyond Stonehenge: essays on the Bronze Age in honour of Colin Burgess*, eds C. Burgess, P. Topping and F. Lynch. Oxford: Oxbow Books, 278–287.

Needham, S. and C. Burgess, 1980. The Later Bronze Age in the Lower Thames valley: the metalwork evidence, in: *Settlement and society in the British Later Bronze Age*, eds J. Barrett and R. Bradley (British Archaeological Reports British Series 83), Oxford: Oxford University Press, 437–469.

Newman, M.E.J., 2010. *Networks. An introduction*. Oxford: Oxford University Press.

Pare, C.F.E., 1991. *Swords and wagon graves of the Early Iron Age in Central Europe* (Monograph 35). Oxford: Oxford University Committee for Archaeology.

Powell, L., forthcoming. *The emergence of metalwork deposition, c. 2300–1500 BC in South England and Northwest France*. Leiden: Sidestone Press.

Roymans, N. and F. Kortlang, 1999. Urnfield symbolism, ancestors, and the land in the Lower Rhine region, in: *Land and ancestors. Cultural dynamics in the Urnfield period and the Middle Ages in the southern Netherlands* (Amsterdam Archaeological Studies 4), eds F. Theuws and N. Roymans. Amsterdam: Amsterdam University Press, 33–61.

Sørensen, M.L.S., 1987. Material order and cultural classification: the role of bronze objects in the transition from Bronze Age to Iron Age in Scandinavia, in: *The archaeology of contextual meanings* (New Directions in Archaeology), ed. I. Hodder. Cambridge: Cambridge University Press, 90–101.

Sørensen, M.L.S., 2015. 'Paradigm lost': on the state of typology within archaeological theory, in: *Paradigm found. Archaeological theory present, past and future*, eds K. Kristiansen, L. Šmejda and J. Turek. Oxford: Oxbow Books, 84–94.

Soroceanu, T., 1995. Die Fundumstände bronzezeitlicher Deponierungen. Ein Beitrag zur Hortdeutung beiderseits der Karpaten, in: *Bronzefunde aus Rumänien* (Prähistorische Archäologie in Südosteuropa 10), ed. T. Soroceanu. Berlin: Spiess Verlag, 15–80.

Stjernquist, B., 1965/1966. Models of commercial diffusion in prehistoric times, *Scripta Minora regiae societatis humaniorum litterarum lundensis* 2.

Sugden, R., 1989. Spontaneous order. *Journal of Economical Perspectives* 3(4), 85–97.

Torbrügge, W., 1970/1971. Vor- und Frühgeschichtliche Flussfunde. Zur Ordnung und Bestimmung einer Denkmälergruppe, *Berichte der Römisch Germanischen Kommission* 51/52, 1–146.

Van der Vaart-Verschoof, S., 2017. *Fragmenting the chieftain. A practice-based study of Early Iron Age Hallstatt C elite burials in the Low Countries* (PALMA 15). Leiden: Sidestone Press.

Vandkilde, H., 1996. *From stone to bronze: the metalwork of the Late Neolithic and Earliest Bronze Age in Denmark* (Jutland Archaeological Society Publications XXXII). Aarhus: Aarhus University Press.

Vandkilde, H., 2014. Breakthrough of the Nordic Bronze Age: transcultural warriorhood and a Carpathian crossroad in the sixteenth century BC, *European Journal of Archaeology* 17 (4), 602–633.

Vandkilde, H., 2016. Bronzization: the Bronze Age as pre-modern globalization, *Prähistorische Zeitschrift* 91(1), 103–123.

Vandkilde, H., 2017. *The metal hoard from Pile in Scania, Sweden. Place, things, time, metals, and worlds around 2000 BC*. Aarhus: Aarhus University Press.

Van Hoof, L.G.L. and L. Meurkens (eds), 2005. Vluchtige huisplattegronden. Erven uit de midden-bronstijd B en nederzettingssporen uit de vroege bronstijd en midden-bronstijd A, *Archol-rapport* 51.

Van Wijk, I.M., H. Fokkens, D. Fontijn, R. de Leeuwe, L. Meurkens, A. van Hilst and C. Vermeeren, 2009. 'Resultaten van het definitieve onderzoek', in: Het grafveld Oss-Zevenbergen. Een prehistorisch grafveld ontleed, *Archol-rapport* 50, 69–139.

Visser, M., forthcoming. *Patterns and practices. The emergence of metalwork deposition in the Netherlands, c. 2300–1500 BC, in North Germany and Jutland*. Leiden: Sidestone Press.

Von Brunn, W.A., 1959. *Die Hortfunde der frühen Bronzezeit aus Sachsen-Anhalt, Sachsen und Thüringen*. Berlin: Akademie Verlag.

Wiseman, R., 2017. Random accumulation and breaking: the formation of Bronze Age scrap hoards in England and Wales, *Journal of Archaeological Science* 90, 39–49.

3

THE VALUE CONUNDRUM

What common things and splendid items share and why their deposition is selective

The introductory chapter argues that the puzzling, selective treatment of metalwork in depositional practices comes from their nature as social valuables. But what does it mean to say something has value? This chapter deals with that question and argues that, contrary to what is usually expected, it is not just insignia of special social or religious statuses that were deposited in such an ordered way. Confusingly, the same is true for many common, commodified items like metal 'currency'. Following the theory of the anthropologist Graeber, I will argue that this is because 'value-as-price' and 'cultural values' are actually variations of the same principle and are conceptually linked. This leads to a discussion that is crucial for this book: how did depositional practices affect perceptions of permanency and circulation?

Introduction

The German Nebra hoard ranks among the most special Bronze Age finds ever discovered in Europe. It consists of a unique bronze-with-gold-inlay disc depicting the night sky, interpreted as a lunar-solar calendar that must have been of great social and ceremonial significance (Meller 2013). It was accompanied by two full-hilted swords, two spiral bracelets, two flanged axes and a chisel – all of bronze – dated around 1600 cal. BC (ibid.; Figure 3.1). Comparable sets, but without the disc, are known from graves in Saxony-Anhalt during the previous centuries, where they were reserved for exceptional occasions, like high status burials beneath monumental mounds (Meller 2004). It is widely agreed that the hoard of Nebra refers to special *socio-religious values*, and that Nebra and earlier assemblages show such a restricted and selective composition for this reason.

Let us now contrast what happened in Nebra with the numerous metalwork hoards of so-called Ösenringe in the northern circum-Alpine regions (south Germany to the Czech Republic) in the first centuries of the second millennium BC

(Pare 2013, 513). These consist of large quantities (often in excess of 100) of similarly looking rings, reminiscent of neck rings (Lenerz-de Wilde 1995, 236). They stand out, not only for their similarity in shape, but also in weight (Lenerz-de Wilde 1995; see Chapter 5). In the circum-Alpine regions, metal depositions display clear selections (Lenerz-de Wilde 1995, 236). Most hoards just consist of dozens of rings and nothing else (Figure 3.2). Contemporary items such as Salez axes were also deposited in large numbers but rarely in association with these rings (Krause 1988 in Vandkilde 2005, figure 5). The explanation is that these rings were exchange items – 'currency' or 'primitive money' (Pare 2013; Primas 1997; Shennan 1993; 1999) – and that their set weight and shape indicates *a specific exchange value*.

Both Nebra and *Ösenringe* are interpreted as assemblages that had 'value', yet they seem to denote and imply very different things. Saying that the items in the Nebra hoard were valuables evokes notions of religion and circumscribed social status; saying that Ösenringe had value refers to a role they supposedly fulfilled in exchange and trade as items of conversion. Whereas the first refers to *cultural qualities*, the latter refers to *economic quantities* (cf. Lambek 2008). A focus on hoards like Nebra makes us consider the Bronze Age as a world that was decisively different from ours; in which religious thought pervaded notions on social order. However, a focus on the ring hoards may evoke a sense of economicity that is more familiar

FIGURE 3.0 Sites mentioned in this chapter: 1. Ommerschans; 2. Grembergen; 3. Nebra; 4. München-Luitpoldpark; 5. Inowrocław.
Source: Drawing by J. Porck, Faculty of Archaeology, University of Leiden.

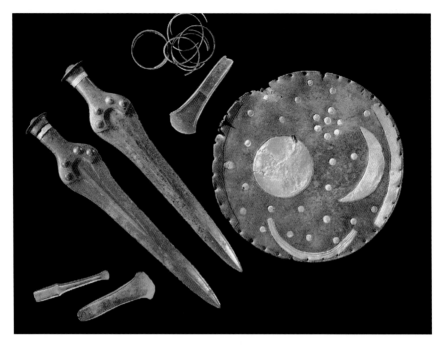

FIGURE 3.1 The Nebra hoard
Source: Photograph by Juraj Lipták, Landesamt für Denkmalpflege und Archäologie Sachsen-Anhalt (State Office for Heritage Management and Archaeology Saxony-Anhalt).

to us and seems in contrast to the 'religiosity' evoked by the Nebra find. How is it possible that we use the same term 'value' in both cases to refer to things that seem so different?

This conundrum is not unique to the Bronze Age – it is a central problem of economic anthropology as a whole and the topic of decades-long debate (Graeber 2005). The ambiguity of the word 'value', referring to both short- and long-term spheres of exchange (Chapter 1), also applies to related terms like 'price' and 'worth' (German: *Wert*; Bazelmans 1998). An additional intriguing point is that the term 'value' is not only used for what seem to be very different concepts (social-religious values as qualities vs. value as quantification) but also to explain why both 'religious' hoards like Nebra *and* 'economic' hoards like those with rings *are both displaying such a strict ordering*. In the first case, because things as cultural valuables are thought to represent important ritual and social meanings which should be maintained by restrictive, selective use. In the second case, because as 'currency' Ösenringe can only represent widely accepted exchange value if they exclude an 'anything-goes' logic. Following the seminal line of thought in the work of Graeber (2001; 2005), I therefore address the same question on these different sorts of value as he did (2005, 439): '*What would it mean to say these are all, ultimately, versions of the same?*'[1]

FIGURE 3.2 *Ösenringe* hoard of München-Luitpoldpark, Archäologische Staatssammlung, Munich
Source: Photograph by M. Kuijpers.

The significance of things and the distinction between alienable and inalienable things

A first step to clarifying this value conundrum is to state that we are not dealing with an abstract concept. Graeber notes that when it comes to value, we tend to have 'things' in mind. 'Importance is always realised through some kind of material token' (Graeber 2005, 451). This seems a relevant point for our case, where we came to discuss notions of 'value' because prehistoric people buried valuable *things* in the landscape. Graeber's term 'token', however, seems inappropriate here, for there are reasons to suggest that things, being both material and visual, do more than merely symbolize something.

For a society to function, Searle (1995) argues, it needs institutional facts: concepts that are socially recognized and capable of being trans-generationally transmitted. These need not necessarily be understood in the same way by everybody, but they have to be 'externally stored': 'anchored' and 'made real' (Renfrew 2001, 95). Renfrew (2001, 97–99) argues that in non-literate societies (like the ones under study here) it is particularly *objects* that make mental concepts real. The notion of weight, for example, is inconceivable without the experience of weighing (ibid., 97). Likewise, he suggests 'it is difficult to conceive "value" without having experience of valuables – that is to say of things to which value may be described' (ibid., 99). So, things not only make concepts concrete and socially effective (Strathern 1999, 15–16), but it is the material world which can make something thinkable in the first place (cf. Olsen 2010). As Durkheim already argued, 'the social fact is sometimes so far materialized as to become an element of the external world' (Durkheim 1951, 313–314 cited in Olsen 2010, 6).

For example: in the Bronze Age, a local community must have had concepts of a broader social world that was perceived as an extension of or linked to local society. That people from different regions used similar valuables (like for example *Ösenringe*) in their exchange transactions may have helped to make such a broader social world *conceivable*. The association in the Nebra hoard of high quality swords deposited together with an object depicting the night sky, might have helped to make it *thinkable* that martiality and leadership were social values that rooted in cosmological notions (cf. Meller 2013).

How significant materiality and visuality was becomes clear from the fact that what we call valuables in shape refer to other things (so-called 'inter-object citation'; Sørensen 2015, 89; Chapter 2). In the Bronze Age, this sometimes leads to absurd enlargements of normal objects like axes or dirks. The Ommerschans ceremonial sword introduced in Chapter 1 (Figure 1.1) is not just some giant sword. It has a very specific shape, carefully crafted to visually refer in all its finer details to a very small group of other ceremonial swords (Butler & Sarfatij 1970–1971). Hansen (2001, 152) refers to a gold version of an Early Bronze Age dagger in Inowrocław (Poland), indicating that both visuality (looking like a dagger) and materiality (gold instead of bronze) mattered to people. That the materiality of 'valuables' was important may also be inferred from the fact that so much of the Bronze Age metal deposited had long histories of use (i.e. evidencing interaction with humans; Fontijn 2002, 212; Knight 2018, 433). Thus, things were effective in their own right and gained value through interaction with humans (Garrow & Gosden 2012, 25; Kopytoff 1986).

A second step is to realize that saying something has 'value' is a statement on how, within a particular practice, the relation between things and persons, or between things and other things emerges and enfolds (cf. Graeber 2001, 45; Gregory 2015).

At a very young age, humans learn to distinguish between persons and things (Hodder 2012, 23), yet at the same time in our encounters with the world, there are things that humans perceive as more linked to persons (or broader, person-derived concepts like society) and those that are less so and more related to other things. This is a vital distinction, for it steers human practices to an important degree. In order for any human society to exist, there needs to be a balance between the way in which people alienate things from the world they live in, and the extent to which they carve out something of their environment that endures (Durkheim 1915 in Kopytoff 1986, 73; Chapter 1). The first is about alienation and things that are alienable. The second is about things one tends to keep, which resist alienation and are therefore inalienable (Godelier 1999; Weiner 1992). These include notions vital to the durability of a given human society in the face of a world that is 'always subject to loss and decay' (Weiner 1992, 7), like notions of social constitution, morals, religion and 'culture' in its broadest sense. However, in a world where all things are inalienably linked to such concepts, nothing can change (Bloch & Parry 1989). But the opposite, a world in which everything is alienable, cannot endure either, as in such a world the social cannot endure and there would be no culture (ibid.). Therefore, in every society alienable things and inalienable things should co-exist, and there need to be procedures to convert alienable to inalienable and vice versa (ibid.). Against the economicity of the world of alienable goods, there is the religiosity and sociality of the inalienable. Next to a short-term notion of value as quantifiable and alienable 'price', there needs to be a long-term notion of values as inalienable cultural qualities (Graeber 2005; Lambek 2008; Chapter 1).

Why inalienable things require specific treatment

Let us now get to the question why the special (selective) treatment of things indicates that they held 'value' to those who deposited them. This seems easiest to understand when the deposited things have taken on a special nature – when they are inalienably linked to persons, identities or to more abstract ideals linked to the social whole (cf. the case of the Nebra hoard mentioned above). Such things are not like any other thing and in some way or another seen as meaningful and to have a certain singularity (Kopytoff 1986, 70), for which people feel they need to be set apart or can only be treated in a particular way (Rowlands 1993, 147). Just as is the case with living persons, there are restrictions and social conventions as to what one can do with personified things (Mauss 1993; Weiner 1992).

As a modern example of how the commensurability of persons and things steers depositional behaviour, think of how difficult it can be to throw away clothes from a beloved one who has passed away. We know they are just clothes, but unlike generic old clothes, if we were to throw them away it would feel like we were rudely throwing out our beloved one with the garbage. We tend to keep these clothes for a much longer time than we would do with normal clothes, or treat them in a special way (for example, pass them on to a relative who had a special relationship to the deceased).

The above mentioned clothes example is about regular things taking on added significance due to a link with a specific individual. In a second modern example, I consider a thing that is by definition not individualized, but integrally linked to the performance of social, representative roles. An appointment as mayor of a town in the Netherlands implies that the one holding that office wears a ceremonial chain during official occasions. In a way, the chain *is* the office and by wearing it an individual *is* the mayor. Unlike the old clothes mentioned before, the chain is not associated with a specific individual but with some supra-personal overarching collective ('the town'), and by wearing the chain the individual temporarily is that collective. Because of this, there are also strict conventions on what to do with the chain, and especially what not to do. It is for example out of the question that someone who was mayor in life is buried wearing that chain. It is by definition a collective possession, inalienably linked to 'the town'. What is generally felt to be the 'appropriate' or 'right' treatment of this chain of office strongly resists permanent identification with one specific individual (as when it enters a coffin and stays there). When the term of office expires, it has to return to the town and be worn by the new mayor.

In both cases, we see that things are treated in restricted ways because they are considered linked to persons or broader social concepts (there is shared feeling on what is 'the right way to act', cf. Kopytoff 1986; Chapter 2). This treatment leads to a certain resistance to alienation: our loved one's clothes are not disposed of like other old clothes (exchangeable with them) and the mayor's chain of office is prevented from association with one particular individual. At the same time, *we also see that it is the very way of treating the thing once its use is considered over that affects its status as an inalienable thing*.

Disposing of the clothes of a deceased loved one may involve special actions on part of the relatives involved. It has to 'feel good' to them. For example, there has to be an appropriate new owner (a family friend or charity), or the disposal has to involve some procedures that comfort those directly involved (cf. Depner (2013), who studied comparable actions when old people move to their final home and have to dispose of treasured possessions). When this is not taken care of properly, it can be a painful process for the mourners. When the disposal of these clothes is done in 'the right way', they may lose their painful association with the beloved one (doing this can even be part of the conclusion of mourning).

If the chain of office is taken up by the new mayor, the institution of mayorhood is restored. If it ends up around the neck of a deceased mayor at a burial, it disappears from society and becomes linked with one specific individual, throwing doubt on the entire system of collective leadership by temporary representatives.

Summing up, we see that things which are linked to persons or social collectives have a certain singularity. If we apply this to the case of the Nebra hoard, we are clearly dealing with the deposition of objects that were already considered singular before deposition, as they referred to overarching, social and religious values like martial leadership (the swords) and notions of the constitution of the cosmos (the disc). Meller (2004) also refers to the idea of objects being like persons, as he argues that the composition of this hoard is highly comparable to that of chiefly graves from previous periods, and suggests that the sky disc itself might have taken the place of the body of a chief here. Allegedly, the sky disc was standing upright in the ground 'and formed a backdrop to the swords and axes which lay across each other' (Meller 2013, 266), reminding us of a human body as it was placed in an Early Bronze Age chiefly tomb.

Thus, it may be relatively easy to understand why objects that were already considered imbued with inalienable values required a selective treatment upon deposition. It is more difficult to comprehend, though, why the same selectivity also applied to things that seem to be more imbued with alienable value.

Why alienable things require special treatment as well

Rethinking the consequences of what was said above, we are confronted with a considerable problem: how are we to explain patterns in depositions of things that are not singular but common? Does the meaningful deposition of social valuables stand *against the meaningless deposition of things stripped of any link to the social or cultural?* Few would argue that the mass deposition of Ösenringe and axes in the Early Bronze Age, or of sickles and fragmented metal in the Middle and Late Bronze Age (Chapter 5) were social 'valuables' akin to the special insignia deposited in hoards like the Nebra one. It seems more apt to qualify them as commodities – common rather than singular things; items linked to or commensurable with other things rather than persons (Gregory 2015, 74–78). Yet, as we have seen above, the deposition of such items also appears to follow certain conventions (Chapter 5). Why is that?

Let us return to things that function as social-religious valuables, things that are inalienably linked to persons, identities or important cultural notions. For a thing to be such a special valuable, it needs to be set apart and made 'non-common'. As argued before, singularization is a means to this end (Kopytoff 1986, 70). According to Graeber (2001, 94), an object can become singular by conveying a distinct history which gives it a special identity which links it to people. Alternatively, there should also be things one can safely alienate – recast and exchange for other things – without directly imbuing them with personal relations or social ideals. Kopytoff (1986, 70) argues that to make things more common is an effective strategy to ease such alienation. The more there is of something, the less special it becomes and the harder it is to link it to 'persons'. Making things visually and materially refer to other things, is another. As Graeber (2001, 94) argues, valuables are 'ranked according to their relative abilities to convey history'. The most singular ones are at the top, and the most generic ones at the bottom (ibid.). The reason why mass-produced identical things can so effectively serve as commodities does not solely lie in their large numbers, but also in the fact that they are identical or standardized – i.e., visually they refer to each other.

With this notion of object appearance we arrive at an important point: that things are alienable does not imply one can do anything with them. Converting or exchanging one thing for another is based on conventions that are socially recognized (Appadurai 1986, 6–16). Bloch and Parry (1989, 16) argue that in non-monetary societies, exchange takes place in separate spheres that are ranked. In each sphere, specific things can only be exchanged against other things. There are clear notions of which things are appropriate to each sphere and which are not (there is a 'right way of acting'; cf. Chapter 2).

Also, not everything can be a commodity; being perceived as a thing with 'commodity potential' is grounded on social agreement; it is an 'institutional reality' (Searle 1995; cf. Appadurai 1986, 13–14). Modern paper money – the ultimate example of a powerful commodity – is a case in point. As Searle (1995, 41–42; also Bloch 2012, 113–114) argues, the acquisitive power of money is purely based on the social recognition that paper money is convertible in an equivalence of other things. The fact that paper money lacks any intrinsic value shows that all parties involved recognize that money derives its acquisitive value from social agreement and shared understanding (Searle 1995, 41–42). Yet, it can only function as such a commodity *because it has a rigidly defined appearance and follows very strict rules of treatment*. Although paper money is purely symbolic, half a ten euro note does not equal five euro. The convention is that it is worth nothing at all. Even though British pounds and euro notes have acquisitive power separately, one cannot not mix them in one transaction. So for things to have acquisitive power as commodities, there also are rules and conventions regarding appearance and how to treat them. This seems to match with items we think fulfilled such roles in the Bronze Age.

Metal can theoretically circulate in any form. What we see in mass depositions of common things like the *Ösenringe* hoards in the North Alpine zone is that *only items with specific shapes and appearances occur* (Chapter 5). Because the perception of things as alienable is based on social recognition, there have to be conventions regarding their appearance and treatment as well. So, even though *Ösenringe* may not be social valuables in the sense that the special items in the Nebra hoard are, we should not be surprised that such rings were selectively treated in the circum-Alpine regions – even if they represent 'payments' or trade stock. This will be the starting point for the discussion on the deposition of 'trade stock' in Chapter 5.

What alienable and inalienable things share and how they are linked

Although alienable and inalienable things are perceived differently, both are constituted in a social context and thus subject to conventions on how they should look and how they are to be treated (Gregory 2015). Both have a social effect: inalienable things evoke links with persons, identities or socio-religious values, whereas alienable things primarily evoke links with other things (Figure 3.3). The former entails cultural qualification, the latter material quantification (Gregory 2015; Lambek 2008). Ultimately, both refer to permanent imaginary notions, an overarching system of meaning, in order to achieve this (Godelier 1999, 28–29, 106, 138, 166; Graeber 2005). Both go back to some imaginary system 'that defines the world in terms of what is important, meaningful, desirable, worthwhile in it' (Graeber 2005, 439). According to Godelier, these are the things that ought to be permanent and define cultural and social identity (1999).

Such a reference to an overarching system of meaning is perhaps easiest conceivable for inalienable things. When these circulate – as gifts – they are not only substitutes for persons, but also for essential, sacred things one keeps (Godelier 1999). These can be perceived as embodied by 'sacred' things, but can also be more abstract cultural ideals. Weiner (1992, 7) argues that every society strives to 'secure permanence' in an ever-changing world. This notion of 'keeping' can be quite literal when it comes to 'sacred things' or *sacra* (Godelier 1999, 59–62). In the

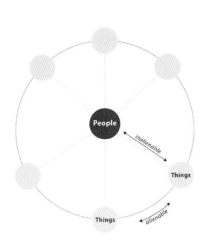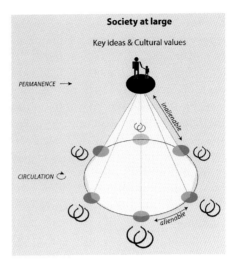

FIGURE 3.3 Schematized presentation of how things can be alienated from persons by conversion into other things, but within a more encompassing cultural framework where such things are always linked to higher ideals and values of society in question through reference with inalienable things and notions
Source: Drawing by J. Porck, Faculty of Archaeology, University of Leiden.

potlatch of Northwest Coast native Americans (the Kwakiutl), there are valuable coppers that circulate which are seen as satellites of very rare, and ultimately sacred coppers that communities try to keep (Godelier 1999, 59). The latter are strongly personified and can have sacred status. Though they do not circulate themselves, they are thought to 'attract' more regular coppers (Mauss 1993, 45). If we follow Meller's (2004) point that the objects accompanying the Nebra sky disc are characteristic for chiefly graves, then the sky disc might have been regarded as equivalent to a high-ranking person. Whereas the sky disc seems to be unique, an interesting point about the potlatch coppers is that those in circulation are comparable in appearance to the highly special one the community keeps, albeit that the latter is of much higher quality – appearances matter (Godelier 1999, 163). This is relevant as it reminds us that negotiating similarity (and differentiation!) in appearance is an important aspect of Bronze Age metalwork (cf. Sørensen 1987; Chapter 2). I mentioned an example with the group of Ommerschans ceremonial swords that mimic each other in the finest details.

However, things made to function as alienable items also refer to an overarching, permanent 'totality'. Money, a commodity par excellence even in our secular times, tends to be decorated with symbols of national identity or religion (like the 'In God We Trust' on American one-dollar bills) (cf. Hart 2005, 170–171).

In the Bronze Age, there are indications that for things to function as commodities, a reference to cultural valuables was important. Theoretically, metal as commodity can have any form, as it can literally be converted by melting it down

(Simmel 2011, 163). What we see in the evidence, however, is that commodities apparently had to have a specific shape and appearance in order to function as such ('the right appearance'; cf. Chapter 2). The Early Bronze Age *Ősenringe* are generally interpreted as exchange items ('currency'). Their appearance evokes the shape of neck rings which were initially valuables of special personal identities, worn on the body and known from graves (Vandkilde 2005, 271–272). The earliest *Ősenringe* were ornaments themselves, and it is only later that they came to have a specialized role as exchange item (Pare 2013, 513). By its appearance, an important commodity refers to an important cultural valuable.

Throughout the entire Bronze Age, we see that metal was exchanged in the form of items having the appearance of specific tools, like axes or sickles (cf. Lenerz-de Wilde 1995; Sommerfeld 1994; see also Chapter 5). To stick with the axe example: the fact that such exchange items specifically mimic axes is significant. Axes appear to have had important social and ritual meaning, as can be deduced for example from the fact that they appear in rare, aggrandized a-functional versions (Hansen 2001). An example is the extravagant, drawn-out Early Bronze Age bronze axe from the river Scheldt near Grembergen (Figure 3.4; Warmenbol 1992, 77–78). Like with the *Ősenringe*, 'currency' axes may have been made with an eye for conversion to other things (facilitated by standardized size and weight). They apparently can only function as such if they also indirectly refer to a broader whole of cultural values (by mimicking the appearance of important social valuables). This role of axes will be explored further in Chapter 5.

Even when fragmented metal circulated as commodity, there are indications that a thing refers to a larger system of meaning, when its exchange is organized on the basis of units of standardized weight (Pare 2013, 520–502). After all, the system only works if all communities involved recognize this weight standard as the right one, implying they shared an overall, abstract system of thought on this. Intriguingly, evidence of early systems of quantification worldwide shows that such systems are often intricately linked to cosmology (Renfrew & Morley 2010). In her study of Late Bronze Age weight systems in the Aegean, Michailidou (2010, 72), for example, remarks that in ancient Egyptian and Greek society, metrological systems were considered to have a divine or mythical origin. Although this requires more research, both Warmenbol (2010) and Kristiansen and Larsson (2005) noted that Bronze Age metalwork in European regions beyond the Aegean was often deposited in specific numbers (namely two, nine and twelve) which they consider to be rooted in broader cosmological notions (cf. also Holst 2015).

So, although singular key socio-cultural insignia like the things in the Nebra hoard and the numerous commodities in Ősenringe deposits around the Alps seem to be each other's opposites, they actually share a fundamental aspect. In both cases prehistoric people made sense of their actions by envisioning it 'as part of some larger whole' (Graeber 2005, 451). Things may be alienable and disconnected from people, but ultimately this takes place in a broader institutional framework set by culture, *where alienable commodities in the end always refer to or are linked with inalienable things and ideas and values* (Figure 3.3; Godelier 1999). Again,

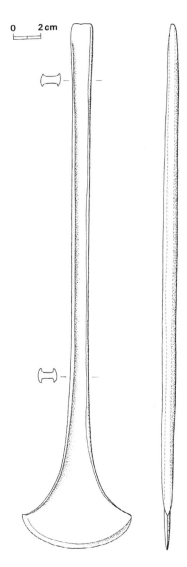

FIGURE 3.4 Elongated bronze axe found in the river Scheldt, Grembergen (Belgium)
Source: From Warmenbol 1992, figure 36.

we see that short- and long-term transactional spheres are always linked (Bloch & Parry 1989; Chapter 1).

Graeber's theory: value as practice

According to Graeber, value is the 'way people's own action become meaningful to them' (.) 'by becoming incorporated into some larger system of meaning' (2005, 453). This may be obvious for insignia of social status (cf. the Nebra hoard with its explicit cosmological references). Commodities may not directly refer to such higher cultural values. They can only function as such provided there is an indirect link to these higher values (such as *Ösenringe* mimicking specific neck rings, see above).

Following Graeber's definition of value, the 'importance' of how one sees one's actions must be comparative (2005, 451). Expressing actions in terms of similarity or difference to each other is crucial. There is a careful balance between the degree to which actions express *sameness with* and *contrast to*.

Aggrandized ceremonial swords of the Ommerschans type are rare but not unique. The six examples now known in Europe appear to have been crafted as '*über*-swords' that closely mimic each other (Fontijn & Amkreutz 2018). They also refer to normal swords by their appearance. However, they are much better made ('virtuoso' crafting; cf. Kuijpers 2018, 264; Figure 3.5), have an exaggerated size and their thinness precludes normal use. They are an other-worldly version of regular swords which occur in much larger numbers (Fontijn 2001). The contrast thus created with regular swords indicates that comparison mattered, but the intention was to have both kinds of swords circulating in different spheres. We see the same concern to 'distance' and 'refer to' normal versions in another item that was mentioned before: the 'overstretched' version of the Early Bronze Age axe that

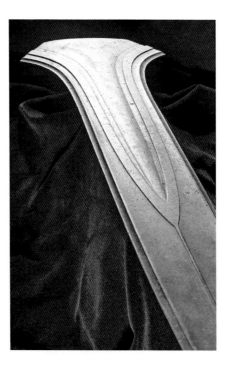

FIGURE 3.5 Detail of sword of Ommerschans, showing its high quality casting
Source: Photo copyright National Museum of Antiquities, Leiden (RMO).

was deposited in the river Scheldt near Grembergen (Figure 3.4; Warmenbol 1992, 77–78).

Next to regular *Ösenringe* that occur in large numbers and have standardized form and weight, there are also singular versions of such rings. These have an exaggerated weight (Lenerz-de Wilde 1995, 243, 255–256, 259, 262). Again, in shape they refer to normal *Ösenringe*, but these are rare, extravagant versions thereof (Figure 3.6). In a pan-European survey, Hansen (2001) argues that such exaggerated versions appear in many parts of Europe during the earlier Bronze Age. They seem to have been essential to how metalwork functioned in exchange.

These examples may remind us of the above mentioned distinction Godelier (1999, 59) recognized for copper shields in the potlatch of the Northwest Native American population. The regular coppers that circulate are seen as 'satellites' of a much smaller group of 'sacred' coppers that were retained. The latter look like those in circulation, but are much better made, abstract (idealized) forms of normal coppers. These '*sacra*' are considered as persons themselves and treated as such (ibid.). Like the potlatch *sacra*, the aggrandized Bronze Age swords, axes and ornaments can be seen as idealized and abstracted versions of normal ones.

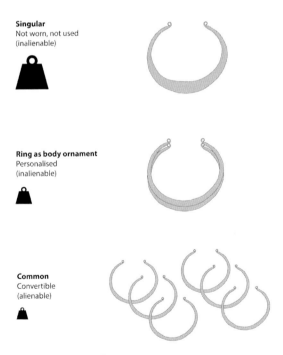

FIGURE 3.6 Model showing how *Ösenringe* as common exchange items refer to neck ornaments as valuables of social status that are worn, and to rare versions with excessive weight

Source: Drawing by J. Porck, Faculty of Archaeology, University of Leiden.

Comparative aspects are again played out with regular *Ösenringe* but now the aim is not to let things stand out, but rather express their sameness. Giving each ring a similar appearance and similar weight creates these rings as a separate class. However, their manufacture does not require exceptional crafting skills. Also, they appear in large numbers in hoards. Manufacture and deposition emphasize that these rings are 'common' things that function in an exchange sphere of their own (cf. Kopytoff 1986, 70). This brings us to an important element of Graeber's theory of value. Value is not an inherent property, but something that is realized in *human practices* (2001, 45). How people crafted things, and what they did with them accordingly, is essential. As Lambek (2008, 133) puts it, 'value is function of acts rather than simply of objects'.

Deposition – the paradox of total alienation and ultimate inalienability

The act of burying objects in the landscape, particularly when these are never to be taken out again, has a special, even paradoxical relation to the entire process of managing value classes described above. This becomes clear when we perceive it from different perspectives: the effect it has on the community involved (human–human relations), on the way in which the people involved relate to the things deposited and things that remain there (human–thing relations), and finally on relations between the community and some imagined (supra-natural) whole whom they perceive to benefit from it.

Human–human relations

When people bury a range of bronze objects in the landscape, from a short-term perspective (Chapter 1), this counts as total alienation. Things – and recyclable material – are removed from human grip in such a way that they can never re-enter the social domain again. From a perspective which only includes living human beings, it is alienation without a human receiver, without an equivalent return, and therewith is tantamount to destruction (Chapter 1).

Human–thing relations

However, if we look at the burial of things from the perspective of relations between humans and things the situation is different. The act of removal alters that relation. First of all, this is because the total amount of comparable things in the community decreases, effectively making deposition an act which creates scarcity, or, phrased *sensu* Kopytoff (1986, 73–77), enhances the singularity of equivalent things still around (Rowlands 1980, 46). Alienation thus makes things still more singular, potentially enhancing their inalienability. Second, destroying things in a performance may also be a way to impress on the onlookers that which is essential. I will explore this point more fully in Chapter 8.

Human–supernatural

But suppose that deposition was seen as a way of giving itself – to gods, ancestors, or more abstract entities thought to be part of the long-term sphere of society (cf. Dumont 1977; Sykes 2009, 159)? As shown before, many depositional acts were interpreted as offerings. Even though we cannot get into people's minds, let us for the sake of the argument suppose this is what people believed depositions to be. How does this alter the picture sketched so far? First of all: it should be realized that if it was a gift, it was a special one. As Mauss emphasized (1993, 8–14), giving comes with the obligation to reciprocate. Mauss (1993, 16) argued that in many non-modern societies spirits of the dead and gods are the true owners of the things and possessions of this world. But as Godelier (1999, 30) took pains to stress, this means that humans are at a disadvantage from the outset, and their gift almost by definition must be small when compared to the counter-gift from the gods and spirits. It also implies people are giving something to gods and spirits that was theirs anyway. Second, unlike human-to-human gift exchange, the thing given no longer circulates – it remains where it is. It is for this reason that offering or sacrifice is permanent – it is 'giving for keeping' (Godelier 1999, 36). As Godelier (1999, 30) states, 'to sacrifice is to give by destroying what is given'. The notion of destruction can be quite literate: the thing itself could be transformed (practically terminating its use life) and/or placed in the landscape in such a way it remains irretrievable for people (e.g. by being thrown in a lake or river). As we have seen, both were common in Bronze Age depositional practices. Therefore, sacrificing to a supernatural being transforms things circulating in life into things permanently kept by these supernatural beings.

If we consider an act of sacrifice from a purely social perspective, another difference between sacrifice and gift exchange between people becomes apparent: with human–supernatural gift exchange, it remains unclear what the counter-gift from the supernatural is. Giving to a greater good therefore may primarily have been conceived of as a moral act: one gave up something because one felt one should. This recalls the notion of moral acts as opposed to those in a political economy (Chapter 1).

As to the counter-gift – it is up to humans to believe whether the good harvest or the success in warfare really comes from the gods or not. Therefore, gifts to 'gods' are open to human interpretation and potentially prone to political manipulation in a way that regular gifts are not, so they are unlike personal gift exchange. Political actions, however, cannot steer the nature of the practice. Dumont (1977) argues that spheres of value are hierarchically ordered, with the most encompassing one at top. Overarching notions on the constitution of the social whole (long-term 'values') are therefore ultimately more important than a political sphere aimed at individual acquisition and maximization (short-term 'value').

At any rate: adding in the human–supernatural or moral perspective resolves the paradox of inalienability by alienation (also: Küchler 1997, 42). Seen from this perspective, all alienable things were linked to higher-order notions from the start:

they were perceived as inalienable possessions of gods or spirits from the very beginning. Permanently removing them from society – as happens in many depositions – then, does not so much work to make them inalienable (from a religious perspective they already were inalienable). It rather imposes 'a sacred character on the prohibition of its alienation' (Godelier 1999, 45).

Summing up

The fact that Bronze Age metalwork was deposited in such a selective way is often seen as indicating that the things buried in the landscape were important social or religious valuables. This chapter, however, argues that more common things, like metal currency, also required social conventions and selections. Following theories from economic anthropology, it is set out why cultural values and value as price are closely linked. Both refer to a broader system of meaning, but in different ways. As something that is produced in practice (Graeber 2001; 2005), how objects were shaped and treated appears to be crucial. Aggrandized, 'other-worldly' versions of regular items indicate that Bronze Age value classes were inextricably linked to each other. The chapter closes by theorizing how deposition may affect the alienable or inalienable status of things and thus their value. The next chapters apply these ideas to empirical cases.

Note

1 Graeber (2005, 439) also mentions value as signifying 'meaningful difference'. I leave this out of the present discussion.

Bibliography

Appadurai, A., 1986. Introduction: commodities and the politics of value, in: *The social life of things. Commodities in cultural perspective*, ed. A. Appadurai. Cambridge: Cambridge University Press, 3–63.

Bazelmans, J., 1998. Geschenken en waren in premodern Europa: enkele gedachten over de waarde van kostbaarheden uit schatvondsten, *LEIDschrift* 13(3), 59–78.

Bloch, M., 2012. *Anthropology and the cognitive challenge*. Cambridge: Cambridge University Press.

Bloch, M. and J. Parry, 1989. Introduction: money and the morality of exchange, in: *Money and the morality of exchange*, eds J. Parry and M. Bloch. Cambridge: Cambridge University Press, 1–31.

Butler, J.J. and H. Sarfatij, 1970/1971. Another bronze ceremonial sword by the Plougrescant-Ommerschans smith, *Berichten van de Rijksdienst voor het Oudheidkundig Bodemonderzoek* 20–21, 301–309.

Depner, A., 2013. Worthless things? On the difference between devaluing and sorting out things, in: *Mobility, meaning and transformation of things: shifting contexts of material culture through time and space*, eds H.P. Hahn and H. Weiss. Oxford: Oxbow Books, 78–90.

Dumont, L., 1977. *From Mandeville to Marx. The genesis and triumph of economic ideology*. Chicago: University of Chicago Press.

Durkheim, E., 1951 [1897]. *The suicide: a study in sociology*. New York: Free Press.
Fontijn, D.R., 2001. Rethinking ceremonial dirks of the Plougrescant-Ommerschans type. Some thoughts on the structure of metalwork exchange, in: *Patina. Essays presented to Jay Jordan Butler on the occasion of his 80th birthday*, eds W.H. Metz, B.L. van Beek and H. Steegstra. Groningen and Amsterdam: privately published by Metz, Van Beek & Steegstra, 263–280.
Fontijn, D.R., 2002. Sacrificial landscapes. Cultural biographies of persons, objects and 'natural' places in the Bronze Age of the southern Netherlands, c. 2300–2600 BC, *Analecta Praehistorica Leidensia* 33/34, 1–392.
Fontijn, D.R. and L. Amkreutz, 2018. Het verzonken zwaard van Ommerschans, in: *Wereldgeschiedenis van Nederland*, eds L. Heerma van Voss, M. 't Hart, K. Davids, K. Fatah-Black, L. Lucassen and J. Touwen. Amsterdam: Ambo/Anthos, 39–43.
Garrow, D. and Ch. Gosden, 2012. *Technologies of enchantment? Exploring Celtic art: 400 BC to AD 100*. Oxford: Oxford University Press.
Godelier, M., 1999. *The enigma of the gift*. Cambridge and Oxford: Polity Press.
Graeber, D., 2001. *Toward an anthropological theory of value: the false coin of our own dreams*. New York: Palgrave.
Graeber, D., 2005. Value: anthropological theory of value, in: *A handbook of economic anthropology*, ed. J.G. Carrier. Cheltenham and Northampton MA: Edward Elgar, 439–454.
Gregory, C.A., 2015 [1982]. *Gifts and commodities*. Chicago: Hau Books.
Hansen, S., 2001. 'Überaustattungen' in Gräbern und Horten der Frühbronzezeit, in: *Vom Endneolithikum zur Frühbronzezeit: Muster sozialen Wandels?* (Universitätsforschungen zur prähistorischen Archäologie, 90), ed. J. Müller. Bonn: Habelt Verlag, 151–174.
Hart, K., 2005. Money: one anthropologist's view, in: *A handbook of economic anthropology*, ed. J.G. Carrier. Cheltenham and Northampton MA: Edward Elgar, 160–175.
Hodder, I., 2012. *Entangled. An archaeology of the relationships between humans and things*. Chichester: Wiley-Blackwell.
Holst, M.K., 2015. Bronze Age geometry and cosmology, in: *Skelhøj and the Bronze Age barrows of southern Scandinavia, Vol. 2* (Jutland Archaeological Society Publications vol. 89), eds M.K. Holst and M. Rasmussen. Højberg: Aarhus University Press, 51–89.
Knight, M., 2018. The intentional destruction and deposition of Bronze Age metalwork in South West England. Unpublished Ph.D. thesis, Exeter University.
Kopytoff, I., 1986. The cultural biography of things: commoditisation as process, in: *The social life of things*, ed. A. Appadurai. Cambridge: Cambridge University Press, 64–91.
Kristiansen, K. and T.B. Larsson, 2005. *The rise of Bronze Age society. Travels, transmissions and transformations*. Cambridge: Cambridge University Press.
Küchler, S., 1997. Sacrificial economy and its objects, *Journal of Material Culture* 2, 39–60.
Kuijpers, M.H.G., 2018. *An archaeology of skill. Metalworking skill and material specialization in Early Bronze Age Central Europe*. London and New York: Routledge.
Lambek, M., 2008. Value and virtue, *Anthropological Theory* 8(2), 133–157.
Lenerz-de Wilde, M., 1995. Prämonetäre Zahlungsmittel in der Kupfer- und Bronzezeit Mitteleuropas, *Fundberichte aus Baden-Württemberg* 20, 229–327.
Mauss, M., 1993 [1923/1924]. *The gift. The form and reason for exchange in archaic societies*. London: Routledge.
Meller, H., 2004. 'Der Körper des Königs', in: *Der geschmiedete Himmel. Die weite Welt im Herzen Europas vor 3600 Jahren*, ed. H. Meller. Stuttgart: Konrad Theiss Verlag, 94–97.
Meller, H., 2013. The Sky Disc of Nebra, in *Handbook of the European Bronze Age*, eds H. Fokkens and A. Harding. Oxford: Oxford University Press, 266–269.
Michailidou, A., 2010. Measuring by weight in the Late Bronze Age Aegean: the people behind the measuring tools, in: *The archaeology of measurements. Comprehending heaven, earth and time in ancient societies*. Cambridge: Cambridge University Press, 71–87.

Olsen, B., 2010. *In defense of things. Archaeology and the ontology of objects*. Lanham MD: AltaMira Press.
Pare, C., 2013. Weighing commodification and money, in: *The Oxford handbook of the European Bronze Age*, eds H. Fokkens and A. Harding. Oxford: Oxford University Press, 508–527.
Primas, M., 1997. Bronze Age economy and ideology: Central Europe in focus, *Journal of European Archaeology* 5(1), 115–130.
Renfrew, C., 2001. Commodification and institution in group-oriented and individualizing societies, in: *The origin of human social institutions* (Proceedings of the British Academy), ed. W.G. Runciman. Oxford: Oxford University Press, 93–117.
Renfrew, C. and I. Morley, 2010. Introduction: Measure: towards the construction of our world, in: *The archaeology of measurement. Comprehending heaven, earth and time in ancient societies*, eds I. Morley and C. Renfrew. Cambridge: Cambridge University Press, 1–4.
Rowlands, M.J., 1980. Kinship, alliance and exchange in the European Bronze Age, in: *Settlement and society in the British Later Bronze Age* (British Archaeological Reports 83), eds J.C. Barrett and R.J. Bradley. Oxford: Archaeopress, 15–55.
Rowlands, M.J., 1993. The role of memory in the transmission of culture, *World Archaeology* 25, 141–151.
Searle, J.R., 1995. *The construction of social reality*. New York: Free Press.
Shennan, S., 1993. Commodities, transactions and growth in the Central European Early Bronze Age, *Journal of European Archaeology* 1(2), 59–72.
Shennan, S., 1999. Cost, benefit and value in the organization of early European copper production, *Antiquity* 73(280), 352–363.
Simmel, G., 2011 [1900]. *The philosophy of money*. London: Routledge.
Sommerfeld, Ch., 1994. *Gerätegeld Sichel. Studien zur monetären Struktur bronzezeitlicher Horte im nördlichen Mitteleuropa* (Vorgeschichtliche Forschungen 19). Berlin: De Gruyter.
Sørensen, M.L.S., 1987. Material order and cultural classification: the role of bronze objects in the transition from Bronze Age to Iron Age in Scandinavia, in: *The archaeology of contextual meanings* (New directions in archaeology), ed. I. Hodder. Cambridge: Cambridge University Press, 90–101.
Sørensen, M.L.S., 2015. 'Paradigm lost': on the state of typology within archaeological theory, in: *Paradigm found. Archaeological theory present, past and future*, eds K. Kristiansen, L. Šmejda and J. Turek. Oxford: Oxbow Books, 84–94.
Strathern, M., 1999. *Property, substance and effect. Anthropological essays on persons and things*. London and New Brunswick NJ: Athlone Press.
Sykes, K., 2009. *Arguing with anthropology. An introduction to critical theories of the gift*. London and New York: Routledge.
Vandkilde, H., 2005. A biographical perspective on Ösenringe from the Early Bronze Age, in: *Die Dinge als Zeichen: Kulturelles Wissen und materieller Kultur* (Universitätsforschungen zur prähistorischen Archäologie 127), ed. T. Kienlin. Bonn: Habelt Verlag, 263–281.
Warmenbol, E., 1992. Le matériel de l'âge du bronze: le seau de la drague et le casque du héros, in: *La collection Edouard Bernays. Néolithique et âge du bronze, époque gallo-romaine et médiévale*, eds E. Warmenbol, Y. Cabuy, V. Hurt and N. Cauwe. Brussels: Musées Royaux d'Art et d'Histoire, 67–122.
Warmenbol, E., 2010. Drowning by numbers: nine lives, twelve deaths in the Bronze Age, in: *Der Griff nach den Sternen. Internationales Symposium in Halle (Saale), 16–21 Februar 2005*. (Tagungen des Museum für Vorgeschichte Halle 5 (I)), eds H. Meller and F. Bertemes. Stuttgart: Landesmuseum für Vorgeschichte Halle/Konrad Theiss Verlag, 563–576.
Weiner, A.B., 1992. *Inalienable possessions: the paradox of keeping-while-giving*, Berkeley CA, Los Angeles CA and Oxford: University of California Press.

4

PRE-BRONZE AGE SELECTIVE DEPOSITION

Was the selective deposition of valuables practised before the Bronze Age? This chapter considers this question by discussing examples of pre-Bronze Age depositional practices in Europe, both of societies with and without metal. It appears that permanently placing things in the landscape was an important social practice already thousands of years before the advent of the Bronze Age. It is argued that it served as a way to re-contextualize valuables that came from afar and as such often became selective in nature. I argue it was a way to create and manage value(s) by depositing valuables, displaying a logic that is time- and culture-transgressive and not unique to metal-using societies.

During the transition from the Late Neolithic to the Early Bronze Age, bronze almost completely replaced other materials in depositions. Bronze objects became dominant: selective deposition contrasts one kind of bronze objects to other ones. One may speak of a system of valuables that is to a great extent 'metallized' (i.e. dominated by metal ones; cf. Kristiansen & Earle 2015). It is in this context that metalwork deposition usually starts to have the specific selective tendencies that are the focus of this book such. First, this is its double exclusivity (specific objects were preferably deposited in specific contexts only). A second feature is that some of these selective preferences were shared at a supra-regional level and had a trans-cultural nature (for example: the tendency to keep gold *lunulae* and bronze halberds out of burials, or the preference to deposit swords in rivers, cf. Chapters 1 and 2). This raises two related questions: was *the kind of* selective deposition known from the Bronze Age a new phenomenon? And if so, is the specific selective nature of Bronze Age deposition linked to the *metallization* of this practice?

In the previous Chapter, I argued that it is to be expected that in prehistoric societies, value as a concept was constituted by objects (Renfrew 2001, 99). It was also explained why the selective treatment of things during deposition relates to the role valuables played in a broader system of value. Graeber (2005, 451) argues that value is referential and comparative. This is an important point for the present book, because a system of valuables dominated by metal may have had a different dynamic than one in which non-metals were crucial. As a material, bronze (or copper, silver or tin) lacks material clues as to provenance visible with the naked eye (unlike stone; Chapter 2). Its capacity to evoke 'value' is very much shape-based (and therewith in the hands of the craftsperson who makes it; cf. Kuijpers 2018). Also, metal introduces a new dynamic to the way valuables related to and could be converted into each other. After all, re-melting and recasting now made it possible to transform a high-order valuable to low-order ones without leaving any trace (Fontijn 2002, 76; Hansen 2011, 138; O'Brien 2014, 271; Simmel 2011, 163). This adds a new tension to the management of value.

This chapter attempts to establish whether Bronze Age selective deposition was a truly new way of dealing with valuables. In the following I consider different examples of pre-Bronze Age systems of deposition in Europe to establish whether these also were (in some way) *selective* in the same way as those from the Bronze Age were.

First, three examples of deposition practices involving stone valuables are discussed to establish whether a deposition system of non-metal valuables can also be selective. Following this, deposition practices in the copper and gold-based system of the eastern European Copper Age are summarized, in order to establish whether it was bronze that made the Bronze Age system selective, rather than just generic metal. Then, I discuss Funnel Beaker (TRB) communities as an example of a pre-Bronze Age case in which both stone and metal valuables featured in deposition practices.

The social fabric of Europe was dramatically altered by the disruptive changes that took place in the third millennium BC. I therefore end by discussing whether the Bronze Age deposition practices were a revival of Neolithic and Copper Age ones, or an entirely new way of dealing with valuables that only emerged out of these third millennium BC social changes.

Late Mesolithic and Neolithic Europe – the west, c. 5600–beginning of the fourth millennium BC

The deposition of stone adzes in Early Neolithic LBK society

Around 5600 BC, Neolithic communities of the so-called Starčevo Culture started to settle in an area previously outside the reach of farming communities: the west Hungarian plain. This area around Lake Balaton saw the formation of a new Neolithic culture that would profoundly change the history of Europe: the Linear Pottery or *Bandkeramik* culture (LBK) (Bánffy & Oros 2010). Firmly rooted in the Neolithic legacy of southeastern Europe, a culture emerged that hallmarked the adaptation to the different (colder and more humid) climatic conditions of temperate Europe (Louwe Kooijmans 2017, 403–404). It came to have a highly distinctive material culture and remarkably uniform cultural practices, linked to its southern legacy, but unique in other ways. LBK communities spread across Europe at an unprecedented rate (Whittle 1996, 146–150). Within 200 years, LBK farming settlements could be found as far west as the Paris Basin and as far east as Moldavia. In most newly settled regions, they were the first farmers (Louwe Kooijmans 2017, 408–409).

For this case study I will focus on the deposition of amphibolite adzes. These played an important part in LBK life. They were tools with which wood was worked and houses were built, but they also must have been held in high social regard. In many parts of the LBK world, they are found in graves of older males and interpreted as signalling important social statuses (Louwe Kooijmans 2017, 447–448). Much like metal millennia later, this stone is not locally available in large parts of Europe where LBK communities lived. Its provenance should be sought in north Bohemia (ibid., 440). Amphibolite adzes were therefore an important item in long-distance exchanges. They are known to have travelled across distances of 800 kilometres (ibid., 440). Adzes ended up in a variety of contexts, ranging from pits alongside houses, burials, but sometimes also in hoards associated with other adzes, stone tools or raw materials (Jeunesse 1998; Raemaekers et al. 2011; Quitta 1955; 1969; Verhart 2012). Imported adzes may have been social valuables. However, this generally did not result in such adzes being deposited in specific kinds of location only; depositional practices were 'fuzzy' rather than selective (Chapman 2000, 114; cf. Figure 2.1, system A rather than B). Yet, there are indications that in some depositional acts, specific adzes and axes were kept apart.

As Jeunesse (1998, 33) and Raemaekers et al. (2011, 15) have argued, objects in hoards are different from those in graves and settlements in that they are larger. When find circumstances allow, there are sometimes also indications that their deposition followed special conventions. This was for example the case at Stein-Berg aan de Maas (NL), where seven adzes were deposited (Bakels & Hendrix 1999). They were placed in a pit, which was situated at a prominent location in the landscape, close to the sharp edge of a terrace overlooking the Meuse valley. The five items that could be researched were all made out of the foreign amphibolite, the sources of which lay 800 kilometres to the east. The adzes are the tallest examples found here, and also the flatter specimens are remarkably large (ibid.). Bakels and Hendrix (1999) argue it was clearly only the blades that were deposited here. Unlike most hoards in Central and Eastern Europe (Jeunesse 1998, 36), there is no evidence that this hoard was located in a settlement, although there may have been one in the vicinity. It is more likely that it was buried at a special, conspicuous location in the landscape at the edge of the inhabited LBK world (there are no LBK settlements on the other side of the river Meuse here). This case may remind us of depositional practices described in Chapter 3 for the Bronze Age: rare, aggrandized versions that in shape refer to regular valuables, were set apart in depositions and left in the earth following specific conventions. Although this requires more in-depth research, Quitta's (1955) and Jeunesse's (1998) inventories of dozens of hoard finds from the LBK and its immediate Danubian successors suggest that the Stein hoard may be part of a larger pattern. Quitta (1955, 57) also notes that particularly along the west and northern edges of the swath of land inhabited by the LBK and their successors, there are hoards with stone tools that seem to be situated beyond settlements. The impression is that this particularly is a feature of later Danubian groups (cf. Jeunesse 1998, 36). Like Stein, the items in stone adze and axe hoards can have a special ordering, such as for example the Wolliner hoard where four tools were ordered in a star shape (Quitta 1955, 58).

The LBK was characterized by a strong tendency to uphold ties, leading to intra-group uniformity and conservatism (Sommer 2001; Whittle 1996, 149). This may be a reason why stone adzes were important valuables in many different regional LBK groups. It may also explain why some of the depositional conventions (such as the separate deposition of enlarged versions of tools in hoards) were shared or 'codified' (Hamon 2008) between farming groups.

The deposition of imported stone adzes and axes among early farmers and foragers

The LBK farming communities settled in parts of Europe that had been inhabited by foragers for millennia. The fifth millennium saw an increasing interaction between farmers and foragers, in the end transforming both and shaping the Neolithic cultures of the fourth millennium BC (Louwe Kooijmans 2017, chapter 8). One way in which this interaction is observable archaeologically is in the exchange of items between farming communities and foragers. The same stone tools that circulated among LBK communities and their immediate successors, were also exchanged with foraging communities. These are so-called LBK adzes and particularly axes or wedges (*Breitkeile*) of LBK successors like Rössen Culture (Klassen 2004; Verhart 2012). *Breitkeile* in particular were objects that apparently were capable of transgressing cultural boundaries, *functioning as a valuable both for farmers and foragers*. They may be the oldest items discussed in this book to have traits of a *transcultural object* (for this term: Vandkilde 2014). How were such valuables included in depositional practices?

Just like LBK farmers, contemporary foragers had practices in which things that were important to them were deposited in the landscape. At the early Holocene site of Lundby, Denmark (Hanssen et al. 2004), carefully arranged remains of slaughtered elk were found in a small bog. Apparently, after slaughter, the remains of elk were time and again piled on a heap and placed in the bog. Not only does this imply discard involved special practices (the 'right way of acting', cf. Chapter 2), but it also means the bog was a zone in the landscape that was apparently regarded as important in its own right.

With the introduction of domesticates, the frequency of depositional practices increased (Louwe Kooijmans 2001). Depositional practices among Late Mesolithic and Early Neolithic foragers are best known from Northwest European continental sites in wetlands, especially from Denmark, northern Germany and the Low Countries. These often include a range of mundane things deposited in bogs like pots, tools, or animal bones, the composition of which may vary from site to site

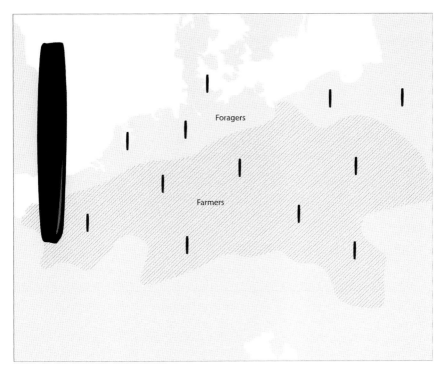

FIGURE 4.1 Area inhabited by early LBK farmers in northern Europe and area inhabited by foragers. Both had the same stone adzes and tools and deposited them in the landscape. Distribution area LBK: based on information in Louwe Kooijmans 2017, 410, shown in simplified form. Adzes symbol is a schematized picture of a generic stone adze.
Source: Drawing by J. Porck, Faculty of Archaeology, University of Leiden.

and was anything but selective (Koch 1998; Figure 2.2). However, from western Poland to the Netherlands, large numbers of stone adzes and axes have also been found in the region occupied by foragers (Amkreutz 2013; Klassen 2004, chapter 2; Raemaekers et al. 2011; Verhart 2012) which were imported from southern farming communities. Although a systematic contextual study is so far lacking, it is interesting to note for regions like Denmark and the Netherlands, that such imports from afar are often found in wetlands, like the pots and animal bones (Karsten 1994, 169; Louwe Kooijmans & Nokkert 2001). However, they are relatively rare in contemporary settlements and graves. When it came to such items from afar, it seems as if most forager groups separated these in depositional practices from other items they considered important.

As described above, stone adzes and axes were also exchanged as valuables among farming communities themselves. Intriguingly, there seems to be a convergence in how both foragers and farmers perceived 'the right ending' for such valuables. Foragers deposited imported 'Neolithic' adzes and axes in wet places, but the same may apply to farmers. As Jeunesse (1998, 32–33) remarked, it is also in regions occupied by farming communities themselves (like in Bavaria or along the river Main in Germany) that single finds of stone adzes and axes and sometimes also hoards are known from wet places like rivers or depressions that once were wet (Jeunesse 1998, 32). This suggests both in farming landscapes and northern foraging ones, that such stone axes were deposited in watery locations. So, when it came to placing exchanged adzes or axes in the ground, *foragers and farmers apparently had comparable ideas on how to position them in the landscape.* This suggests a transcultural valuable was deposited following conventions that were transculturally shared.

Jade Europe: transcultural views on the other-worldly ending of special objects

Above, it was described how in the late 6th and early 5th millennium BC, stone adzes and axes were important, perhaps even transcultural valuables in prehistoric societies inhabiting parts of Europe. There are indications that aggrandized versions of regular adzes were subject to selective depositions in farming groups themselves (cf. the Stein-Berg-aan-de-Maas hoard). There are also hints that their nature as an import from a distant place may have steered a selective treatment in depositional practices (deposition of *Breitkeile* among foragers in northern Europe). Lack of research leaves many uncertainties on this topic and it remains unclear whether deposition of imported adzes and axes really represents a system of selective deposition as in the Bronze Age. More can be said on the deposition of axe heads made of special, restricted Alpine stone sources, in particular jade.

From about 5300 BC, Early Neolithic communities in Italy started using a rare shiny green stone to make adzes and arm rings from, a repertoire familiar to contemporary Neolithic communities elsewhere (Pétrequin et al. 2012a; 2012c, 22; Pétrequin et al. 2013, 68). Towards the end of the sixth millennium BC, they also produced much larger axe heads of this stone, too large to be functional (examples with lengths of 46.6 cm are known; Pétrequin et al. 2013, 69). These non-functional axes in particular started to circulate widely – especially in the second half of the fifth millennium BC. Such axe heads ended up as far east as the coast of the Black Sea, and in Ireland and Scotland in the northwest – travelling over distances in excess of 1,700 kilometres (Pétrequin et al. 2002, 72–73; 2012c, 24).

The emergence of jade exchange added an entirely new dimension to how *things* shaped prehistoric worldviews. While jade was exchanged on a vast scale – similar to the non-local materials discussed above – its use was far more restricted and primarily non-functional. Jade was mined on highly inaccessible and difficult to reach locations in the Italian Alps (Monte Viso and Monte Beigua; Pétrequin et al. 2012c, 23). Like elsewhere in the world, it seems to have been valued for its conspicuous, luminous, shiny colour (Bradley 2017, 112–115). But beyond its inherent properties and special acquisition history, jade's singular character was

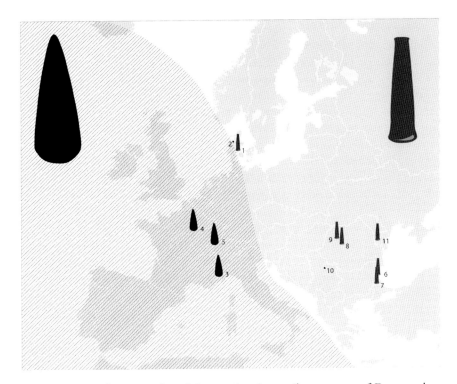

FIGURE 4.2 Part of Europe where jade axes (west) prevail versus part of Europe where copper objects occur (east), simplified after information in Pétrequin et al. 2002, figure 12. Sites mentioned in the text are indicated. 1. Bygholm; 2. Mollerup; 3. Monte Viso; 4. Vendeuil; 5. Ostheim; 6. Durankulak; 7. Varna; 8. Vâlcele; 9. Moigrad; 10. Čoka; 11. Cărbuna. There is an overlap between jade and copper distributions in Denmark. Symbols: schematized drawings of generic objects that give an impression what a jade and copper axe may look like.

Source: Drawing by J. Porck, Faculty of Archaeology, University of Leiden.

enhanced by being crafted into exceptional things. Very long axe heads were made – evoking some idealized, 'not of this world' notion of an axe, rather than a functional tool. The enlarged LBK adzes as in the Stein-Berg-aan-de-Maas hoard already had such traits. With the jade axe heads, however, people went one step further. Jade axe heads were often extensively polished, which worked to amplify and emphasize their material and perhaps other-worldly character even more (Pétrequin et al. 2013, 69–71). They have all the characteristics of the key valuables or *sacra* described by Godelier (1999; see Chapter 3). There is visual referencing to regular items (axes), but at the same time jade axe heads are set apart by visual aggrandizement, a sense of abstraction and contrasting materiality and quality. The Bronze Age examples of exceptionally well-crafted gold daggers or aggrandized swords and axes quality come to mind as comparable (Chapter 3).

By the middle of the fifth millennium BC, Europe must have been a patchwork of different cultural groups, each with their own regional networks of supply and material culture production. It is therefore all the more significant to note that non-functional jade axe heads from the Italian Alps apparently were desired in societies living as far away from each other as Scotland and Italy. As Pétrequin et al. (2002) demonstrate, jade axe heads were the key valuable in western Europe, being rare but important in ceremonial exchanges for people living in all regions of the west – *to a previously unseen extent.*

Jade is important for the present discussion not only because it formed a transcultural valuable in an unprecedented, 'European' way, but also because it is the first thing for which there was an equally transcultural perception of what should be its 'right ending'. Regardless whether one inspects sites in France or east Germany – when something is known on find circumstances, especially from the second half of the fifth millennium BC, it is clear that jade axe heads generally were often deposited away from settlements and graves, which has been argued to be deliberate (Pétrequin et al. 2002, 86; 2013, 73).[1] They tend to be deposited singly, but also occur in pairs (Pétrequin et al. 2012b, figure 13). Jade axes are rarely associated in such contexts with anything other than jade axes (Pétrequin et al. 2012b). There is evidence from remote places that axe heads were ordered in circles, or in a vertical position with their cutting edges up (e.g. at Vendeuil and Ostheim (F); ibid., figure 20). Of those axes with known find contexts, 79 per cent were deposited in a wet environment (ibid., figure 21). There are also examples of intentional destruction by burning or breaking (ibid., 1370). They were buried in conspicuous places, often in marshy areas, at the banks of rivers, springs or near rocks (ibid.). The distancing and singularization (cf. Kopytoff 1986) that marked their production seems to culminate in an equally distanced and other-worldly ending. Crucial is that this singular treatment is not just something observed for adjacent areas in Italy and France, or remote ones like Scotland, but was practised in large parts of 'Jade Europe'. This suggests there was a shared world view, not just on the interpretation of these axe heads as social and ritual valuables, and on how to treat them right, *but also on the places in the landscape where they were allowed to end their life.*

Copper Europe – the east, c. 5000–2900 BC

When jade axes became important valuables everywhere in western Europe, objects made of copper, but also gold and occasionally (somewhat later) silver acquired comparable roles in the east (Hansen 2013). Copper was already won by the sixth millennium BC in the Balkans (O'Brien 2014, 38). In the first centuries of the fifth millennium BC, casting techniques became widespread (Boroffka 2009; Pernicka & Anthony 2010). This meant that, unlike jade, copper and gold had the potential to be worked into a much broader variety of shapes – and this is indeed what happened. Copper was originally in use as one of the materials decorating bodies of the deceased as beads or small rings. For example, this is known from

Lengyel Culture (successor to LBK groups) cemeteries in Hungary, but also from cemeteries like Varna II and Durankulak much further to the south in Bulgaria (Hansen 2013, 139). With the improvement of metalworking techniques, copper and gold were elevated from two of the non-local materials for adornment to materials that facilitated a profusion of new valuables, ranging from tools and weapons to complex social insignia. Case in point is the famous Bulgarian cemetery of Varna, dating to 4600/4300 BC (Slavchev 2010, with further references). In the Varna graves, there are new kinds of objects made of metal, creating distinctions between the deceased with a previously unseen complexity. Copper objects now include shaft-hole axes, and spear or dagger-like items. With the abundant use of gold to adorn bodies, there are novel objects like gold pendants depicting animals, gold sceptres, or discs that were probably attached to garments (cf. Slavchev 2010, figure 9.7: 8–11; Hansen 2013, 141). New metal paraphernalia of personal status were combined with those of other materials, like Spondylus shells, or exceptionally long flint blades (ibid.). Hansen (2013, 143) argues that, although exceptional in its quantity and profusion of gold objects, what is observable in Varna reflects a broader social phenomenon. Pendants like those found in Varna are also known from graves elsewhere, in for example the Carpathian Basin and Slovakia (often in later burials). Such metal objects, but also copper axes, adzes and bracelets are consistently found in a minority of graves. These items are therefore interpreted as insignia of special and restricted (male) statuses (ibid.).

The question arising from these examples of deposition practices in 'Copper Europe' is whether this pre-Bronze Age usage of metalwork for valuables had consequences for the way they were deposited (cf. Taylor 1999). Was there a pre-Bronze Age 'metallization' of depositional practices? First of all: Neolithic communities in eastern Europe already deposited valuable things in settlements and beyond them in considerable quantities. In one of the hoards from Čoka (no. I), thousands of beads made of different materials and other items were buried (Chapman 2000, app.; Raczky 1994). However, comparable to what would happen with the adoption of bronze much later, with the transition to the Copper Age the number of hoards increased (cf. Chapman 2000, app.; Hansen 2013, 145).

Second, metal facilitated the creation of new kinds of valuables. This extended the Neolithic notion to adorn the bodies of deceased individuals to refer to a non-local world (cf. Borić et al. 2013; Chapman 2000, 117). However, key valuables in graves apparently could also 'act' in their own right. One of the fascinating aspect of the Varna cemetery is that it not only contains bodies with artefacts, but also many pits that have the same outline as graves but which lack bodies (Slavchev 2010, figure 9.10). These are generally regarded as cenotaphs, and are quite numerous (47 out of 310; ibid., 198). In these pits, objects have been found that are comparable to those in graves with bodies and in the same position, but without a body. What is relevant for this discussion is that this implies that *objects apparently could represent the concept of a person by themselves*. This suggests these metal objects were regarded as singularized to such an extent that they could only be deposited in a specific, selective way.

The selective treatment of metal valuables in depositions applied to other kinds of objects as well. When placing certain metal objects in the ground, Copper Age communities often consistently preferred certain contexts to the exclusion of others (Hansen 2011, 146). For example, Chapman (2000) argues there is a tendency for specific copper objects to be buried outside of the settlement. These include copper axe-adzes, but also some axe types (Banyabik and cruciform ones) and ornaments like spiral-wire bracelets (Chapman 2000, 119). Hansen (2011, 145–146) shows that copper hammer axes in the fifth millennium BC were deposited in graves along the coast of the Black Sea. However, further to the northwest, in the Carpathian Basin, they were usually *not* given with the dead in graves, but deposited singly or in hoards.

Hansen argues that there are reasons to suppose that there was more to these objects that were buried in the landscape than just a different preference for a place to end their circulation in daily life. For example: the gold pendant deposited in the landscape of Moigrad in the Carpathian Basin in weight equals 200 small pendants that adorn the dead or were buried in settlements elsewhere in southeast Europe (Hansen 2013, 145). He argues that this is also true for copper axes. Those found in hoards or singly in special landscape settings are significantly heavier than the ones found in graves like those of the Varna cemetery (ibid.). This is reminiscent of what happened with stone adzes of the LBK, where it also seems to have been the aggrandized forms that ended up in hoards. Placing oversized axes in the landscape outside graves and settlements was done in the east with ones made of copper, while in contemporary western Europe jade examples were used. This indicates that objects placed in the landscape visually referred to social valuables that figured in daily life, but were by their appearance nonetheless regarded as of a different kind and deposited in a different way.

As a practice, depositing in the land could also stand out by sheer quantity. Hansen (2013, 145) refers to the Cărbuna hoard in Moldavia which contained no fewer than 444 copper objects and 407 items of other materials. In Transylvania, metal is hardly known from other contexts. This suggests the burial of metalwork in the landscape had become a significant and exclusive social practice in its own right, containing evidence of spectacular events like the burial of 43 axes in Vâlcele (Romania; Hansen 2011, 146).

Copper vs. jade

Summing up, in Copper Age East Europe in the 5th and 4th millennium BC metal valuables increasingly came to dominate certain depositional contexts (graves and hoards: 'metallization'). Depositional practices emerged that surpassed Neolithic ones in quantity and frequency. Metal objects now became the main players, and their deposition seems to have been driven by conventions regarding where to deposit certain objects (and where not). There are clear differences between what happened with comparable objects in different regions (cf. axes in graves in the Circum-Pontic region vs. shaft-hole axes in hoards in Transylvania; Hansen 2011, figure 14). This suggests that they primarily reflected regional rather than supra-regional or transcultural conventions.

The circulation of jade in the west and copper in the east is often seen as reflecting two exclusive systems (Pétrequin et al. 2002). Although jade axe heads were occasionally deposited in the east and copper in the west (cf. Bradley 2017, 114), the distributions of jade and copper items indeed barely overlap (cf. Pétrequin et al. 2002). Whereas jade was particularly used to make aggrandized versions of axes, metal was used to make a broad variety of valuables ranging from ornaments to tools and weapons. As such, the jade and copper systems are not comparable. In the east, with the widespread adoption of metalwork a new value system came into being in which different objects could fulfil different social roles. Jade axe heads, however, were mostly imported items from afar that stood out among local and regional axes by their quality, origin and 'other-worldly' nature. However, when these different prehistoric communities decided to deposit such items in the earth, there are interesting similarities (cf. Pétrequin et al. 2002). In both the west and the east, the singular nature of some items often steered an exclusive treatment in most regions. Jade axe heads and several kinds of copper and gold items in the east seem to have been deliberately kept out of graves and settlements and were buried in the landscape instead. Often, such items were non-functional (enlarged, too heavy) versions of normal objects (like the Moigrad gold ornament or overweight copper axes (Hansen 2013, 145)).

How TRB depositions worked to keep stone, jade and copper valuables apart

Above, deposition systems with and without metal valuables were compared that were almost 'mutually exclusive' (Bradley 2017, 112). As a last example of a pre-Bronze Age deposition practice, the following section discusses Funnel Beaker (TRB) societies of the fourth millennium BC in which jade and copper occurred together between c. 3800 and 3300 BC, alongside a range of valuables made out of other materials. How did this affect depositional practices?

TRB material culture is found in a vast area, stretching from the northern Netherlands in the west, to beyond the river Bug in Ukraine in the east, southern Scandinavia in the north and Bohemia in the south (Müller 2009, figure 75). It coincides with fully-fledged subsistence farming. Klassen (2004) argues that the TRB came into existence under the influence of both the western and the eastern European realm. Participating in long-distance exchange of valuables like stone axes from southern farming worlds (Lengyel IV and regional Michelsberg groups) is thought to have been pivotal and even to have influenced their adoption of the farming way of life (Klassen 2004, 334–5). During the fourth millennium BC, complex 'ritual' TRB landscapes emerged, involving the building of thousands of megalithic tombs (Klassen 2000, 300; Müller 2009). But there are indications that the uncultivated landscape had special connotations as well. All kinds of things were purposefully inserted in the land. This happened in a selective manner.

First of all, pots, bone and other artefacts have been found in watery places like bogs, sometimes called 'mixed bog deposits'. Koch (1998) has provided extensive arguments that these represent items that were deliberately sacrificed. Assemblages are variable, and paraphrasing Ebbesen (1993), Louwe Kooijmans (2001) states that it seems as if 'nothing was too humble' for a deposition.

Second, *flint axes* played an important role in TRB depositional practices. They are often found in the same bogs that have pot deposits, though rarely in association (Koch 1998, 141). TRB people did differentiate between axes in a way that recalls patterns detected before in Copper Age Europe. In the TRB West Group, axes of both Nordic and Atlantic origin were deposited in graves (Wentink 2006; Wentink & Van Gijn 2008, 30). Axes accompanying the dead, however, tend to be used and worn axes. There is a second group of aggrandized axes (length >20 cm) which are too large for practical use. They are in mint condition and sometimes not or hardly polished (ibid., 35). In many cases their cutting edges were covered with red ochre and there are indications that they were wrapped in soft material during life (ibid., 38). These were not deposited in graves but mainly in peat bogs, where they occur singly or in hoards with comparable axes or with raw or half-finished flint (Wentink 2006, 43). There is a comparable contrast between regular items in graves (and settlements) vs. enlarged versions deposited in the landscape for much older and different societies like the LBK, groups depositing jade axes and aggrandized Copper Age metal in eastern Europe.

Third, there is a small group of *jade axe heads* in the North Group (Klassen 2004, 83–89; *Fundliste* 9). Although these are types mainly dated to late 5th/early 4th millennium BC, Klassen (2004, 87) suggests several of them must have been in circulation for centuries and may have been used by TRB communities. Like aggrandized flint axes, they were not made to be used and some are also very large (length 36 cm; Klassen 2004, 89). Nevertheless, there is no evidence that enlarged flint axes and jade axes were deposited together. The depositional context of jade axes is poorly known: most are single finds without clear context, and there is one bog find (ibid., *Fundliste* 9).

Fourth, there are *copper* items, a foreign material like jade, but with different social and depositional trajectories.[2] Copper flat axes from the Balkans or Carpathians incidentally reached Late Mesolithic communities in the north during the fifth millennium BC (Klassen 2000, 298). Copper items, now from eastern Alpine sources, more frequently figure in TRB communities between 3700 and 3300 BC (Klassen 2000). Unlike jade, there are indications that this foreign material was worked locally (ibid., 218–219, 225–232). It came in various forms (axes and a variety of ornaments). Ornaments figure in hoards, but also adorned the dead in graves in association with other materials. Axes, however, are unknown from burial contexts – this implicates that it was shape and what this evoked that was decisive for how objects ended their life. Like enlarged flint axes and jade ones, copper axes were often not used (Visser forthcoming). Yet, when deposited in hoards they are not associated with either flint axes or jade ones. In hoards, they are associated with other copper items and with ceramic vessels, like in the Bygholm hoard (Klassen

2000, 351–352). Although contextual information is poor, Visser (forthcoming) suggests copper items tend to be placed not in bogs but on dry land, possibly in the vicinity of burial monuments.

Fifth, *amber* ornaments (especially beads) are another prominent group of deposited items. Unlike jade or copper, they are of regional provenance. Like copper, they are known both from burials (where pots and copper also figure) and hoards. Of the latter, some 50 are known from Denmark, mostly from bogs from c. 3500–3000 BC (like the Mollerup hoard; Jensen 2013, 211–214). Obviously, bogs were seen as the 'right' recipients for both foreign and local and regional items. In amber hoards there is the same tendency towards multiplication as seen before in hoards of Neolithic and Copper Age southeast Europe (like Čoka or Cărbuna, see above). The amber hoard of Mollerup contains 12,849 beads, the one from Hvilshøj c. 3600 and Lille Ajstrup 8092 beads (Jensen 2013, 211–212). Apparently, in each case, material for several necklaces was surrendered – suggesting these were practices evoking communal rather than personal identities. The observation that the Mollerup beads were not or hardly used implies the emphasis seems to have been on their transformative potential as constituents of personal identity.

Taken together, this reflects a system of selective deposition in which people systematically and consistently kept certain things apart from others by depositing them in a particular way in the landscape. Specific valuables seem to be regarded as different from others (like aggrandized flint axes and copper axes) even though both are non-functional. In some cases, materials seem to matter (flint axes apparently were not on par with jade axes), in others they do not (both local amber and copper ornaments went in graves). This suggests it was their role in body adornment that was decisive. Bogs were apparently the 'right' receptacle for large axes and amber items, but not for copper ones. The evidence covered so far is probably not complete (cf. the poor contextual information on both copper and jade finds), mainly based on the TRB north and west group, and in need of further investigation (systematic surveys of ornament deposition are so far lacking). Yet, the outline of a truly selective system of deposition is recognizable.

Selective deposition: different societies, same solutions?

The above survey shows that an emergent selective deposition can already be demonstrated for societies that did not have metalwork. The similarities in the way jade axe heads were deposited in large parts of Europe is the best example thereof. More tentatively, the treatment of *Breitkeile* in depositional practices among farmers and Late Mesolithic foragers suggests that the phenomenon of selective deposition was not unique to a particular culture or way of life.

In the pre-Bronze Age metal cultures of the East European Copper Age, on the other hand, different kinds of important social valuables were made out of metal. In depositional practices, some of them were kept apart from others. As such, it foreshadows the 'metallized' kind of selective deposition that would characterize the Bronze Age. Among the TRB communities, however, stone and copper items were partly separated on the basis of material, and partly on the basis of their relation to the constitution of personhood. Here, copper was just one of the materials valuables were made of.

Furthermore, the extended system of selective deposition in the TRB also indicates that selective deposition was not simply about separating imported and locally made things. The strictest distinction made in depositional acts in the TRB West group (that can be observed by us), is between items that were entirely made of non-local flint: the deposition of oversized, unused flint axes in peat bogs, and regular, used ones in graves (Wentink & Van Gijn 2008).

If anything, the understandings on which pre-Bronze Age societies based their selective treatment of certain items in depositional practices defy a simple categorization like metal & non-metal or foreign & local. Nevertheless, a remarkably stable pattern can be seen. In many cultures and periods, there are regular objects and other-worldly, rare, exaggerated, singular versions thereof. The latter category tends to be strictly dissociated from the former in depositions. This recalls the difference made by Godelier (1999; see Chapter 3) between valuables that circulate *en masse*, and rare *sacra* that a society keeps. It reflects ranked spheres of exchange that are linked by object citation and separated by the creation of distanced or singular versions (Chapter 3; cf. Hansen 2001; Helms 1993; Sørensen 2015; Wentink 2006).

All this implies that selective deposition was *not* a feature unique to one particular culture, way of living or period. Rather, it seems to have been a practice steered by a time-transgressive logic that has to do with how value and valuables were created, upheld, contrasted and ranked in a particular social act. In this case, this was a deposition – an act in which things were displayed before they were hidden from view forever (cf. Rowlands 1993; more on this in Chapters 2 and 8).

The disruptive third millennium BC – did landscape-bound deposition disappear?

If the above holds true, a crucial issue remains. The upholding and ordering of valuables happened during acts in which things were buried in the ground. Chapter 2 emphasized that this is a quite specific social context. There are many cultures in which valuables were never systematically buried in the ground, but where value creation or conversion for example happened only during exchange. Archaeologically, those resulting in frequent deposition are the only ones that are directly researchable to us (Chapter 2). LBK farmers and Copper Age groups may have been very different cultures. Both, however, buried important valuables in the landscape. The first half of the third millennium BC is a problematic period, because it seems as if the habit of burying such things in the landscape decreases or even disappears (Hansen 2012, 32–36). This fits with broader theories that see this period as one that heralded a decisive break in European prehistory, both culturally and socially (Kristiansen et al. 2017).

Key evidence for this view is provided by the appearance of a new way of burying associated with the Corded Ware Culture (CWC). From c. 2850 BC, in many parts of continental Europe people started to bury their dead in a way that contrasts markedly with existing Neolithic burial traditions. Individuals were placed on their side in a crouched position associated with objects from a limited, yet widely shared set of valuables like a decorated vessel, flint knife and stone 'battle' axe (Bourgeois & Kroon 2017). There is evidence that variations in such practices emphasized male–female differences (indicating different ideas on gender). The burial tradition is remarkably homogeneous, to the extent that it is difficult to distinguish a grave from Danish Jutland from one in the central Netherlands (Bourgeois & Kroon 2017).

This correlates with aDNA evidence that indicates people buried in this CWC tradition differ genetically from those from the Neolithic, but do have great similarity to older graves from the Pontic-Caspian steppes (the so-called Yamnaya cultural horizon; Haak et al. 2015). It has therefore been argued that CWC graves are proxies for a 'massive migration' from the steppes (Kristiansen et al. 2017), partly replacing an already declining Neolithic population. These immigrants are also held responsible for the introduction of proto-Indo-European languages, almost entirely erasing previous 'Neolithic' ones (Iversen & Kroonen 2017). As far as we know, people using Yamnaya material culture did not deposit material in hoards in the landscape. Intriguingly, hoards and other kinds of depositions outside graves also seem to cease in regions where CWC settled. Does this mean such landscape-based depositions were not part of CWC cultural practices? Given the now accepted overriding importance of the CWC legacy for the Bronze Age, how is it possible that depositional practices again came to play such a prominent role towards the end of the third millennium BC?

Until recently, no answer could be suggested. There was a general decline in landscape-bound depositional activity in regions where CWC burials were found. However, an important point of critique is that certain CWC objects like battle axes did occur in hoards or in rivers (Hansen 2012, 32). Iversen's recent study (2015; 2016) on eastern Denmark sheds new light onto this problem.

Iversen (2015, 82–88) shows TRB depositional practices were already declining before the onset of CWC graves. He also emphasizes that characteristic CWC burials are indeed known from Denmark but then particularly from Jutland (2016, 168–169). He argues that the Danish isles remained inhabited by several Neolithic groups, including late TRB communities during the first half of the third millennium BC. CWC artefacts apparently did reach these islands, and occasionally figured in the kind of (wet place) depositional practices that are so characteristic of TRB culture (Iversen 2015, 91).

But there are not only indications that CWC artefacts were deposited by what were essentially Neolithic communities; it may also be suggested that CWC itself transformed or at least incorporated TRB-like depositional practices. In the northern Netherlands, a region known for the many CWC barrows, no less than nine hoards are known that contain what are considered characteristic CWC artefacts (Wentink et al. 2011, 404–405).

The legacy of the Corded Ware world view for Bronze Age depositional practices

Whether CWC originally included ideas on landscape-bound deposition or not, one aspect of CWC would have important repercussions. With the CWC world view came a belief – repeated in thousands of burial practices across Europe – *that only a circumscribed set of valuables was allowed in the construction of the ancestral persona in the grave*. This automatically means that there were other objects that apparently were considered *not* appropriate. Although previous Neolithic communities (e.g. the TRB) also had specific ideas on what not to deposit with the dead, it is with the CWC that ideas of a restricted and specific notion of personhood came to be held across Europe on an unprecedented scale (Bourgeois & Kroon 2017).

This almost pan-European sharing of ideas on which objects were appropriate to adorn the deceased was taken to a new level in the Bell Beaker grave ritual (c. 2500–2000 BC) that in many European regions replaced CWC burial practices and had a comparable broad distribution. New aDNA evidence suggests that deceased buried in such graves may be genetically considered as offspring of marriages between Neolithic and CWC people (Olalde et al. 2018). The portrayal of the dead in such graves, however, was markedly different from CWC norms. There was a stronger emphasis on bodily ornamentation, on dressing them in 'connectivity' (Fontijn 2002, 80–82; Van der Beek 2004; Wentink forthcoming). Ornaments in supra-regional styles (like gold basket-shaped hair rings; Fontijn 2002, 66–67) signalled a reach to a wider world, and the outlook of the famous Amesbury Archer grave in England is so similar to graves in the Netherlands that Wentink (forthcoming) suggests that Bell Beaker people from the Dutch side of the North Sea would have recognized the roles and status of the man buried at Amesbury. As Harris et al. (2013) put it, the decorated body was not meant to let the deceased stand out, but rather to have them blend into a supra-regional whole of *personae*. 'Parity', not individuality was the ideal strived for (ibid., 71). This new emphasis on embodied connectivity makes sense in a Europe where long-distance exchange networks became increasingly important. There is ample reason to argue that this was indeed happening by that time: it is this period that heralds the emergence of the first European-wide exchange networks for metals (Roberts et al. 2009).

Bell Beaker (BB) burial practices required a shared mind set on what objects can do to people, but also on their appropriate resting place once their role among the living society was considered over. Importantly, this also applies to things that were consistently *kept out* of the graves but had to be deposited in specific places of the landscape (Figure 4.3). Such landscape-focused perceptions on 'the right ending' (Chapter 2) were important among Neolithic cultures like the TRB. They start to gain significance at the end of the third millennium BC and now increasingly involved objects made of metal. Gold *lunulae*, gold 'precious cups', copper-alloy

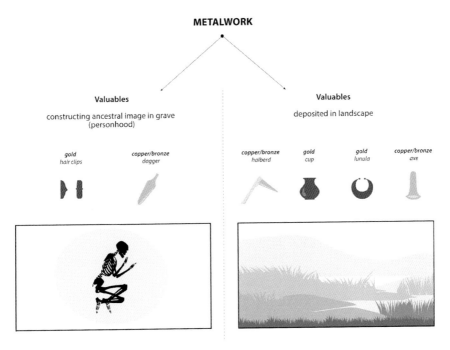

FIGURE 4.3 Model of selective deposition showing how from the Bell Beaker period onwards, particular objects were deposited in graves, whilst others were deposited in different locations in the landscape. Objects shown are simplified versions of real ones and only serve to give some impression of what they may look like.
Source: Drawing J. Porck, Faculty of Archaeology, University of Leiden.

axes and halberds were hardly ever given to the dead, but copper daggers, awls, gold earrings and diadems, as well as metalworking implements (cushion stones) were (Needham 1989; Needham et al. 2006).

Like the ideas on bodies of connectivity evidenced in Bell Beaker burials, the landscape-destined items are usually rather rare but found in large parts of Europe. Halberds – a new weapon without precursors in other materials – in particular can be seen as the first metal item that became important almost everywhere in Europe (Genz 2004) and so are conventions on their proper deposition.

With bronze objects becoming dominant valuables, selective deposition increasingly was about associating and dissociating specific bronze items. The unprecedented broad scales at which bronze economies operated apparently had a counterpart in the sometimes transcultural nature of some depositional conventions.

Conclusion

This chapter established that selective deposition is not unique to Bronze Age society, nor is it characteristic of societies in which important valuables were made of recyclable and therewith convertible metal. I argued it also existed in non-metal-using Neolithic societies where deposition of things in the land was an important social practice. It was a time-and culture-transgressive practice. The examples discussed show that deposition of things in hoards or graves could work to reify value(s) by first displaying and then concealing valuables (cf. Rowlands 1993). Doing this repeatedly, excluding things from one depositional act and including them in others can have the effect of reifying a certain ordering among valuables (more on this in Chapter 8). In different, culturally unrelated examples, selective deposition had the effect of distancing aggrandized objects from their regular counterparts.

In the cases discussed, selective depositional practices recontextualized valuables from distant places. This suggests that burial in the land or with the dead may have had the effect of appropriating and recontextualizing foreign things with local ideas and values at home (Bloch & Parry 1989, 23). However, there was more to things than their 'foreignness'. Examples from the TRB north and west group show their use life was a factor as well.

With the BB culture, valuables creating a body that signals a sense of supra-regional personhood become more important than before (Harris et al. 2013). It hallmarks a period in which selective deposition was increasingly about emphasizing distinction between items related to the construction of personhood and those that were not (cf. Fontijn 2002, 218; Vandkilde 1996, 267–268). From the beginning of the second millennium BC, a now fully metallized selective deposition took shape following these distinctions. It will be central in the discussions of the next three chapters.

Notes

1 A notable exception is the situation in Brittany, where jade axe heads were also included in megalithic tombs (Bradley 2017, 114; Petréquin et al. 2002, 87).
2 Copper finds are particularly frequent in the North group, but lacking in the West one.

Bibliography

Amkreutz, L., 2013. *Persistent traditions: a long-term perspective on communities in the process of Neolithisation in the Lower Rhine area (5500–2500 cal BC)*. Leiden: Sidestone Press.

Bakels, C.C. and W. Hendrix, 1999. Ein bandkeramisches Dechseldepot aus Stein-Berg-aan de Maas, Niederlande, *Archäologisches Korrespondenzblatt* 29, 317–324.

Bánffy, E. and K. Oros, 2010. The earlier and the earliest phase of the LBK in Transdanubia, in: *Die Neolithisierung Mitteleuropas* (RGZM Tagungen 4), eds D. Gronenborn and J. Petrasch. Mainz: Schnell & Steiner Verlag, 255–272.

Bloch, M. and J. Parry, 1989. Introduction: money and the morality of exchange, in: *Money and the morality of exchange*, eds J. Parry and M. Bloch. Cambridge: Cambridge University Press, 1–31.

Borić, D., O.J.T. Harris, P. Miracle and J. Robb, 2013. The limits of the body, in: *The body in history. Europe from the Palaeolithic to the future*, eds J. Robb and O.J.T. Harris. Cambridge: Cambridge University Press, 32–63.

Boroffka, N., 2009. Simple technology: casting moulds for axe-adzes, in: *Metals and societies. Studies in honour of Barbara S. Ottaway* (Universitätsforschungen zur prähistorischen Archäologie 169), eds T.L. Kienlin and B. Roberts. Bonn: Habelt Verlag, 246–257.

Bourgeois, Q. and E. Kroon, 2017. The impact of male burials on the construction of Corded Ware identity: reconstructing networks of information in the 3rd millennium BC, *PLOSone* 12(10): e0185971. https://doi.org/10.1371/journal.pone.0185971.

Bradley, R., 2017. *A geography of offerings. Deposits of valuables in the landscapes of ancient Europe* (Oxbow Insights in Archaeology). Oxford: Oxbow Books.

Chapman, J., 2000. *Fragmentation in archaeology. People, places and broken objects in the prehistory of South Eastern Europe.* New York: Routledge.

Ebbesen, K., 1993. Sacrifices to the powers of nature, in: *Digging into the past: 25 years of archaeology in Denmark*, eds S. Hvass and B. Storgaard. Aarhus: Aarhus University Press, 122–125.

Fontijn, D.R., 2002. Sacrificial landscapes: cultural biographies of persons, objects and 'natural' places in the Bronze Age of the southern Netherlands, c. 2300–2600 BC, *Analecta Praehistorica Leidensia* 33/34, 1–392.

Genz, H., 2004. Stabdolche – Waffen und Statussymbole, in: *Der geschmiedete Himmel. Die weite Welt im Herzen Europas vor 3600 Jahren*, ed. H. Meller. Stuttgart: Konrad Theiss Verlag, 160–161.

Godelier, M., 1999. *The enigma of the gift*. Cambridge and Oxford: Polity Press.

Graeber, D., 2005. Value: anthropological theory of value, in: *A handbook of economic anthropology*, ed. J.G. Carrier. Cheltenham and Northampton MA: Edward Elgar, 439–454.

Haak, W., I. Lazaridis, N. Patterson, N. Rohland, S. Mallick, B. Llamas, G. Brandt, S. Nordenfelt, E. Harney, K. Stewardson, Q. Fu, A. Mittnik, E. Banffy, Ch. Economou, M. Francken, S. Friederich, R. Garrido Pena, F. Hallgren, V. Khartanovich, A. Khokhlov, M. Kunst, P. Kuznetsov, H. Meller, O. Mochalov, V. Moiseyev, N. Nicklisch, S.L. Pichler, R. Risch, M.A. Rojo Guerra, Ch. Roth, A. Szecsenyi-Nagy, J. Wahl, M. Meyer, J. Krause, D. Brown, D. Anthony, A. Cooper, K. Werner Alt and D. Reich, 2015. Massive migration from the steppe was a source for Indo-European languages in Europe, *Nature* 522, 207–211.

Hamon, C., 2008. The symbolic value of grindingstones hoards: technical properties of Neolithic examples, in: *Hoards from the Neolithic to the Metal Age. Technical and codified practices* (British Archaeological Reports International Series 1758), eds C. Hamon and B. Quilliec. Oxford: Archaeopress, 19–28.

Hansen, S., 2001. 'Überaustattungen' in Gräbern und Horten der Frühbronzezeit, in: *Vom Endneolithikum zur Frühbronzezeit: Muster sozialen Wandels?* (Universitätsforschungen zur prähistorischen Archäologie, 90), ed. J. Müller. Bonn: Habelt Verlag, 151–174.

Hansen, S., 2011. Metal in South-Eastern and Central Europe between 4500 and 2900 BCE, in: *Anatolian Metal V. Veröffentlichungen aus dem Deutschen Bergbau-Museum Bochum, Nr 180*, ed. Ü. Yalçin. Bochum: Bergbau-Museum, 137–149.

Hansen, S. 2012. Bronzezeitliche Horte: Zeitliche und räumliche Rekontextualisierungen, in: *Hort und Raum Aktuelle Forschungen zu bronzezeitlichen Deponierungen in Mitteleuropa* (Berlin Studies of the Ancient World 10), eds S. Hansen, D. Neumann and T. Vachta. Berlin: De Gruyter, 23–48.

Hansen, S., 2013. Innovative metals: copper, gold and silver in the Black Sea region and the Carpathian Basin during the 5th and 4th millennium BC, in: *Metal matters. Innovative technologies and social change in prehistory and antiquity* (Menschen-Kulturen-Traditionen; Forschungscluster 2, Bd 12), eds S. Burmeister, S. Hansen, M. Kunst and N. Müller-Scheessel. Rahden: Marie Leidorf Verlag, 137–167.

Hanssen, K.M., E. Brinch Petersen and K. Aaris-Sørensen, 2004. Filling the gap: early preboreal magelmose elk deposits at Lundby, Sjælland, Denmark, in: *Hunters in a changing world: environment and archaeology of the Pleistocene-Holocene transition (ca. 11000–9000 BC) in Northern Central Europe*, eds T. Terberger and B. Valentin Eriksen. Rahden: Marie Leidorf Verlag, 75–84.

Harris, O.J.T., K. Rebay-Salisbury, J. Robb and M.L.S. Sørensen, 2013. The body in its social context, in: *The body in history. Europe from the Palaeolithic to the future*, eds J. Robb and O.J.T. Harris. Cambridge: Cambridge University Press, 64–97.

Helms, M.W., 1993. *Craft and the kingly ideal: art, trade, and power*. Austin: University of Texas Press.

Iversen, R., 2015. *The transformation of Neolithic societies. An eastern Danish perspective on the 3rd millennium BC*. Aarhus: Aarhus University Press.

Iversen, R., 2016. Was there ever a single grave culture in East Denmark? In: *Transitional landscapes? The 3rd millennium BC in Europe* (Universitätsforschungen zur Prähistorischen Archäologie 292), eds M. Furholt, R. Grossmann and M. Szmyt. Bonn: Habelt Verlag, 159–169.

Iversen, R. and G. Kroonen, 2017. Talking Neolithic: linguistic and archaeological perspectives on how Indo-European was implemented in Southern Scandinavia, *American Journal of Archaeology* 121(4), 511–525.

Jensen, J., 2013. *The prehistory of Denmark. From the Stone Age to the Vikings*. Copenhagen: Gyldendal.

Jeunesse, Chr., 1998. A propos de la signification historique des dépôts dans le Néolithique danubien ancient et moyen, in: *Tradition und Innovation. Prähistorische Archäologie als historische Wissenschaft. Festschrift für Christian Strahm*, eds B. Fritsch, M. Maute, I. Matuschik, J. Müller and C. Wolf. Rahden: Marie Leidorf Verlag, 31–50.

Karsten, P., 1994. Att kasta yxan i sjön. En studie över rituell tradition och förandring utifrån skånska neolitiska offerfynd, *Acta Lundensia* 8(23). Stockholm.

Klassen, L., 2000. *Frühes Kupfer im Norden* (Jutland Archaeological Society 36). Aarhus: Aarhus University Press.

Klassen, L., 2004. *Jade und Kupfer. Untersuchungen zur Neolithisierungsprozess im westlichen Ostseeraum unter besonderer Berücksichtigung der Kulturentwicklung Europas 5500–3500 BC* (Jutland Archaeologcial Society 47). Aarhus: Aarhus University Press.

Koch, E., 1998. *Neolithic bog pots from Zealand, Møn, Lolland and Falster* (Nordiske Fortidsminder Serie B Vol. 16). Copenhagen: Nordiske Fortidsminder.

Kopytoff, I., 1986. The cultural biography of things: commoditisation as process, in: *The social life of things*, ed. A. Appadurai. Cambridge: Cambridge University Press, 64–91.

Kristiansen, K., M. Allentoft, E. Morten, K. Frei, M. Karin, R. Iversen, N.N. Johannsen, G. Kroonen, L. Pospieszny, T.D. Price, S. Rasmussen, K.-G. Sjoegren, M. Sikora and E. Willerslev, 2017. Re-theorising mobility and the formation of culture and language among the Corded Ware culture in Europe, *Antiquity* 91(356), 334–347.

Kristiansen, K. and T. Earle, 2015. Neolithic versus Bronze Age social formations. A political economy approach, in: *Paradigm found. Archaeological theory. present, past and future. Essays in honour of Evžen Neustupný*, eds K. Kristiansen, L. Šmejda and J. Turek. Oxford: Oxbow Books, 234–247.

Kuijpers, M.H.G., 2018. *An archaeology of skill. Metalworking skill and material specialization in Early Bronze Age Central Europe*. London and New York: Routledge.

Louwe Kooijmans, L.P., 2001. Vroeg-neolithische offerplaatsen, de wortels van bronstijddeposities? In: *Edelpatina. 2 toespraken tot Jay J. Butler gehouden op 12 april 2001 ter gelegenheid van de overhandiging van Patina*, ed. J. Steegstra. Groningen: privately published by Steegstra, 9–15.

Louwe Kooijmans, L.P., 2017. *Onze vroegste voorouders. De geschiedenis van Nederland in de steentijd van het begin tot 3000 V.C.* Amsterdam: Bert Bakker.

Louwe Kooijmans, L.P. and M. Nokkert, 2001. Sporen en structuren, in: *Een kampplaats uit het Laat-Mesolithicum en het begin van de Swifterbant-cultuur (5500–4450 v. Chr.)* (Rapportage Archeologische Monumentenzorg 88), ed. L.P. Louwe Kooijmans. Amersfoort: Rijksdienst voor Cultureel Erfgoed, 75–115.

Müller, J., 2009. Die Jungsteinzeit, in: *Atlas der Vorgeschichte, in Europa von den ersten Menschen bis Christi Geburt*, ed. S. Von Schnurbein. Stuttgart: Konrad Theiss Verlag, 60–105.

Needham, S., 1989. Selective deposition in the British Early Bronze Age, *World Archaeology* 20, 229–248.

Needham, S., K. Parfitt and G. Varndell (eds), 2006. *The Ringlemere Cup. Precious cups and the beginning of the Channel Bronze Age.* London: British Museum Press.

O'Brien, W., 2014. *Prehistoric copper mining in Europe, 5500–500 BC.* Oxford: Oxford University Press.

Olalde, I., S. Brace, M.E. Allentoft, I. Armit, K. Kristiansen, T. Booth, N. Rohland, S. Mallick, A. Szécsényi Nagy, A. Mittnik, E. Altena, M. Lipson, I. Lazaridis, T.K. Harper, N. Patterson, N. Broomandkhoshbacht, Y. Diekmann, Z. Faltyskova, D. Fernandes, M. Ferry, E. Harney, P. de Knijff, M. Michel, J. Oppenheimer, K. Stewardson, A. Barclay, K. Werner Alt, C. Liesau, P. Ríos, C. Blasco, J. Vega Miguel, R. Menduiña García, A. Avilés Fernández, E. Bánffy, M. Bernabò-Brea, D. Billoin, C. Bonsall, L. Bonsall, T. Allen, L. Büster, S. Carver, L. Castells Navarro, O.E. Craig, G.T. Cook, B. Cunliffe, A. Denaire, K. Egging Dinwiddy, N. Dodwell, M. Ernée, C. Evans, M. Kuchařik, J. Francès Farré, C. Fowler, M. Gazenbeek, R. Garrido Pena, M. Haber-Uriarte, E. Haduch, G. Hey, N. Jowett, T. Knowles, K. Massy, S. Pfrengle, P. Lefranc, O. Lemercier, A. Lefebvre, C. Heras Martínez, V. Galera Olmo, A. Bastida Ramírez, J. Lomba Maurandi, T. Majó, J.I. McKinley, K. McSweeney, B. Gusztáv Mende, A. Mod, G. Kulcsár, V. Kiss, A. Czene, R. Patay, A. Endrödi, K. Köhler, T. Hajdu, T. Szeniczev, J. Dani, Z. Bernert, M. Hoole, O. Cheronet, D. Keating, P. Velemínsky, M. Dobeš, A.-M. Herrero-Corral, S. Tusa, E. Carnieri, L. Lentini, A. Valenti, A. Zanini, C. Waddington, G. Delibes, E. Guerra-Doce, B. Neil, M. Brittain, M. Luke, R. Mortimer, J. Desideri, M. Besse, G. Brücken, M. Furmanek, A. Hałuszko, M. Mackiewicz, A. Rapiński, S. Leach, I. Soriano, K.T. Lillios, J. Luís Cardoso, M. Parker Pearson, P. Włdarczak, T. Douglas Price, P. Prieto, P.-J. Rey, R. Risch, M.A. Rojo Guerra, A. Schmitt, J. Serralongue, A.M. Silva, V. Smrčka, L. Vergnaud, J. Zilhão, D. Caramelli, T. Higham, M.G. Thomas, D.J. Kennett, H. Fokkens, V. Heyd, A. Sheridan, K.-G. Sjögren, P.W. Stockhammer, J. Krause, R. Pinhasi, W. Haak, I. Barnes, C. Lalueza-Fox and D. Reich, 2018. The Beaker phenomenon and the genomic transformation of Northwest Europe, *Nature* 555, 190–196.

Pernicka, E. and D.W. Anthony, 2010. The invention of copper metallurgy and the Copper Age of Old Europe, in: *The lost world of Old Europe. The Danube Valley, 5000–3500 BC*, eds D. Anthony and J.Y. Chi. Princeton NJ and Oxford: Princeton University Press, 162–177.

Pétrequin, P., S. Cassen, Chr. Croutsch and M. Errera, 2002. La valorisation sociale des longues haches dans l'Europe néolithique, in: *Matériaux, productions, circulations du Néolithique à l'Âge du Bronze*, ed. J. Guilaune. Paris: Éditions Errance, 67–98.

Pétrequin, P., S. Cassen, E. Errera, L. Klassen and A. Sheridan, 2012a. Des choses sacrées … fonctions idéelles des jades alpins en Europe occidentale, in: *Jade. Grands haches alpines du Néolithique européen*, eds P. Pétrequin, S. Cassen, E. Errera, L. Klassen, A. Sheridan and A.-M. Pétrequin. Besançon: Presses Universitaires de France-Comté, 1354–1422.

Pétrequin, P., S. Cassen, E. Errera, L. Klassen, A. Sheridan and A.-M. Pétrequin, 2012b. *Jade. Grands haches alpines du Néolithique européen.* Besançon: Presses Universitaires de France-Comté

Pétrequin, P., M. Errera, S. Cassen, E. Gauthier, L. Klassen, A.-M. Pétrequin and A. Sheridan 2012c. Austausch auf europäischer Ebene: alpine Jade des 6. Bis 4. Jahrtausends v. Chr, *Archäologie in Deutschland* 2, 22–25.

Pétrequin, P., S. Cassen, M. Errera, L. Klassen, A.-M. Pétrequin and A. Sheridan, 2013. The value of things: the production and circulation of alpine jade axes during the 5th–4th millennia in a European perspective, in: *Economic archaeology: from structure to performance in European archaeology*, eds T. Kerig and A. Zimmerman. Bonn: Habelt Verlag, 65–82.

Quitta, H., 1955. Ein Verwahrfund aus der bandkeramischen Siedlung in der Harth bei Zwenkau, in: *Festschrift zum 70. Geburtstag von Friedrich Behn* (Beiträge zur Vor- und Frühgeschichte), ed. R. Weinhold. Leipzig: Barth, 20–59.

Quitta, H., 1969., Zur Deutung bandkeramischer Siedlungsfunde aus Auen und grundwassernähen Standorten in: *Siedlung, burg und Stadt. Studien zu ihren Anfängen* (Schriften der Sektion für Vor- und Frühgeschichte 25), eds K.M. Otto and J. Hermann. Berlin: Akademie Verlag, 42–54.

Raczky, P., 1994. Two late Neolithic 'hoards' from Csóka (Čoka)-Kremenyak in the Vojvodina, in: *A kőkortól a középkorig: Tanulmányok Trogmayer Ottó 60. Születésnapjára*, ed. G. Lőrincy. Szeged, Hungary: Mora Ferenc Múzeum, 161–172.

Raemaekers, D.C.M., J. Geuverink, M. Schepers, B.P. Tuin, E. van der Lagemaat and M. van der Wal, 2011. *A biography in stone. Typology, age, functio and meaning of Early Neolithic perforated wedges in the Netherlands* (Groningen Archaeological Studies 14). Groningen: Barkhuis and Groningen University Library, 1–53.

Renfrew, C., 2001. Commodification and institution in group-oriented and individualizing societies, in: *The origin of human social institutions* (Proceedings of the British Academy), ed. W.G. Runciman. Oxford: Oxford University Press, 93–117.

Roberts, B.W., C.P. Thornton and V.C. Pigott, 2009. Development of metallurgy in Eurasia, *Antiquity* 83(322), 1012–1022.

Rowlands, M.J., 1993. The role of memory in the transmission of culture, *World Archaeology* 25, 141–151.

Simmel, G., 2011 [1900]. *The philosophy of money*. London: Routledge.

Slavchev, V., 2010. The Varna Eneolithic Cemetery in the context of the Late Copper Age in the East Balkan, in: *The lost world of Old Europe. The Danube Valley, 5000–3500 BC*, eds D. Anthony and J.Y. Chi. Princeton NJ Oxford: Princeton University Press, 193–210.

Sommer, U., 2001. Hear the instruction of thy father, and forsake not the law of thy mother. Change and persistence in the European Early Neolithic, *Journal of Social Archaeology* 1(2), 244–270.

Sørensen, M.L.S., 2015. 'Paradigm lost': on the state of typology within archaeological theory, in: *Paradigm found. Archaeological theory present, past and future*, eds K. Kristiansen, L. Šmejda and J. Turek. Oxford: Oxbow Books, 84–94.

Taylor, T., 1999. Envaluing metal: theorizing the Eneolithic 'hiatus', in: *Metals in antiquity* (British Archaeological Reports 792), eds S.M.M. Young, A.M. Pollard, P. Budd and R. A. Ixer. Oxford: Archaeopress, 22–32.

Van der Beek, Z., 2004. An ancestral way of burial. Late Neolithic graves in the southern Netherlands, in: *Graves and funerary rituals during the Late Neolithic and Early Bronze Age in Europe (2700–2000 BC). Proceedings of the international conference held at the Cantonal Archaeological Museum, Sion (Switzerland) October 4th–7th 2001* (British Archaeological Reports International Series 1284), eds M. Besse and J. Desideri. Oxford: Archaeopress, 157–194.

Vandkilde, H., 1996. *From stone to bronze: the metalwork of the Late Neolithic and Earliest Bronze Age in Denmark* (Jutland Archaeological Society Publications XXXII). Aarhus: Aarhus University Press.

Vandkilde, H., 2014. Breakthrough of the Nordic Bronze Age: transcultural warriorhood and a Carpathian crossroad in the sixteenth century BC, *European Journal of Archaeology* 17 (4), 602–633.

Verhart, L., 2012. Contact in stone: adzes, *Keile* and *Spitzhauen* in the Lower Rhine Basin, *Journal of Archaeology in the Low Countries* 4(1), 5–35.

Visser, M., forthcoming. *Patterns and practices. The emergence of metalwork deposition in the Netherlands, c. 2300–1500 BC, in North Germany and Jutland*. Leiden: Sidestone Press.

Wentink, K., 2006. *Ceci n'est pas une hache. Neolithic depositions in the Northern Netherlands*. Master's thesis, Leiden University. Leiden: Sidestone Press.

Wentink, K., forthcoming. *The social identity of burials in Late Neolithic barrows in the Netherlands* (working title). Leiden: Sidestone Press.

Wentink, K. and A. Van Gijn, 2008. Neolithic depositions in the Northern Netherlands, in: *Hoards from the Neolithic to the metal ages. Technical and codified practices* (British Archaeological Reports International Series 1758), eds C. Hamon and B. Quilliec. Oxford: Archaeopress, 29–43.

Wentink, K., A.L. van Gijn and D.R. Fontijn, 2011. Changing contexts, changing meanings: flint axes in Middle and Late Neolithic communities in the Northern Netherlands, in: *Stone axe studies III*, eds V. Davis and M. Edmonds. Oxford: Oxbow Books, 399–408.

Whittle, A., 1996. *Europe in the Neolithic. The creation of new worlds*. Cambridge: Cambridge University Press.

5

TRADE HOARDS

The un-economic nature of the Bronze Age metal economy

This chapter focuses on one of the most puzzling aspects of metalwork depositions. Why was what seems to be straightforward 'economic' trade stock treated in such an 'un-economic' way, by placing it permanently in the landscape? By reviewing some of the evidence of so-called trade hoards, this chapter will demonstrate that objects placed in such hoards indeed had commodity potential and reflect convertibles used in specific spheres of exchange. I argue that deposition was a way to emphasize such separations and anchor these in special social actions. The insertion of trade stock in the landscape must have been elemental in Bronze Age economies, regardless of whether or not material was later taken out.

Introduction

In Aschering (Bavaria) a hoard consisting of c. 100 rings was found, dating to the Early Bronze Age (c. 2000–1750 BC; Lenerz-de Wilde 2002, 14, 16; Stein 1979, nos. 56, 184). These so-called *Ösenringe* are reminiscent of neck rings in shape and size, but were never used as such. Because of their homogeneity in shape and weight, such rings are generally seen as currency in trade, or even as primitive money (Chapter 3; Lenerz-de Wilde 1995).

In Voorhout, close to the Dutch coast, 18 bronze palstaves and one lugged chisel were found in a Middle Bronze Age (c. 16th–15th century BC) hoard (Butler 1990, 78–84). The fact that they were buried in a 50×50 cm pit indicates this was a hoard of axe blades, not of axes as tools. Just like in the case of the Aschering ring hoard, the similarity of the axe blades evokes notions of bulk items circulating in trade. Research by Butler (1990) and others shows the majority of the objects were produced in northern Wales and must have been transported overseas. The Voorhout hoard therefore has always been interpreted as a classic example of trade stock that was buried in the ground.

Finds like Aschering and Voorhout are examples of so-called 'trade' or 'merchant's' hoards, a find category archaeologists have recognized all over Europe and for every period of the Bronze Age and Early Iron Age (Butler 1963, 59–62). Such assemblages typically consist of large numbers of similar objects and are usually interpreted as stores or caches in which trade material was temporarily kept.

Buried collections consisting of large numbers of similar items give rise to a sense of bulk trade[1] of commodities and economicity that feels familiar to us. As a ubiquitous find category, 'trade hoards' support the perception of the Bronze Age as a period in which a new, more familiar, economic rationality emerged (cf. Chapter 1). That objects in such hoards are often interpreted as currency or early money is case in point (Kienlin 2010).

Paradoxically, these same 'trade hoards' render our understanding of a Bronze Age 'economy' problematic. The reason for this is that the trade stock of hoards like Aschering and Voorhout was never taken out again – which must never have been people's intention if the material indeed represented a temporary store of material. What's more, in both cases we are dealing with material that was placed in a peat bog – not the most obvious context to store precious trade stock. As a matter of fact, it is precisely because of their inaccessibility that hoards from watery places have long since been interpreted as representing 'ritual' 'gifts to gods' rather than rational-economic acts (Chapter 1). Was trade stock sacrificed, or does the trade content imply that we underestimate prehistoric people's capacity to store material in all sorts of places? Can we reconcile the contradiction between hoard content and context?

This chapter focuses on depositions known as 'classic trade hoards' to establish what Bronze Age economy actually entailed. What does it reveal of this economy if sizeable proportions of trade stock were repeatedly inserted in the landscape and never re-entered the short-term economy again? Can we resolve the paradox that information on such economies comes from a context that seems profoundly un-economic?

What makes a thing a commodity?

In my opinion, the widespread occurrence of hoards containing 'trade stock' is problematic, but also holds the key for understanding how the circulation of bulk metal relates to permanent deposition. Making sense of patterns in depositions of such material is central in this chapter. Before introducing these, it is important to first answer a crucial question: why is it that we almost immediately associate hoards with massive numbers of similar objects with trade? What exactly is it about the objects that makes archaeologists interpret them as a collection of *commodities*?

According to Appadurai (1986, 6–16), commodities are things with a social potential for acquiring other things without excessive cultural or social 'costs'. As discussed in more detail in Chapter 3, this implies that in order to function in such a way, things should not or only be weakly be linked to persons; they are alienable (Gregory 2015). This allows more kinds of usage, makes it easier to appropriate or transform things in anonymous units. As Appadurai (1986, 16) points out, things can be commodities by destination and/or acquire that status in the course of their use life. One way to have 'commodity candidacy' (ibid., 15) is to avoid hints at a unique, singular nature. In other words: to make them common. This can be achieved by avoiding use of rare materials or non-normative appearances and emphasizing object similarity and reference at large scale (cf. Kopytoff 1986, 68–70). Hoards containing large numbers of similar, perhaps even serially produced items as mentioned above, have all of this.

Chapter 3 argued that perceiving something as a commodity takes place in a social context. Its appearance often refers to things that have long-term socio-cultural value: axes may function as commodities, but they also are important social valuables (Chapter 3). An effective commodity is a socially recognized one (Appadurai 1986, 6). In trade, this means two things.

- The first is that among trade partners, there has to be a shared feeling on which object is accepted to act as a commodity and which are not (Harding 2013, 370–371). This comes down to exchange items having 'the right appearance' (Chapter 2).
- Second, regardless of how the things are perceived in each community, things can only function as a commodity once they are successful in obtaining other things. This means one particular thing is regarded as commensurable to other things (they are convertibles, Gregory 2015, 74–80; cf. Chapter 3).

The way in which a thing can be a *convertible* (its exchange value or 'price'; ibid.) is situated in a social setting, and subject to conventions accepted by the people involved. There are different ways in which a commodity can have such exchange value. As these matter for the material under discussion here, they will be briefly summarized. Going back to a distinction made by Aristotle between use value and immaterial or referential value (cf. Graeber 2005, 441–442) the following distinction Pare (2013) made for types of value conversion between metal items is useful for the present discussion.

1. The objects themselves have a good potential for use (evidenced by use wear, sharpening). This means that the object itself can immediately be converted to new use by its recipient.
2. The objects received can be shaped into a 'useable thing', but need not necessarily be used themselves. Conversion often only takes place after re-melting and re-shaping the objects into new ones. That the exchanged object has an axe shape indicates that the bronze affords a conversion into a new axe (cf. Borgna 1992; Pearce 2007, 88–91).
3. The object lacks both functional properties and the necessary intrinsic quality for being shaped into a useable thing. The metal, for example, is not suitable. It refers to normal tools/ornaments but cannot function as such. It is a token instead of tool. Recipients of such tokens trust the token to have further acquisitive power in other trade transactions.
4. Appearances of things do not matter, but only quantities of material that can be converted into other quantities following an abstract system of

measurement that exists outside the object (like one based on standardized weight; Rahmstorf 2010).

Type 2 in this system represents a situation where the shape of an object is important as it informs of its potential.[2] If such a system is shape- rather than weight-based, this is termed an *aes formatum* system (Haeberlin 1910). When the object is merely a token (Type 3), we are still dealing with a shape-based system. In the Bronze Age, there are many examples where a specific shape (important for 2 and 3) is coupled to a standardized weight (important in Type 4 conversions). It is unclear whether the European Bronze Age had a value conversion system for bronze that was entirely based on an overarching abstract weight system, as known from the Middle East or East Mediterranean Bronze Age (Rahmstorf 2010; Pare 2013, 524).

Ranging from the concrete to the abstract, types 1 to 4 are known from non-monetary societies all over the world (cf. Renfrew & Morley 2010), and they are usually seen as steps on an evolutionistic ladder towards the emergence of money (Simmel 2011). This may be misleading as it could blind us from studying the system in its own right. In what follows, I use Pare's classification, refraining, however, from using terms like currency or money that may be anachronistic or teleological (cf. Kienlin 2010, 175–176). To concentrate on what these things do – or are supposed to do – the term 'convertible' will be used. There are 'tool' and 'ornament convertibles' (Types 1 and 2), token convertibles (Type 3) and system convertibles where conversion refers to an abstract system in the mind (Type 4).

Axes in as-cast state or miniature token versions of axes could have functioned as Type 2, resp. Type 3 convertibles in short-term exchanges. The question is, however, whether the way they were deposited in the ground is also in line with this. In what follows, I describe how convertibles ended up in deposition. The case studies discuss the deposition of large numbers of rings, ribs and axes in Early Bronze Age Central Europe, and of large numbers of axe blades in the Middle Bronze Age and Early Iron Age of western Europe.

Example 1 – Early Bronze Age Central Europe: rings, ribs and axes as convertibles

Two convertibles became important in Central European exchanges from c. 2000 BC up until the 17th/16th century BC (Pare 2013, 513–514). These are rings (later ribs) and axes (Figure 5.1). They are all made of multi-impurity coppers and predate the full introduction of tin-bronze metal (ibid.).

Rings have been studied thoroughly by Lenerz-de Wilde (1995; 2002) and it is her seminal work that will provide the basis for what follows. She argues that a particular kind of looped neck-ring (*Ösenringe*), initially used as body ornament and known from lavish graves, over time became shaped in standardized forms with standardized weight (such as 45–50 g; 85–100 g; 175–200 g; 881–994 g; Pare 2013, 513; Lenerz-de Wilde 1995). In a vast area north of the Alps, from Bavaria

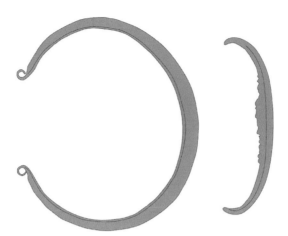

FIGURE 5.1 Figures showing a generic *Ösenring* ('ring'; left) and *Rippenbar* ('rib'; right). Such a ring usually has a length of c. 12 cm.
Source: Drawing by J. Porck, Faculty of Archaeology, University of Leiden.

to the Czech Republic, rings were deposited in massive hoards. Although in appearance similar to neck rings known from graves, these examples occur in 'every state of finish' (Vandkilde 2005, 271–272). Because of their similarity in weight, size and occurrence in large one-typed assemblages, Lenerz-de Wilde (1995) argues they were ring-*money*. In the terminology used here they are Type 2 convertibles with standardized weight as they essentially allow conversion to real use directly or after re-melting. In later phases, abstraction of appearance took place. Instead of rings, there now are 'ribs' (*Rippenbarren*) or clasp-ingots (Liversage 2001), and miniature versions thereof. They are interpreted as partial versions of rings (Hensel 2015), indicating that reference to 'ring-appearance' still mattered. These also tend to be of standardized weight (Pare 2013, 513), though of smaller weight units. Intrinsic quality of these rings and ribs declines (Liversage 2001), indicating that it apparently was no longer important whether a convertible itself could be used (after re-melting). They therefore are interpreted as tokens (Type 3 above) rather than tool convertibles.

Metallurgical research shows that both rings and ribs are made out of a type of copper alloy that is different to that from which contemporary axes were made (Junk et al. 2001: '*Ösenring* metal'). Pare (2013, 514) takes this to mean that ribs, but probably earlier rings as well, were not meant to be re-melted and re-shaped, but *were tokens in exchange that functioned in their own right*.[3] By about the 17th/16th century BC, rings and tokens feature less prominently in hoards, whilst fragment metal becomes more prominent. This coincides with the period in which tin-bronzes become dominant (Pare 2013, 514). This is interpreted as an indication that metal itself (raw and scrap) now became the main convertibles (Primas 1997, 123).[4]

Axes are the other item that is thought to have functioned as a convertible in exchanges (Lenerz-de Wilde 1995, 301–310). This is mainly derived from the fact that, like rings, they also occur in massive one-type hoards in the same region where rings and rib hoards are found. Like rings, it seems to have been important that the axe had a particular appearance, though for axes there seems to be more variety in size and shape (different 'types' of axes exist alongside each other; ibid.). Like rings and especially the younger rib variety, the casting quality of axes could be bad (Zabel in Hänsel & Hänsel 1997, 107), implying showing off the metal had 'axe potential' was more important than whether the object itself could be converted to practical use.

All this indicates that, above all, it was 'axe shape' that mattered. The fact that some show traces of basic preparation (Kienlin 2010, 175), implies that proven workability was important as well and that they were not merely ingots. Taken together, axes in such hoards are Type 2 tool convertibles or *aes formatum*, rather than tools in their own right (cf. Pearce 2007, 88–91). It is unclear whether weight standardization also was relevant to such axes.[5]

Thus, both ring/rib and axe hoards indicate convertibles were organized following a shape-based system. At least for rings and ribs, there was an underlying measurement system of conversion, but it remains unclear whether ring/rib weight units were meaningful for metal conversion in a broader sense.

Placing rings and axes in the landscape: depositional conventions in three zones compared

Rings and ribs may once have been produced with the intention of functioning as convertibles for certain socio-economic transactions. This does not mean that their role could not change. Rings are to be found in a vast area, from Bavaria to southern Scandinavia. By charting how rings ended up in the archaeological record, Vandkilde (2005, 268–271) was able to argue that the economic role of rings in northern regions was different from that in southern regions. An important addition to this statement is: *as appears from how they were finally deposited in the landscape*. Following Vandkilde (2005; also Krause 1988) three zones are to be distinguished – in each, rings were deposited following different patterns (Figure 5.2).

Zone I. In the north Alpine, Danubian zone, ranging roughly from Bavaria in the west to parts of the Czech Republic in the east, rings usually occur in large hoards that consist solely of such rings.[6] They usually were neatly ordered, and Lenerz-de Wilde (1995, 244–245) argues that there sometimes are sub-groups of five, which she interprets as indicating that hand-counting systems were used to organize large assemblages of rings. For the later ribs, Liversage (2001, 390) suggests that the total weight of buried items is often the same. He sees this as an argument that when burying material, people had clear understanding of appropriate quantity. All this implies that in Zone I, the totality of what was buried mattered and was meaningful and functional in itself. In Zone I, hoards consisting of many axes like those of type Salez that were buried in the same period are also known (Vandkilde 2005, figure 5; Krause 1988). However, axes and rings/ribs are usually not found together in one deposition. Rings/ribs and axes may have been made to

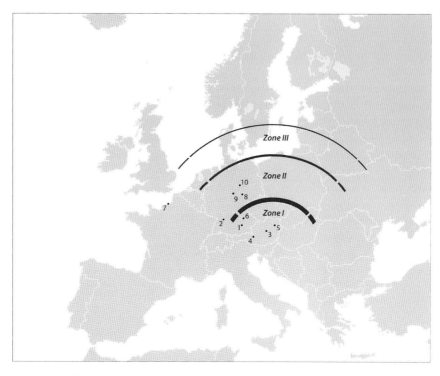

FIGURE 5.2 Schematized figure showing approximate position of Zones I–III in Europe and sites mentioned in the text. 1. Aschering; 2. Pfedelbach; 3. Riedl; 4 Obereching; 5. Ragelsdorf; 6. Haag a.d. Amper; 7. Cap Hornu; 8. Dieskau; 9. Gröbers-Bennewitz; 10. Schkopau.
Source: Drawing by J. Porck, Faculty of Archaeology, University of Leiden.

function as different kinds of convertibles in systems of exchange. What kind of transactions these were, we do not know. It may have differed from region to region. Ethnographical case studies suggest we need not just think of basic barter practices, but also of social transactions like the exchange of marriage partners (bride price), or to compensate for killings (e.g. Platenkamp 2016). The selections made when depositing such items, seems to have upheld and emphasized their separate roles.

Zone II. In central and northern Germany and Poland (the region inhabited largely by people of the northern Únětice Culture) comparable axes and rings were deposited as well. However, in this region, single-ring depositions are unknown (Vandkilde 2005, 268–270). Rings tend to be part of large hoards that contain other items like axes, ornaments or halberds (like in the large hoard of Dieskau II; Von Brunn 1959, 55–56). Also, the rings occur in smaller numbers (Lenerz-de Wilde 1995, 321–323). On the other hand, large hoards that exclusively consist of axe blades of a single type do exist. In Chapter 1, I mentioned the famous example of the east German Gröbers-Bennewitz hoard with 297 axe blades in a pot (Von

Brunn 1959, 57–58; Zabel in Hänsel & Hänsel 1997, 107), or the 124 axe blades in Schkopau (Von Brunn 1959, 66). These are often of low quality, and unfinished and finished ones co-occur in hoards. Axe blades, then, may have functioned as Type 2 (*aes formatum*?) convertibles in exchanges; their deposition in such large axe hoards indicates they were also deposited referring to this role.

Zone III. In southern Scandinavia, rings probably only rarely figured in depositions. Large hoards solely consisting of metal axes as in Zone II are also rare. There only are cases of rings and metal axes that were singly deposited in bogs (Vandkilde 2005, 275), or in exceptional hoards like Pile and Skeldal (ibid., 275–276). Rings and metal axes may have functioned as convertibles, but they were never deposited in ways that refer to such a function.[7]

One-offs. Finally, there is the case of a sizeable hoard that in content is consistent with depositions in Zone I. However, it is a one-off in the region where it was found. A collection of 71 ribs was found in western France at Cap Hornu, by the bay of the river Somme (Blanchet in Talon 2012, 80). Such ribs are extremely rare in this part of Europe. Such a hoard, however, would not be out of place in Central Europe, some 1000 km to the east. It suggests that ribs circulated as packages far beyond the circum-Alpine region (but were usually *not* deposited?). This is an example of what was termed the 'small-world effect' in Chapter 2. An indirect hint that *Ösenringe* circulated far outside their core region, but were not deposited, is that an axe found in the Netherlands was made of metal that is very similar to *Ösenring* metal (Butler 1995/1996, 166).

Ritual offerings that are like trade stores and vice versa

Many hoards of rings and ribs in Zone I come from dry contexts (Lenerz-de Wilde 2002, 16). 'Dry' is usually regarded as equivalent to 'potentially retrievable', which is what one would expect for a store. The majority are known to have been situated in settlements, like the neatly ordered ring packages found at Ragelsdorf (Austria; Lenerz-de Wilde 2002, 14). At Obereching (Austria), no fewer than four rib hoards were found in a settlement area. One of these was situated within a house (ibid., 14). This recalls actions where convertibles were stored underground, to be taken out at some later moment. As the settlement was probably destroyed by fire, the presence of these hoards may never have been intentional (ibid.). However, in total more than 1,100 rings/rib varieties were found in sixteen hoards in settlements (Lenerz-de Wilde 2002, 16). It is harder to accept that *all* of these represent forgotten or never retrieved collections of trade stock. This is particularly so if it is realized that another 218 rings come from hoards in wet contexts like peat bogs, rivers or lakes (ibid.). It is much harder to retrieve material from such contexts and therefore less likely that they represent temporary stores. Just like 'stores' in settlements, such wet depositions can consist of large numbers as well, like the c. 100 rings in Aschering, or the 60 ribs deposited in a river at Haag-an-der-Amper (ibid.). In Pfedelbach (southwest Germany) 21 rings were inserted into rock cavities along a high and steep bluff (Krause 1996). Some of the rings were ordered in

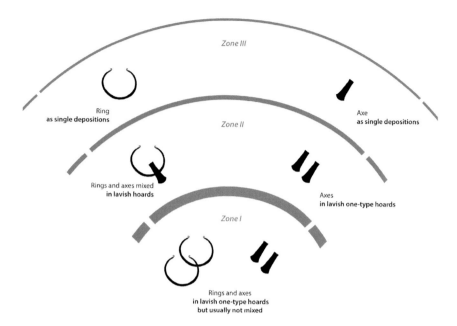

FIGURE 5.3 Zones I–III as different regimes of selective deposition for Early Bronze Age *Ösenringe* and axes
Source: Drawing by J. Porck, Faculty of Archaeology, University of Leiden.

bundles of two or three. This bluff setting is also a context from which retrieval is difficult. Lenerz-de Wilde (2002, 16) sees the settlement hoards as profane and those in wet places or dry ones like Pfedelbach as ritual.[8] If anything, these cases exemplify how problematic ritual–profane distinctions may be (cf. Chapter 1). Material deposited in an irretrievable 'ritual' setting, is actually very similar to what was deposited in a retrievable 'profane' setting. This at least implies that temporary storage need not always have been what motivated people to bury trade stock in the land. Rather, it suggests Bronze Age people *perceived such acts as important in their own right*.

Example 2 – palstave hoards in the Middle Bronze Age North Sea and Channel zone (c. 16th–13th century BC)

Hoards consisting of numerous axes (palstaves) are found in the Channel zone, stretching from southern England to northwest France during the Middle Bronze Age (in about the 16th–13th century BC; Figure 5.4). At least 23 palstave hoards are recorded in England (O'Connor 1980, 319–332) and 44 in northwest France (Gabillot 2003, table 15). Reference will also be made to such hoards in the Low Countries, as this region was closely connected to both by metal exchange. Unfortunately, find circumstances of most hoards in this area are poorly recorded (Gabillot 2003, 15), and therefore my review on depositional practices will be limited to a few general remarks.

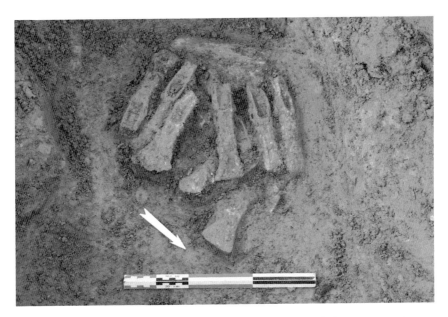

FIGURE 5.4 The Gatteville palstave hoard (Normandy, France) during its excavation
Source: Photograph by C. Marcigny.

There is no evidence for Type 3 token convertibles in this period. However, many large axe hoards consisting of finished, unfinished and sometimes as-cast axe blades are seen as arguments that metal at least circulated as axes (Barrett 1989, 315; Bradley 1990, 118–121). Absence of standardization in weight suggests they functioned as *aes formatum* (cf. Fontijn & Roymans forthcoming). Charting how axes were deposited, it is possible to recognize something reminiscent of Vandkilde's (2005) 'Zone II situation' described above.

First, there is the south English–northwest French zone in which axe blades were deposited individually or with other objects in a variety of contexts like rivers. There are also many hoards that consist almost entirely of axes (palstaves; Gabillot 2003; O'Connor 1980, 319–332). Axes occur in different (regional) varieties but British and French types were clearly affiliated (Butler & Steegstra 1997/1998). Although this has not been systematically verified, well-studied finds demonstrate as-cast, finished and unfinished palstaves were deposited together (Fontijn & Roymans forthcoming; Verney 1991), supporting the view they were deposited referring to a role as *aes formatum*. This is particularly clear for certain palstaves from Brittanny. Gabillot shows these were produced in large quantities in standardized shape. Even though they were often finished, they show many casting errors, suggesting appearance mattered more than practical use potential (Gabillot 2003, 99; 2006).

Second, beyond the south English–northwest France Channel region, in the northern Low Countries, as-cast or unfinished palstaves of similar shape rarely figure in depositions (Fontijn 2002, 315–320). Axe types that are prevalent in northwest France (type Normand) or southern Britain (e.g. Acton Park palstaves)

96 Trade hoards

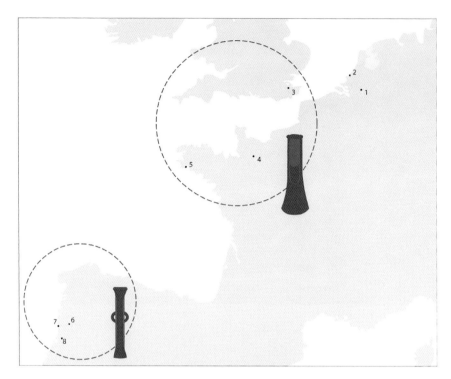

FIGURE 5.5 Schematized figure showing zone with many palstave hoards (encircled) and comparable finds outside the concentration mentioned in the text for Middle Bronze Age south England and northwest France and Late Bronze Age northwest Iberia. 1. Hoogeloon; 2. Voorhout; 3. Birchington; 4. La Chapelle; 5. Saint-Thois; 6. Gingleta; 7. Cobidalto; 8. Abelheira.
Source: Drawing by J. Porck, Faculty of Archaeology, University of Leiden.

are rare in the Low Countries (Fontijn 2002; Verlaeckt 1996) and so are hoards of axes in general (Butler 1990). This reminds us of Vandkilde's 'marginal' Zone III (cf. Figure 5.6). This makes the hoards from Voorhout at the Dutch coast (referred to in the introduction) and the one recently discovered at Hoogeloon in the southern Netherlands all the more exceptional. Voorhout mainly consists of Acton Park palstaves imported from Wales, and Hoogeloon of type Normand (-related) palstaves and one British one (Butler 1990, 78–84; Fontijn & Roymans forthcoming). Except for these hoards, such palstaves are hardly known from finds in the Low Countries and one-offs. Yet, in composition and nature (finished and unfinished axes of French-British style) the Voorhout and Hoogeloon finds are consistent with what is found in palstave hoards in northwest France and (southern) Britain. This is another example of the 'small-world effect' (see above and Chapter 2).

Contextual information is only poorly recorded and/or published. For some, it is clear that only axe blades were deposited. The Birchington hoard (UK), for example, consists of 14 palstaves which were placed in a pot – something which is

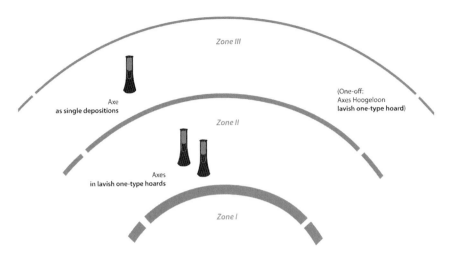

FIGURE 5.6 Zones I–III as different regimes of selective deposition for Middle Bronze Age palstave depositions in the south England–northwest French Channel zone. A situation similar to that of Zone I (token versus other axes) does not exist. There is patterned deposition of one-type *aes formatum* axes (Zone II), as well as deposition of single axes outside these areas (Zone III).
Source: Drawing by J. Porck, Faculty of Archaeology, University of Leiden.

only possible if there were no shafts attached (O'Connor 1980, 324). The same is true for many French hoards (e.g. the Gatteville hoard; Figure 5.4; Le Carlier & Marcigny 2011). For French hoards in particular, it has been recorded that many were buried in dry ground. In some cases, axe blades were ordered in a specific way (Gabillot 2003, 14). This is for example the case for the French hoard of La Chapelle-du-Bois-des-Faulx (Normandy; Verney 1991), where two axe hoards were found close to each other. In one, the axes were neatly stacked in a pit, and there are indications that they were bundled in groups of two or three (Verney 1991, 119). At Saint-Thois, 155 axe blades were found in an organic bag which was placed in a cache where the wall and floor were plastered with clay (Gabillot 2003, 14). Both situations give the impression that packages of blades were carefully stored. Something similar may have happened at the Dutch site of Voorhout, where 18 British and French palstaves were placed in a small pit. However, as mentioned in the introduction to this chapter, this pit was located in a peat bog. Such a location is a far less logical place to temporarily store material. At Hoogeloon in the Netherlands, a collection of palstave blades that is very similar to those of La Chapelle-du-Bois-des-Faulx in Normandy, was thrown as a package into a pool (Fontijn & Roymans forthcoming). This is also not a practical location for a cache.

Poor as the contextual evidence may be, it is clear that 'trade stock' was deposited in different contexts in the landscape, including watery ones from which actual retrieval would be hard. The settings often suggest material was being stored (cf. Birchington or Saint-Thois). However, as this is also true for material from inaccessible settings (cf. the peat bog hoard of Voorhout) it is doubtful whether later recovery was always intended. The large numbers of hoards that remained in the ground and the sizeable quantity of material again make it hard to conceive of all these hoards as material that was unintentionally left in the ground.

Summing up, in the northwest French–south British zone, packages of (*aes formatum*, Type 2) axes were regularly deposited (cf. the Zone II situation above). North of it (Low Countries) the same axes were rarely deposited, although exceptional finds indicate that they did reach the area. In this region, single deposition of regional palstaves in wet places was the general pattern (cf. the Zone III situation mentioned above; Fontijn 2002, 119–125).

Example 3 – axe hoards in the Late Bronze Age Iberian northwest

As a comparison, in this section I briefly consider hoards with Late Bronze Age palstaves in northwest Iberia (Portugal and part of Galicia). Like the northwest European region discussed above, palstaves were the most common type of bronze deposited, occurring in many kinds of depositions. In appearance, we are dealing with quite a different looking axe, evidencing cultural differences with northern societies. Casting cones are usually still present on such axes, and many have casting errors or are unfinished as well as often unused (Sampaio 2015, 60, figures 2, 4, 6, 8). The often high percentage of lead in the metal composition (sometimes in excess of 50 per cent; Sampaio 2015, table 2) also makes these unsuitable for practical use. All this indicates they were made as token axes (Type 3 convertibles). Similarly looking (but not identical) axe blades were deposited together in numbers ranging from a few to 34. Sampaio's (2015) contextual study shows axe blades were deposited in small pits in dry land and covered by a slab (like at Abelheira – S. Martinho do Bougado), but also in cavities in rocks (Cobidalto hoard) and in watery locations (Gingleta-Ganfei: alluvial margin of river, ibid., 57–65). Sampaio argues that palstave hoards were buried away from domestic contexts. Rather, they were located along routes, corridors and rivers, observing, as it were, such routes (ibid., 65). Some were close to watercourses that are rich in alluvial cassiterite (SnO_2) – zones that possibly held special significance as places where rare tin could be won (ibid., 66).

So, even though the appearance of the axes is entirely different from those in the northwest-French–south English region, their deposition has similarities. Palstaves of comparable appearance were deposited together. This happened both in accessible locations and those that are harder to access. Again, this depositional pattern brings Vandkilde's (2005) Zone II depositions to mind, where one kind of convertible was deposited in one-type hoards separately from other metalwork.[9]

Example 4 – deposition of axes and token axes in Early Iron Age northwest Europe

In the Early Iron Age (800–500 BC), there were many functional axes, but also large numbers of objects that look like axes but cannot be used. Huth (2003, 48)

FIGURE 5.7 One of the two Agneaux token axe hoards during the excavation
Source: Photograph by C. Marcigny.

interprets the latter as ingots (Type 2 convertibles). For many types, however, this is unlikely and they are better interpreted as tokens (Type 3; Roberts et al. 2015, 387). For practical use, they either are too thin, have an unsuitable metal composition, are miniatures or all of that together (Huth 2003, 44–49). They are known in many regions of Europe from Portugal up to southeast Europe (ibid., figure 4). Their precise use is unknown, but given the fact that they were produced in large quantities, they must have figured in regular and important social transactions. Focusing on evidence from northwest Europe, I will chart whether, and if so how, token and regular axes were used in depositional practices. Token axes are known from some regions in northwest Europe (southern England, northwest France and the Belgian-Dutch-German Meuse-Rhine region). Their appearance is different for each region, which may be explained from the fact they probably mimic axes current in their region.

The Belgian and Dutch Geistingen axes are a thin-walled and relatively well-made token socketed axe. Butler and Steegstra (2001/2002, 309) argued that they were modelled after regular Wesseling axes. Most Geistingen axes were part of hoards in (semi-) dry ground that seem to have consisted exclusively of such axes (Fontijn 2002, 161). The eponymous hoard contained 26 or 28 axes of which it was recorded that they were placed as a package in a circle, tied up with a rope (Butler & Steegstra 2001/2002, 304). Their regular, useable counterpart (Wesseling axes) occurs in hoards as well, but there is no evidence that regular and token axes were deposited together (Fontijn 2002, 162). In the same region, at least one other token axe was in circulation: the equally well-made thin-walled axes of type

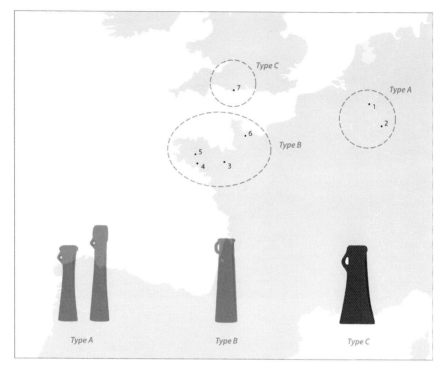

FIGURE 5.8 Simplified picture of regions where clusters of Early Iron Age token axe hoards occur. Symbols of axes are simplified and only serve to give an impression of their appearance. A. Belgian-Dutch-German Meuse-Rhine region: Amelsbüren and Geistingen token axes; B. northwest France: Armorican token axes; C. southern England: Portland token axes; 1. Geistingen (Belgium); 2. Amelsbüren (Germany); 3. Maure-de-Bretagne; 4. Menez-Ru; 5. Guesman; 6. Agneaux; 7. Langton Matravers (UK).
Source: Drawing by J. Porck, Faculty of Archaeology, University of Leiden.

Amelsbüren (Fontijn 2002, 164; Kibbert 1984, 168). Some of them are known from peat bogs, and there is at least one hoard.

A comparable selective deposition of token axes is represented by the so-called Armorican axes of Lower Normandy and Brittany. Unlike carefully finished Geistingen axes, Armorican axes look as if they came straight from the mould, rarely showing any kind of secondary working. They often show casting errors and stand out markedly from contemporary bronzes by the unusually high percentages of lead (Briard 1965, 259). By sheer quantity they out-rival token axes in all the other regions. For the latest part of the Late Bronze Age and particularly the Early Iron Age, an estimated 32,500 axes are known (Briard 1965, 242). In form, they share traits with regular linear axes (cf. O'Connor 1980, 232), but they occur in a variety of shapes, including miniatures, suggesting that they were a distinct class of valuable (Briard 1965, 247–271). In Normandy and Brittany, they were buried in equally impressive numbers. The Maure-de-Bretagne hoard consists of 4,000 miniature axes (ibid., 242), and at least six others are known that contain between 500 and 1,000. More common hoards are still impressive, containing between 100 and 300 axes (ibid., 242–243). Although hoards may contain different kinds of Armorican axe, they are only rarely associated with other axes or items. In some cases, broken metal of other Armorican axes was placed in their sockets (Marcigny & Verney 2005). Within Armorica, they thus represent an extravagant, but strictly selective kind of deposition. At Menez-Ru, axes were placed in such a way as to create a triangle. At Guesman, axes were placed in circles and ten rows of axes were stacked on top of each other (Briard 1965, 243). In some cases, axes were placed in a ceramic or bronze vessel, and curiously, a second but empty vessel was placed close to it. Axe packages tend to be buried in dry locations. Some were buried close to rock outcrops or Neolithic megaliths, or contemporary cremation graves (though not in graves; Briard 1965, 245). At Marchésieux, at least eight such hoards were deposited. They were placed along an 80 metre axis in a humid area (perhaps along a path?) that lacks traces of other contemporary activities. For one hoard, it is clear that it was deposited at the banks of a swamp (Verron 2005). At Agneaux, two hoards were found in pits close to a barrow landscape that had been in use since the Middle Bronze Age (Marcigny & Verney 2005). All cases where find circumstances are recorded indicate we are dealing with carefully stacked, ordered and buried groups of material that were neatly kept separate from other objects in circulation. Although they may appear to us as the apex of the bizarre wastefulness of prehistoric people, there is nothing which indicates material was dumped or left because it lost its meaning and value.

In the Early Iron Age of southern England, Armorican axes were also deposited, albeit in much smaller numbers. Other axes that were placed in the landscape are regular ones (type Sompting) and so-called linear faceted axes of which there are several sub-groups (O'Connor 1980, 231–233; Roberts et al. 2015, 373). The so-called Portland variety is of particular interest here, as like Armorican ones, these are non-functional axes. Their metal contains high tin levels, which renders them unsuitable for practical use and gives them a silvery colour. They are also poorly finished and many axes from the Langton Matravers hoard still contained their casting cores and were in as-cast condition (Roberts et al. 2015). In depositions, Portland axes in general were separated from other objects (like Armorican axes were). It is clear that different production batches were present in one hoard (ibid.), indicating that people by all means strived to reproduce self-referential items with a standardized appearance. This is also a feature of Armorican axes. Hoards consisting of Portland axes are usually located on high ground, away from settlements (Yates & Bradley 2010), either overlooking the Channel or close to rivers. For these token axes there was also a tendency towards mass deposition. One of the largest bronze finds of the UK, the Langton Matravers find consisted entirely of such axes (373 intact and 404 fragments; Roberts et al. 2015), which were distributed across four adjacent pits. These were situated in a location overlooking the sea. According to Roberts et al. (2015), this is a characteristic location for hoards containing Portland axes.

102 Trade hoards

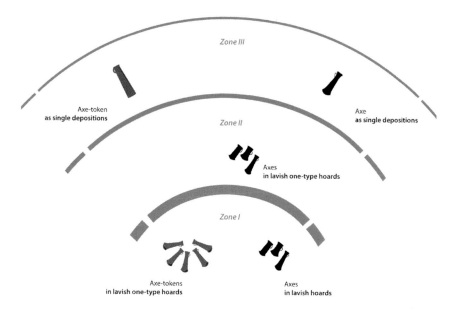

FIGURE 5.9 Zones I–III as different regimes of selective deposition for Early Iron Age axes. There are areas where token axes and other axes are deposited in axe hoards, but separately (Zone I). The latter also occur outside of that zone (Zone II). Beyond, there is deposition of single (token) axes outside these areas (Zone III).
Source: Drawing by J. Porck, Faculty of Archaeology, University of Leiden.

Summing up, at the transition from the Bronze Age to the Iron Age token axes start to function alongside more regular ones. It is only in a few regions that they are found in some numbers, and in all we are dealing with tokens that are characteristic of the region. Sometimes, even more than one kind of token axe was in use (Meuse-Rhine area: Geistingen vs. Amelsbüren token axes). At the beginning of the Iron Age in northwest Europe, a similar development took place in regions that were not always closely connected (e.g. Meuse-Rhine vs. northwest France): the mass burial in the ground of token axes. Everywhere, this happened in a selective way – token axes were buried with token axes of the same shape (even when in fragments; cf. the Agneaux hoard), and not with regular axes. Especially in northwest France, it seems to have been common practice to deposit hundreds of token axes at the same time. It is unknown in what social contexts and for what reasons such depositions took place. The 'line' of token axe hoards at and along the Marchésieux swamp suggests there was a concern to 'mimic' previous depositional actions (Verron 2005; cf. Løvschal & Fontijn 2018 for other examples of such pit alignments). This implies it was a social event that was important enough to repeat.

According to Huth (2003, 48), it is not this massive deposition that should surprise us. He argues societies always have to create stores of material for future use: it is rather their non-retrieval which indicates something special was going on. His explanation is that at the transition to the Iron Age, supplies of bronze alloys were shifting and collapsing. Stored material devaluated, lost its meaning and caches were not opened again. As Huth (2003, 48) puts it: 'there was a sudden surplus (…) which could no longer be exchanged'. As a general explanation, this is not entirely convincing. In the Meuse-Rhine region, for example, the unprecedented lavish metalwork depositions in Hallstatt C graves defies any hint at there being a crisis or stagnation in the supply of bronze (Van der Vaart-Verschoof 2017). In France, the almost 300 known hoards of Armorican axes represent the same number of individual depositional events, done by communities everywhere in the region. Token axes clearly had an important significance to these people. The fact that they were carefully buried in massive numbers at specific places in the landscape, time and again, suggests that this act of burial was equally important. A supra-regional comparison as done here strengthens Roberts et al.'s (2015) view that these hoards represent 'lavish' depositions rather than 'collapsing commodities'.

Conclusion: deposition as 'objectifying' spheres of exchange

The above overview shows a few remarkable time-transgressive traits in how bronze-using people interacted with bronzes.

1. Time and again, people buried massive numbers of uniform objects in the landscape. It did not happen everywhere, but only in certain regions during certain periods. In western Europe, for over a millennium, it was axe blades that were buried in such large numbers.
2. In regions where this happened, there is evidence that different types of convertibles were kept separate in deposition (e.g. *aes formatum* Type 2 convertibles vs. tokens (Type 3) in Zone I situations).
3. Through time, we see that the objects tend to be carefully deposited. This often happened in locations that were potentially accessible, but also in ones from which it would have been hard to retrieve them.
4. Though they look like stores or caches, the fact that they were only opened by modern archaeologists demonstrates that they did not function as such.

Such finds are conventionally called 'trade hoards', but how do they relate to metal trade? For a commodity exchange to function there have to be shared conceptions on how one particular valuable can be converted into others (e.g. 1 X = 2 Y; cf. Gregory 2015, 74–78). As explained in Chapter 4, metal adds an entirely new dimension to such transactions. The re-melting option potentially allows far more possibilities for conversion of metal than just the exchange of one object X for two Ys. Finds of large collections of heterogeneous, partly fragmented metalwork from cargoes in the sea like Salcombe or Langdon Bay (Needham et al. 2013) indeed suggest metal circulated as scrap metal, at least in the later Bronze Age. This implies that there were other systems of value conversion in use as well (such as by weight units; Primas 1997). However, in Early Bronze Age central

Europe and western Europe up until the Early Iron Age, the above overview indicates metal circulated – at least partly – *as axes* (Barrett 1989, 315). It follows that *aes formatum* axes were a specific kind of valuable, probably used for restricted social transactions only. This is even more clear when there are also bronze tokens, as the Early Bronze Age ribs or the Early Iron Age token axes. Because of their composition, they can no longer be converted into useable metal tools. This means that the commodity exchange system relied more on 'trust': shared beliefs of what could be obtained in exchange for such tokens. So, it is not so much trade in general that 'trade hoards' are linked to. Massive deposition of similarly-looking items are rather related to a specific *class* of valuables and convertibles in such transactions.

The fact that we have evidence for both the circulation of scrap metal and convertibles with a specific appearance implies there were separate 'spheres of exchange' or 'value classes' (Kopytoff 1986, 70; Vandkilde 2005). Within a particular sphere, there are conventions on which things can be exchanged for or converted into other things (Bohannan 1959). Spheres are morally ranked, and this makes it hard to exchange something from a higher sphere with something from a lower one. As Kopytoff (1986, 70) argues, such separate spheres exist in every society. They provide means to manage value between one extreme where everything is alienable and exchangeable for everything else, and the other extreme where every object is of singular cultural value and cannot change ownership (is inalienable; ibid.).

A 'sacrificial economy'

The 'trade hoards' discussed here are usually interpreted as storage. There is no doubt that storing metal must have been common practice in the Bronze Age. Communities in non-metalliferous regions in particular must have had metal surpluses that they could rely on when needed. Wiseman (2017) models that 85–95 per cent of metal in Late Bronze Age Britain must have been hoarded to create sustainable metal stock. He argues that this involved random accumulation and breaking of bronze objects and hoards. The examples discussed in this chapter, however, are not random but selective. In my opinion we are dealing with 'stores' of commodities aimed at specific exchange transactions only: objects meant to function in one specific sphere of exchange.

This implies that there was more going on than just 'storage'. There is not only a tendency to bury certain valuables separately from others. Some of the above examples also show that the act of burial was sometimes a performance in itself involving some kind of 'ritualization' (Bell 1997). As described above, there are examples of axes laid out in circles or triangles. There are indications that such acts were repeated, or simultaneously carried out in each other's vicinity (e.g. the eight hoards from Early Iron Age Marchésieux). Particularly for the Early Iron Age cases, the huge quantities deposited on a single occasion (like the hundreds at Langton Matravers or the 4,000 token axes at Maure-de-Bretagne) make it clear that their burial must have been impressive for onlookers. Doing this at special locations may have further imbued the act with special significance (cf. burial at the margin of a river (Gingleta-Ganfei), in or alongside swamps (Marchésieux), or close to burial mounds (Agneaux)). Such actions suggest that if temporary storage was the intention, it was surrounded by ceremony and special performance. As Needham (2001, 294) suggests, this may have been to ritually ensure their safekeeping. But by such qualities of human performance (Lambek 2008), 'commodities' become linked more strongly to persons and to cultural values. To a certain extent, commodities acquired a certain inalienability.

This raises an important question: what does it do to 'commodities' if they are removed from circulation and made invisible in general? Simmel (2011, 147), recalling Aristotle's philosophy, wrote that 'an unsold commodity is merely a possible commodity'. What we find in 'trade' hoards has commodity potential, and in the emphasis on generic qualities, mutual commensurability by identical appearance seen in such depositions, it is commodity qualities that are referred to. But this was done in an act *that precluded the very circulation that would have made them into real commodities*. Placing this material in the ground transformed the very nature of the material. From something that was visible and useable in life, it became an invisible 'out there'. Writing on hoarding money, Marx (cited by Graeber 2001, 100–101), states that concrete coins become abstract money when hoarded and hidden from view. They represent a 'capacity to act' (cf. Graeber 2001, chapter 4; Brandherm et al. 2018, 5). In the Bronze Age, carefully selecting and arranging specific convertibles in a deposition pit may have had the effect of first to emphasize and make concrete (to 'objectify'[10]) the valuables operating in a specific sphere of exchange, before they were hidden from view. Whether this was explicitly intended or not, when repeated over and over again such acts have the effect of conveying memory on the right order of things in the minds of onlookers and participants. When sealed, the memory of such an act may have lived on (cf. Rowlands 1993). The act of deposition itself thus was an important act in which the right *order* of things (the different spheres of valuables) was socially 'anchored' by a special performance (cf. Wengrow 2011). This becomes particularly clear from the fact that 'trade stock' was deposited in similar ways in locations where retrieval was difficult or impossible, rendering obsolete the entire idea that retrieval was the only aim.

By burying material referring to a commodity status, material that functioned in or was destined for short-term economic transactions effectively became part of a long-term sphere of exchange (Chapter 1). Above I gave examples for different regions and periods where trade stock was deposited at specific locations in the landscape (bluffs, peat bogs, lakes, near barrow landscapes). Using economic terminology, it is as if trade stock was *given* to the landscape. In Chapter 1, I argued that it is crucial that the flow of alienable goods should always be connected with the long-term sphere of inalienable cultural ideas and values (Bloch & Parry 1989). As De Coppet (1985) argues, in non-modern society the landscape (and all the imagined entities supposed to live in it) tends to be seen as the ultimate owner of society (Chapter 7). Depositing material acquired in acquisitive, short-term transactions in the landscape may therefore have been regarded as re-contextualizing it within the long-term order of local society, by making it part of what outlasts everything: the local landscape (Fontijn & Roymans forthcoming; cf. Shennan 1993).

As Needham (2001) argues, such a deposition need not have been permanent. As happened in Greek and Roman temples, commodities intended for specific social transactions might have been temporarily 'ritualized' and forfeited but could be recovered at a later stage and re-enter short-term circulation (ibid.; Hansen 2016, 186). If this was regular practice, such hoards were not supposed to remain in the ground permanently. Hoards of trade stock that are unique in their region may represent situations where the majority of imported material was indeed recycled and only a *pars pro toto* permanently deposited in the landscape to make the entire exchange transaction morally acceptable (e.g. one-offs like the Central European rib tokens at French Cap Hornu, or the French palstave package of Hoogeloon in the Netherlands; also Hansen 2016). However, as long as the general recycling cannot be attested this explanation remains hypothetical. If anything, the above review demonstrates that later recovery was optional. It is not just that commodities were often *not* retrieved. It is also that for different periods we see that the same material was also deposited in inaccessible locations, indicating it was meant to remain part of the landscape. This implies that placing trade material in the ground was a more encompassing practice than storage or safe-keeping. Later recovery could have been one of the intentions, but this in itself does not explain the particular selectivity regarding content and location where it was carried out (cf. Needham 2001). In a way, spheres of value were 'created' or 'made real' by the very act in which valuables were hidden from view. So, valuables were not merely 'consumed' in deposition (Vandkilde 2005, 268), but *deposition itself was an act that created meaning and value*. I will return to this in Chapter 8.

The conclusion is inescapable that the 'un-economic' giving-up of commodities by burial in the landscape *was an integral part of what a Bronze Age economy was about*. Adopting a phrase from Küchler (1997), the Bronze Age economy was a 'sacrificial economy'.

Notes

1 The term 'trade' is used here as is conventional in Bronze Age archaeology – referring to exchange of commodities in general (cf. Gregory 2015). It is sometimes understood as specifically referring to commodity exchange in a monetary system with markets (Harding 2013, 370). Such a system did not exist in Bronze Age Europe.
2 Kienlin (2010, 175) argues that this is also true for things usually designated as ingots. The fact that some 'ingots' had basic preparation after casting indicates that showing off affordance was important for them as well. They were more than just unworked rough-outs.
3 There is some discussion on whether this is correct. It has been suggested there is an example of an axe of *Ösenring* metal (see further in text; Butler 1995 and 1996, 166).
4 Whether this implies that a new system emerged in which reference to a weight system existing outside of the objects (Type 4 mentioned here; cf. Primas 1997, 123), remains

to be investigated. So far, there are no indications for adherence to standard weight units at a supra-regional scale in Europe (Pare 2013, 517).
5 Lenerz-de Wilde (1995) argues that there is no weight standardization among axes as we have it with rings and ribs. Whether this still stands up to scrutiny is currently being investigated by Catalin Popa and Maikel Kuijpers (Leiden).
6 This is average behaviour (Chapter 2). There certainly are exceptions, for example Riedl (Bavaria): 15 rings with one flanged axes and four arm spirals (Weihermann in Hänsel & Hänsel 1997, 183); Ragelsdorf 1 (Austria): four flanged axes, one complete and ten fragmented rings, one arm spiral, 14 arm spiral fragments; Ragelsdorf 2: 150 rings and a few arm spirals (Lenerz-de Wilde 2002, 5–6).
7 Vandkilde (2005, 275) argues flint daggers played such a role in south Scandinavia, because these do occur in massive one-type hoards and are rarely deposited together with metalwork.
8 'Im Rahmen von Kulthandlungen deponiert' (Lenerz-de Wilde 2002, 16).
9 Not much is known on deposition of such Iberian axes beyond this region.
10 Thomas 1996, 169.

Bibliography

Appadurai, A., 1986. Introduction: commodities and the politics of value, in: *The social life of things. Commodities in cultural perspective*, ed. A. Appadurai. Cambridge: Cambridge University Press, 3–63.

Barrett, J., 1989. Food, gender and metal: questions of social reproduction, in: *The Bronze Age–Iron Age transition in Europe. Aspects of continuity and change in European societies c. 1200 to 500 B.C.* (British Archaeological Reports International Series 483), eds M.L.S. Sørensen and R. Thomas. Oxford: Archaeopress, 304–320.

Bell, C., 1997. *Ritual. Perspectives and dimensions*. New York and Oxford: Oxford University Press.

Bloch, M. and J. Parry, 1989. Introduction: money and the morality of exchange, in: *Money and the morality of exchange*, eds J. Parry and M. Bloch. Cambridge: Cambridge University Press, 1–31.

Bohannan, P., 1959. The impact of money on an African subsistence economy, *Journal of Economic History* 19, 491–503.

Borgna, E., 1992: *Il ripostiglio di Madriolo presso Cividale e I pani a piccone del Fruili-Venezia Giula* (Studi e ricerche di Protostoria mediterranea 1). Rome: Quasar.

Bradley, R., 1990. *The passage of arms. An archaeological analysis of prehistoric hoards and votive deposits*. Cambridge: Cambridge University Press.

Brandherm, D., E. Heymans and D. Hofmann, 2018. Introduction: comparing currency and circulation systems in past societies, in: *Gifts, goods and money. Comparing currency and circulation systems in past societies*, eds D. Brandherm, E. Heymans and D. Hofmann. Oxford: Archaeopress, 1–8.

Briard, J., 1965. *Les dépôts Bretons et l'Âge du bronze Atlantique* (Travaux du Laboratoire d'Anthropologie Préhistorique). Rennes: Faculté des Sciences de Rennes.

Butler, J.J., 1963. Bronze Age connections across the North Sea. A study in prehistoric trade and industrial relations between the British Isles, The Netherlands, North Germany and Scandinavia, c. 1700–1700 B.C, *Palaeohistoria* IX, 1–286.

Butler, J.J., 1990. Bronze Age metal and amber in the Netherlands (I), *Palaeohistoria* 32, 47–110.

Butler, J.J., 1995/1996. Bronze Age metal and amber in the Netherlands (II:1). Catalogue of the flat axes, flanged axes and Stopridge axes, *Palaeohistoria* 37/38, 159–243.

Butler, J.J. and J. Steegstra, 1997/1998. Bronze Age metal and amber in the Netherlands (II:2). Catalogue of the palstaves, *Palaeohistoria* 39/40, 163–275.

Butler, J.J. and J. Steegstra, 2001/2002. Bronze Age metal and amber in the Netherlands (III: 2). Catalogue of the socketed axes, Part A, *Palaeohistoria* 43/44, 263–319.

De Coppet, D., 1985. ... Land owns people, in: *Contexts and levels. Anthropological essays on hierarchy*, eds R.H. Barnes, D. de Coppet and R.J. Parkin. Oxford: JASO, 78–90.

Fontijn, D.R., 2002. Sacrificial landscapes. Cultural biographies of persons, objects and 'natural' places in the Bronze Age of the southern Netherlands, c. 2300–2600 BC, *Analecta Praehistorica Leidensia* 33/34, 1–392.

Fontijn, D.R., 2008. 'Traders hoards': reviewing the relationship between trade and permanent deposition: the case of the Dutch Voorhout hoard, in: *Hoards from the Neolithic to the Metal ages in Europe: technical and codified practices* (British Archaeological Reports International Series 1758), eds C. Hamon and B. Quillec, Oxford: Archaeopress, 5–17.

Fontijn, D.R. and J. Roymans, forthcoming. Branded axes, thrown into a pool? The Hoogeloon hoard and the shape-based bronze economy of the Northwest European Bronze Age, *Oxford Journal of Archaeology*.

Gabillot, M. 2003. *Dépôts et production métallique du Bronze moyen en France nord-occidentale* (British Archaeological Reports international Series 1174). Oxford: Archaeopress.

Gabillot, M. 2006. Les manipulations après la fonte des objets en alliage cuivreux: caractéristique sociale, éonomique, culturelle? L'exemple des haches à talon du Bronze moyen du Nord-Ouest français, in: *Normes techniques et pratiques de la simplicité des outillages pré- et protohistoriques (Antibes, XXVIe rencontres internationals d'archéologie et d'histoire d'Antibes)*, eds L. Astruc, L. Bon, V. Léa, P.-Y. Milcent and S. Philibert. Antibes: Editions APDCA, 287–295.

Godelier, M., 1999. *The enigma of the gift*. Cambridge and Oxford: Polity Press.

Graeber, D., 2001. *Toward an anthropological theory of value: the false coin of our own dreams*. New York: Palgrave.

Graeber, D., 2005. Value: anthropological theory of value, in: *A handbook of economic anthropology*, ed. J.G. Carrier. Cheltenham and Northampton MA: Edward Elgar, 439–454.

Gregory, C.A., 2015 [1982]. *Gifts and commodities*, Chicago: Hau Books.

Haeberlin, E.J., 1910. *Aes Grave. Das Schwergeld Roms und Mittelitaliens einschliesslich der ihm Vorausgehenden Rohbronzewährung, vol. 1*. Frankfurt am Main: J. Baer & Co.

HänselA. and B. Hänsel (eds), 1997. *Gaben an die Götter* (Seminar zur Ur- und Frühgeschichte der Freien Universität). Berlin: Museum für Vor- und Frühgeschichte.

Hansen, S., 2016. A short history of fragments in hoards of the Bronze Age, in: *Materielle Kultur und Identität im Spannungsfeld zwischen Mediterraner Welt und Mitteleuropa* (Akten der Internationalen Tagung am Römisch-Germanischen Zentralmuseums Mainz, 22–24 Oktober 2014), ed. H. Baitinger. Mainz: Verlag des Römisch-Germanischen Zentralmuseums, 185–208.

Harding, A., 2013. Trade and exchange, in: *The Oxford handbook of the European Bronze Age*, eds H. Fokkens and A. Harding. Oxford: Oxford University Press, 370–381.

Hensel, M., 2015. Untersuchungen zum Konsum einer archäologischen Objektgruppe über die Grenzen von Zeit, Raum und Kontext, in: *The limits of change. Was ist der Wert der beständigen Dinge?*, eds L. Picht, K. Schmidt, G. Schmitz and L. Wiggering. Berlin: Neofelis Verlag, 215–234.

Huth, C., 1997. *Westeuropäische Horte der Spätbronzezeit. Fundbild und Funktion* (Regensburger Beiträge zur prähistorischen Archäologie III). Bonn: Habelt Verlag.

Huth, C., 2003. Poor Belgium, rich Belgium. Reflections on the nature of metalwork depositions in the Late Bronze Age and Early Iron Age, in: *Exchange and interaction. The role of the Scheldt and Meuse during the Bronze Age and the iron Age,*. eds. J. Bourgeois and I. Bourgeois. Brussels: Vlaams Kennis- en Cultuurforum, 39–60.

Junk, M., R. Krause and E. Pernicka, 2001. Ösenringbarren and the classical Ösenring copper, in: *Patina. Essays presented to J.J. Butler on the occasion of his 80th birthday*, eds W.H. Metz, B.L. van Beek and H. Steegstra. Groningen and Amsterdam: privately published by Metz, Van Beek & Steegstra, 353–366.

Kibbert, K., 1984. *Die Äxte und Beile im mittleren Westdeutschland II* (Prähistorische Bronzefunde IX: 13). Munich: C.H. Beck.

Kienlin, T., 2010. *Traditions and transformations: approaches to Eneolithic (Copper Age) and Bronze Age metalworking and society in Eastern Central Europe and the Carpathian Basin* (British Archaeological Reports International Series 2184). Oxford: Archaeopress.

Kopytoff, I., 1986. The cultural biography of things: commoditisation as process, in: *The social life of things*, ed. A. Appadurai. Cambridge: Cambridge University Press, 64–91.

Krause, R., 1988. *Die endneolithischen und frühbronzezeitlichen Metallurgie Grabfunde auf der Nord-stadtterrasse von Singen am Hohentwiel* (Forschungen und Berichte zur Vor- und Frühgeschichte in Baden-Württemberg 32). Stuttgart: Konrad Theiss Verlag.

Krause, R., 1996. Deponiert und vergraben: ein frühbronzezeitliches Ösenringdepot von Pfedelbach, Hohenlohekreis, *Archäologische Ausgrabungen in Baden-Württemberg*, 60–63.

Küchler, S., 1997. Sacrificial economy and its objects, *Journal of Material Culture* 2, 39–60.

Lambek, M., 2008. Value and virtue, *Anthropological Theory* 8(2), 133–157.

Le Carlier, C. and C. Marcigny, 2011. Nouveaux travaux sur les dépôts de l'âge du bronze dans la Manche, *Bulletin du Groupe de Recherches Archéologiques du Cotentin* 14, 28–31.

Lenerz-de Wilde, M., 1995. Prämonetäre Zahlungsmittel in der Kupfer- und Bronzezeit Mitteleuropas, *Fundberichte aus Baden-Württemberg* 20, 229–327.

Lenerz-de Wilde, M., 2002. Bronzezeitliche Zahlungsmittel, *Mitteilungen der Anthropologischen Gesellschaft in Wien* 132, 1–23.

Liversage, D., 2001. Riddle of the ribs, in: *Patina. Essays presented to J.J. Butler on the occasion of his 80th birthday*, eds W.H. Metz, B.L. van Beek and H. Steegstra. Groningen and Amsterdam: privately published by Metz, Van Beek & Steegstra, 377–398.

Løvschal and D. Fontijn, 2018. Directionality and axiality in the Bronze Age: cross-regional landscape perspectives on 'fire pit lines' and other pitted connections, *World Archaeology*, doi:10.1080/00438243.2018.1488609.

Marcigny, C. and A. Verney, 2005. La nécropole d'Agneaux (Manche) et ses dépôts, in: *La Normandie à l'aube de l'histoire, les découvertes archéologiques de l'âge du Bronze 2300–800 av. JC.*, eds C. Marcigny, C. Colonna, E. Ghesquière and G. Verron. Paris: Somogy Éditions d'Art, 120–121.

Marx, K., 1967 [1867]. *Capital* (3 vols). New York: New World Paperbacks.

Needham, S., 2001. When expediency broaches ritual intention: the flow of metal between systemic and buried domains, *Journal of the Royal Anthropological Institute incorporating Man* 7, 275–298.

Needham, S., D. Parham and C. Frieman (eds), 2013. Claimed by the sea: Salcombe, Langdon Bay, and other marine finds of the Bronze Age, *CBA Research Reports* 173.

O'Connor, B., 1980. *Cross-Channel relations in the Later Bronze Age. Relations between Britain, North-Eastern France and the Low Countries during the Later Bronze Age and the Early Iron Age, with particular reference to the metalwork* (British Archaeological Reports International Series 91). Oxford: Archaeopress.

Pare, C., 2013. Weighing commodification and money, in: *The Oxford handbook of the European Bronze Age*, eds H. Fokkens and H. Harding. Oxford: Oxford University Press, 508–527.

Pearce, M., 2007. *Bright blades and red metal. Essays on north Italian prehistoric metalwork* (Accordia Specialist Studies on Italy 14). London: Accordia Research Institute.

Platenkamp, J.D.M., 2016. Money alive and money dead, in: *The archaeology of money. Proceedings of the workshop 'Archaeology of Money', University of Tübingen, October 2013* (Leicester Archaeology Monographs), eds C. Haselgrove and S. Krmnicek. Leicester: University of Leicester, 161–181.

Primas, M., 1997. Bronze Age economy and ideology: Central Europe in focus, *Journal of European Archaeology* 5(1), 115–130.

Rahmstorf, L., 2010. The concept of weighing during the Bronze Age in the Aegean, the Near East and Europe, in: *The archaeology of measurement. Comprehending heaven, earth and time in ancient societies*, eds I. Morley and C. Renfrew. Cambridge: Cambridge University Press, 88–105.

Renfrew, C. and I. Morley, 2010. Introduction: Measure: towards the construction of our world, in: *The archaeology of measurement. Comprehending heaven, earth and time in ancient societies*, eds I. Morley and C. Renfrew. Cambridge: Cambridge University Press, 1–4.

Roberts, B.W., D. Boughton, M. Dinwiddy, N. Doshi, A.P. Fitzpatrick, D. Hook, N. Meeks, A. Mongiatti, A. Woodward and P.J. Woodward, 2015. Collapsing commodities or lavish offerings? Understanding massive metalwork deposition at Langton Matravers, Dorset during the Bronze Age–Iron Age transition, *Oxford Journal of Archaeology* 34(4), 365–395.

Rowlands, M.J., 1993. The role of memory in the transmission of culture, *World Archaeology* 25, 141–151.

Sampaio, H. A., 2015. Late Bronze Age monotypical deposits of palstave axes between the hydrographic basins of rivers Minho and Ave (Iberian northwest): spatial contexts and interpretations, *Estudos do Quaternáro* 13, 55–67.

Shennan, S., 1993. Commodities, transactions and growth in the central European Early Bronze Age, *Journal of European Archaeology* 1(2), 59–72.

Simmel, G., 2011 [1900]. *The philosophy of money*. London: Routledge.

Stein, F., 1979. *Katalog der vorgeschichtlichen Hortfunde in Süddeutschland* (Saarbrücker Beiträge Altertumkunde 24). Bonn: Habelt Verlag.

Talon, M., 2012. Trade within the English Channel/North Sea region, in: *Beyond the horizon. Societies of the Channel and North Sea 3,500 years ago*, eds A. Lehoërff, J. Bourgeois, P. Clark and M. Talon. Paris: Somogy Art Publishers, 74–81.

Thomas, J., 1996. *Time, culture and identity. An interpretive archaeology*. London and New York: Routledge.

Van der Vaart-Verschoof, S., 2017. *Fragmenting the chieftain. A practice-based study of Early Iron Age Hallstatt C elite burials in the Low Countries* (PALMA 15). Leiden: Sidestone Press.

Vandkilde, H., 2005. A biographical perspective on Ösenringe from the Early Bronze Age, in: *Die Dinge als Zeichen: Kulturelles Wissen und materieller Kultur* (Universitätsforschungen zur prähistorischen Archäologie 127), ed. T. Kienlin. Bonn: Habelt Verlag, 263–281.

Verlaeckt, K., 1996. *Between river and barrow. A reappraisal of Bronze Age metalwork found in the province of East-Flanders (Belgium)* (British Archaeological Reports International Series 632). Oxford: Archaeopress.

Verney, A., 1991. La production en série d'objets métalliques à l'Age du Bronze: les dépôts de la Chapelle-du-Bois-des-Faulx (Eure) (Matières et figures, etudes et travaux ecole du Louvre Ecole du Patrimoine). Paris: La Documentation Francaise, 117–135.

Verron, G., 2005. Les dépôts de l'âge du Bronze et leur signification, in: *La Normandie à l'aube de l'histoire, les découvertes archéologiques de l'âge du Bronze 2300–800 av. JC.*, eds C. Marcigny, C. Colonna, E. Ghesquière and G. Verron. Paris: Somogy Éditions d'Art, 118–119.

Von Brunn, W.A., 1959. *Die Hortfunde der frühen Bronzezeit aus Sachsen-Anhalt, Sachsen und Thüringen*. Berlin: Akademie Verlag.

Weiner, A.B., 1992. *Inalienable possessions: the paradox of keeping-while-giving*. Berkeley CA, Los Angeles CA and Oxford: University of California Press.

Wengrow, D., 2011. 'Archival' and 'sacrificial' economies in Bronze Age Eurasia: an interactionist approach to the hoarding of metal, in: *Interweaving worlds. Systemic interactions in Eurasia, 7th to the 1st millennia BC*, eds T.C. Wilkinson, S. Sherratt and J. Bennet. Oxford: Oxbow Books, 135–144.

Wiseman, R., 2017. Random accumulation and breaking: the formation of Bronze Age scrap hoards in England and Wales, *Journal of Archaeological Science* 90, 39–49.

Yates, D. and R. Bradley, 2010. The siting of metalwork hoards in the Bronze Age of southeast England, *Antiquaries Journal* 90, 41–72.

6

GIFTS TO FAMILIAR GODS?

Instead of hallmarked by the rise of 'rational' economies, the European Bronze Age can also be seen as a period of profound religiosity. From this perspective, selective deposition of metalwork is explained as gifts offered to different gods. This chapter argues that such views are based on problematic assumptions and not supported by archaeological evidence. It often leads to a conception of the Bronze Age as a forerunner of the religions of younger civilizations that we feel more familiarity with, playing down the special characteristics of Bronze Age practices. I argue that the evidence of Bronze Age depositions informs us on how people used objects to conceptualize supernatural things in relation to themselves and to other humans. Not much is learnt about how Bronze Age people perceived the supernatural. Rather, evidence suggests that transgressive objects conventionally interpreted as 'religious' were used to impersonate and stage cosmological narratives.

Introduction

Interpreting metalwork deposition as gifts to supernatural entities is a radical move away from the economic-rationality that many scholars associate with the Bronze Age. As it offers an explanation for selective deposition it deserves special attention. In what follows, I will scrutinize this view by laying bare four assumptions that usually go with it. This is done in order to broach the essential question: what can one learn of religion by studying metalwork deposition?

Assumption 1: deposition represents gifts

Working from the assumption that people always have some notion of the supernatural powers governing their world, it is often argued that people have a general wish to communicate with those powers to ask for their favours and help in order to overcome the uncertainties and hardships of life (e.g. Hänsel 1997, 12). Presenting gifts to those powers would be one way to achieve this. Metalwork deposited in the ground, then, would be the tangible proof of such offerings (Hansen 2013; Kristiansen & Larsson 2005; Randsborg 1995).

Assumption 2: there was a concept of gods and these were like humans

In the choice of goods offered, Hänsel (1997, 13) argues, we not only see what was important to the giver, but also what was thought to please the recipient higher powers. The assumption is that these were perceived as gods. Such gods, so his argument goes, must have been like humans, as they apparently valued the same goods. As such gift giving to higher powers was practised for long periods of time almost everywhere in Europe, it is thought to reflect a widely-shared belief that it was generally beneficial to society. There must have been a social belief that the gods reciprocated in some way and therefore entertained the same moral codes (the *do ut des* logic; ibid.,15; Hansen 2013). As gift-giving, the metalwork deposition not only reflects what befits both the giver and the receiving 'god'. There is also the element of material wealth involved that may support this notion that the deposition was like a gift (Hänsel 1997, 17). Several scholars emphasize that what is

FIGURE 6.0 Sites mentioned in this chapter: 1. San Sosti; 2. Gela; 3. Bloody Pool hoard; 4. Staffordshire; 5. (East-)Rudham; 6. Ommerschans; 7. Nebra; 8. Egtved; 9. Rørby; 10. Grevensvaenge; 11. Viksø; 12. Trundholm; 13. Simris. 14. Olympia.
Source: J. Porck, Faculty of Archaeology, University of Leiden.

given also had material, economic value, just like in a transaction between humans (Hänsel 1997, 17; Innerhofer 1997; Menke 1978/1979). This evokes an aspect of offering that is familiar to modern scholars. The notion of the material wealth and transactional proportionality, for example, is known from the Bible. When King David refuses to sacrifice cattle and objects he was given by Araunah to God, he says: 'I will not offer burnt offerings to the Lord my God which cost me nothing' (2 Samuel 24:24).

Assumption 3: there were functional differences between gods and these resulted in depositions that were selective

The next assumption that matters here is that there were several gods to whom offerings were made during the Bronze Age and that particular things were offered to particular gods. This is an important point for this book, as it offers a general explanation for the fact that metalwork deposition was selective. When one accepts the point that offerings were made to gods, it follows that there was a Bronze Age pantheon, where individual gods or supernatural entities could be distinguished on the basis of functional properties reflected in the objects 'given' to them in depositions (Hänsel 1997, 19–20.; Randsborg 1995, 114–119).[1]

Assumption 4: these gods were forerunners of gods known from later historical periods

This line of thinking could have taken many courses. The notion that supernatural forces (in a variety of guises) manifest themselves in the landscape, is attested in cultures all over the world. Ethnographic and archaeological studies of the native inhabitants of arctic Europe and Asia, for example, show that specific locations were associated with specific supernatural forces or entities (not necessarily conceptualized as gods). This led to different sacrifices being made at different places (Manker 1957; Mulk 1997; Ovsyannikov & Terebikhin 1997). As Bradley (2000, 36–37, 48–50) pointed out, such practices have similarities to Bronze Age selective deposition. What often happened though, is that the presumed Bronze Age pantheon was regarded as a forerunner of gods from another European past: the Greek and Roman pantheons that are central in the prevailing discourse on European civilization. In Germany and southern Scandinavia, links were laid with Germanic and Viking Age society that are equally important in modern national myths (cf. Randsborg 1995, 84). It has also been argued that characteristics of divinities may even go back to more fundamental shared notions that originated in proto-Indo-European cultures. Randsborg (1995, 84) argues that the thunderbolt of Zeus and the hammer of Thor indicate that axes were symbols of celestial gods. The preference since the Neolithic to deposit axes would evidence the deep traditionality of offerings to sky powers (ibid.). The Bronze Age gods, then, supposedly were gods that are 'familiar' to us.

Bronze Age 'pantheons' and the notion of functional gods

It has been argued that humans in general tend to see things around them as imbued with 'agency' and human qualities (Guthrie 1993) on 'the flimsiest of pretext' (Whitehouse 2004, 190). Seeing one's landscape as imbued with anthropomorphic but non-human powers, or objects as 'doing things', then, is universally human (Guthrie 1993). That Bronze Age supernaturals would have been perceived as having certain human qualities or shapes is therefore relatively easy to accept. However, the same ethnographic sources suggest that this does not automatically mean the supernatural was conceptualized as anthropomorphized gods. Ethnographic and historical sources show that there is a bewildering variety of ways in which such supernatural beings can be conceptualized. They can be like spirits of ancestors, superhuman beings, but also elements of the landscape itself like mountains, rivers or more abstract entities or forces (e.g. Oosten 1985, 25; Mulk 1997). There are also examples of religious people who believe in the supernatural but not in divine beings (e.g. Buddhists; Pals 2006, 95). Thus, there is no compelling reason to suppose Bronze Age supernatural entities were necessarily conceptualized as (anthropomorphic) *gods*.

For the Bronze Age, the notion of there being different functional gods to whom different offerings were made, was modelled on Greek & Roman and Germanic & Viking historical examples. There are reasons to doubt, however, whether such a view does justice to how Greek or Roman communities themselves perceived their gods. In his study of gods and temples in Roman Gaul, Derks (1998, 78; based on Oosten 1985) doubts this. He remarks that in the case of war, there is evidence of Roman generals invoking no less than 15 different gods to help them on the battlefield (Derks 1998, 81), debunking the notion that there ever was one specialized 'god of war'. On a more general level, Oosten (1985, 25–26) argues that most Indo-European gods 'represented many functions at the same time'. Combinations of functions are essential to their significance (ibid., 25). A war god could also be a fertility god (e.g. Viking Age Thor; ibid., 26). This makes any assumption about there having been, for example, a single god of smithing or war problematic even for the Graeco-Roman or Viking world. Supposing that Bronze Age people had a single and exclusive god of war, for example, is therefore just as unlikely.[2]

If we were to accept that metalwork depositions represent 'gifts to gods', it would therefore be very difficult to identify such a god on the basis of the attribute offered – as acknowledged by both Hänsel (1997, 20) and Randsborg (1995, 115). Hänsel, for example, is confronted with such problems when he discusses the example of an axe found in San Sosti (Italy) that carries an inscription reading 'Hera'. Does this imply that the axe is seen as an attribute of Hera (which according to Hänsel is not in line with general notions on what ought to be Hera's attributes)? Or is it the offering of a tool that was used to kill animals that were sacrificed to Hera? In the latter case, the link between the nature of the god and what is offered to her is only an indirect one, and it is primarily the human participant and the use-life of the object that we should take into account.

Summarizing, the association between the thing offered and the god to whom it is offered is problematic on both theoretical and empirical grounds.

The problem with historical comparison

The same holds true for the assumption that ideas of the role of and nature of gods were rooted in assumptions with a deep history, going back to one original proto-Indo-European pantheon that came into existence among the first proto-Indo-European speakers (cf. Glob 1970 cited in Kaul 1998, 55). Whereas historical linguistics has shown that there are conspicuous similarities in certain myths and notions of the divine among early Indo-European speakers (cf. Fortson 2010; Oosten 1985), historical sources also demonstrate that notions of the supernatural world were highly variable from region to region and anything but stable through time. Many Indo-European languages have related words for a sky god who wields a weapon or a hammer (Fortson 2010, 26). As said, axe depositions are interpreted as offerings made to such a god (cf. Randsborg 1995, figure 32). However, Chapter 4 showed that axe depositions already feature in Early Neolithic societies that inhabited Europe long before the spread of Indo-European languages! This is at least inconsistent with the identification of such deposits with an Indo-European 'sky god'. Similarly, the ritual significance of the solar disc – that is so prominent in Nordic Bronze Age material culture – cannot be an exclusive Indo-European phenomenon either, as it for example also features strongly in Ancient Egyptian cults (Kristiansen & Larsson 2005, 69–75). Although some notions of the supernatural do seem to have the broad distribution and extensive time-depth argued for by comparative linguistics (like there being a 'sky god'), there are many others that seem to be tied to particular periods only. There is hardly any archaeological source, for example, that suggests that the solar disc which was so central in the northern Bronze Age iconography, had the same relevance in the Iron Age (Kristiansen & Larsson 2005, 297). Kaul (1998, 13) notes other changes when he compares historical sources on Iron Age Germanic tribes recorded by Tacitus to those of the Viking age. The Roman author Tacitus[3] describes how several tribes in Danish Jutland had a cult of the goddess Nerthus, associated with a sacred chariot. On linguistic grounds, the Viking Age god Njord should be a younger version of that same god's name, but Njord is a male god and his cult is not associated with a chariot. In the Viking Age, chariots, however, are now linked to another goddess, Freya – rendering assumptions of a long-term stability in gods' concepts problematic. So, siding with Kaul (1998), I argue that if we wish to interpret deposition of Bronze Age materials in relation to a divine world, notions based on historical accounts of later periods are unhelpful.

The Bronze Age gods delusion[4]

If the evidence from historical sources is already inconsistent, the situation only gets more confusing when we confront the evidence of depositions with notions of cults as derived from historical sources from a later period. Hänsel (1997, 19), following the work of Orlandini (1965/1967), argues that at Gela, Sicily, there was a Greek sanctuary dedicated to Demeter dating to the second half of the sixth century BC. At the same location, no less than 30 Bronze Age metalwork hoards have been found, dating from the 10th to the 7th century BC. He suggests that such a continuity in ritual use might imply that Bronze Age people were already venerating some prehistoric version of a Demeter-like goddess here. But this would entirely disregard even the possibility that perception of place could have changed over time (something which may be expected as we are dealing here with a colonial appropriation of a native location). It would also go against his own view that the nature of depositions would represent attributes of the god to whom it was offered. Hänsel is aware of this, as he emphasizes that at Gela, hoards have a content that does not seem to directly correspond with a cult of a chthonic, fertility goddess. They contain amongst other things complete and broken rings, and fragments of a variety of objects such as metal vessels, axes, ingots, sickles and needles (ibid., 19). Orlandini, argues that we are to interpret such scrap hoards as representing currency, or scrap money, in this case offered to a divinity (cf. Chapter 5). If we follow this train of thought, any link between the content of a hoard and a supposed divinity to whom it is supposedly offered is obscured to us. After all, when we find scrap hoards, or hoards with commodities (Chapter 5) in locations elsewhere in Europe where cult places from historical periods are lacking, how are we then ever to identify whom they were dedicated to?

So by trying to identify 'gods' to whom metalwork was supposedly offered in the Bronze Age on the basis of attributes that 'befit the god', we are over-simplifying matters. If we accept cases like Sicilian Gela where there might be continuity between prehistoric and historical cult places, such sites only serve to show how difficult it is to identify metalwork hoards with familiar gods of historical periods. At a more fundamental level, it has been argued that the entire notion of a pantheon of gods differentiated on the basis of functions and attributes does not even hold true for the 'familiar' gods of the Graeco-Roman world that are often seen as equivalents or successors to earlier ones. So, by trying to get at a Bronze Age pantheon by means of a study of the content of depositions, I argue we are chasing something that probably never existed as such.

Giving, keeping and 'keeping-while-giving' in depositions

It may be very difficult to infer what Bronze Age people believed, and as selective deposition is a phenomenon emergent from many individual actions, there will probably be an equal number of beliefs involved. Archaeology is better equipped to discover what people were doing when they deposited metalwork and the context in which this took place. Although the notion of gifts-to-gods may be problematic, metalwork deposition does have similarities to gift-giving among humans, and it may be worthwhile to explore this further.

Giving

Deposited metalwork very often consists of objects that travelled or ones that refer to notions of travelling and (supra-regional) exchanges. For many objects that were placed in the landscape it is likely they circulated in exchange before that time. The notion of travelling, exchange and circulation is also objectified in the composition of depositions. Hoards often consist of a range of foreign things that must have come from different directions, all showing the connectivity of a community to distant regions (so-called *Mappa Mundi* hoards; Chapter 2). That a deposition is like a transaction among humans is also suggested by the fact that it can contain commodities or exchange token convertibles (Chapter 5). The 'staging' of objects, by for example displaying them in special orderings recalls a feature that is specific for *gift*-giving – it tends to take place in special, ceremonial settings, involving specific gestures and acts (cf. Bazelmans 1999; Lambek 2008). Chapter 5 shows that this was – paradoxically – also the case for material that refers to commodity-potential. I interpreted this as an indication that the very act of deposition led to a transformation in which alienable things acquired a certain inalienable status. A modern example would be gift-wrapping things to make items bought in commercial transactions (commodities bought in shops) acceptable as gifts to friends at birthday parties. Another observation that matches with the notion that deposition is a bit like gift-giving can be found in the recurrent observation that in the Bronze Age, objects were often deposited in as-used form. In regions like the Low Countries, axes and swords from wet places are often sharpened and prepared as if they still have to be used – demonstrating their usefulness at a moment when they in fact would disappear from daily life forever (Fontijn 2002, 212).

Keeping

But there is also an element of 'keeping' observable. What deposition in inaccessible zones like lakes or rivers brings about, is that – if indeed it were perceived as a gift – the act of 'giving' is practically irreversible. The thing can no longer return, so it represents the ultimate way of 'giving', and – regarded from the side of presumed supernatural recipients – as the ultimate way of 'keeping'. If gift-giving is about retaining inalienability, here ultimate inalienability seems to be achieved (cf. Bazelmans 1999, figure 2.3; Chapter 3).

Keeping-while-giving

In a literal way, a deposition can also represent 'keeping-*while*-giving' (Weiner 1992; Chapter 3). This may be the case when only parts of objects are given (deposited) – and thereby only parts are kept. This seems to play a role in some hoards consisting of fragments, for example. As breaking of bronze is necessary for re-melting, collections of fragmented bronzes are usually seen as material awaiting recycling – so-called founder's or scrap hoards (Wiseman 2017). There are reasons why this is not always likely. As with so-called trade hoards, it is remarkable that such assemblages were never retrieved (Chapter 5). Fragmented objects, for example, were deposited in inaccessible wet locations, like the Late Bronze Age Bloody Pool hoard (Devon, England; Knight 2018, 353–361). Broken, incomplete items were sometimes placed in burials (Brück 2016, 80–82; Van der Vaart-Verschoof 2017). Vachta (2016) argues that large Late Bronze Age 'scrap' hoards in Bohemia contain fragments from only a selection of items, implying it was only specific kinds of objects the fragments of which mattered. Dietrich (2014) shows how in many parts of Europe fragments were placed in sockets of Late Bronze Age axes. It is not always clear whether this was done just for re-melting, particularly not when the socket was sealed with organic material and the axe thrown in a river (Hansen 2016, 186–187). Although there are also cases where no selection or special treatment was carried out (Brandherm 2018; Wiseman 2017), there is at least reason to believe bronze was often intentionally broken for reasons other than re-melting. This implies that the process of breaking itself was meaningful, but if so, what was done with the fragments afterwards? If only a part of the object was deliberately deposited at a location, this means it was apparently seen as important that the other parts were distributed by participants (to further circulate? Figure 6.1). This would fit best with a view that emphasized that deposition aimed at creating relations between participants (including supernatural ones). Thus, relational identities were constructed (Brück 2004; Brück & Fontijn 2013). Identities were distributed, shared and mapped across several individuals and places (ibid.). Deposited items then, are some kind of *pars pro toto*, where the 'whole' is expressed by linking activities aimed at the human (further circulation of parts) and the supra-human realm (parts that were deposited in the landscape; Chapter 3). In giving up a part, and retaining the rest, a new link was forged between participants and places in the landscape. Or presumably, with the supernatural forces, however perceived, that are supposed to reside there. Hansen (2016, 186) compares this to what happened at the early Greek sanctuary of Olympia (11th–8th century BC). Fragments from bronze tripods were offered to gods there, but the majority of fragments were withheld (presumably entering circulation as bronze for re-melting).

An irreversible gift?

Depositions have an element of irreversibility to them that is unknown with gifts between humans. This can be inferred from the fact that objects were often placed in inaccessible locations. There are also numerous examples where objects underwent irreversible physical transformation (cf. Fontijn et al. 2012; Knight 2018; Nebelsick 2000). They sometimes were bent, smashed, broken, or burnt. This occasionally involved violence, as if to underline the definitive nature of such acts. One of the six ceremonial swords of the Ommerschans-Plougrescant series, the one found in East-Rudham, was also bent.[5] As this was already a sword that was unuseable by nature, it underscores the symbolic nature of the additional bending as an act that emphasized termination and transformation of status upon deposition.

120 Gifts to familiar gods?

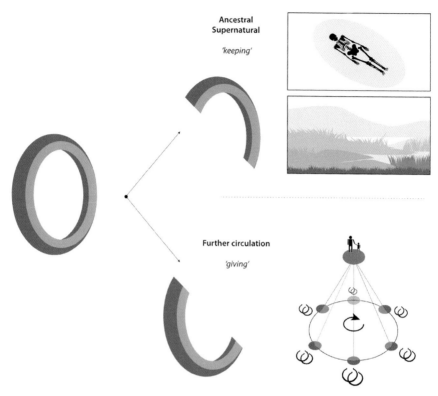

FIGURE 6.1 Model showing possible life-cycles of a fragmented object (in this case a bracelet)
Source: Drawing by J. Porck, Faculty of Archaeology, University of Leiden.

Things may be transformed during exchanges in general, often marking the change in status of the thing given – from a commodity to thing imbued with personal qualities (e.g. the modern gift-wrapping). Transforming it to such an extent that it can no longer continue its previous function is an extreme form thereof, but it is precisely such 'destructive' acts that are known from ethnographical and historical accounts on offerings and sacrifice world-wide (Burkert 1983). It underscores the special, other-worldly or transgressive nature of an act whereby things are given by humans to supernatural beings. As Lambek (2008, 150) puts it: 'Sacrifice also exemplifies the power of transvaluation in which the act of destroying something of one kind of value is actually productive of some other kind of value.'

Deposition: dissolution *and* construction of personhood and social wholes

So, even though the identity of the perceived supernatural recipients may escape archaeology, what people did when they were depositing objects shares some of the characteristics of gift-giving, implying that such acts were a bit like gifts. Other traits (like irreversible physical transformation), however, indicate that depositions represent a special form of giving, different from how objects circulate among people. This is perhaps the most obvious in the one feature that led me to write a book on depositions in the first place – the fact that objects were placed in the land forever.

It has been argued that exchange, not kinship, forms the basis of society (Mauss 1993). Preventing things from circulating, then, can potentially be seen as a threat to social cohesion, hallmarking the dissolution of communal bonds (Platenkamp 2016). Yet, this is precisely what happened in depositional practices on a huge scale. This can be conceptually remedied by assuming that society comprises more than just living human beings, but includes ancestral spirits and the supernatural as well (Dumont 1977) – entities supposed to reside in the landscape where objects are given to. Backgrounding such notions is Mauss' (1993, 16) point that in non-modern society, all life and matter ultimately belongs and comes from gods, ancestors and spirits (see also Chapter 3). This is why, according to Hubert and Mauss (1964) there should always be some form of exchange between living humans and the ancestral and supernatural realm (however these were perceived). The notion that things in the world come from the supernatural seems to be an almost universal one in non-modern belief systems, a notion that only gave way to a more anthropocentric, individual one with the introduction of the three world religions (Sahlins 1996). The assumption that matter and people 'come from' a supernatural realm, overarching living society, implies people inherit a world that is owned by ancestral societies and that their life might be only a faint mirror of what once was there (cf. De Coppet 1985). Restoring and reiterating the deeds of past society, then, may in their eyes be a logical step, and according to some this is why like burials or offerings tend to focus on the past rather than look towards the future (Eliade 2005). As Lincoln (1986) puts it, ritual actions therefore may involve ideas that are central to the ideas and values of the broader whole and to how it emerged. They may refer to cosmogenesis, sociogenesis (the constitution of people's own community), anthropogenesis (the constitution of personhood) or the genesis of the landscape (Derks 1998, 74; Lincoln 1986).

Applying to the Bronze Age

One may wonder whether it is possible to recognize prehistoric notions of the genesis of the cosmos and the world in Bronze Age depositional acts. It might well be that we are pressing the evidence too hard. Regarding the notion that such deeds relate to the constitution of personhood, or communal identity, however, I see the evidence has potential. After all, things directly relating to personal identity, like body ornaments or dress items (Harris et al. 2013), are prominent among the items Bronze Age people placed in the land.

According to Mauss (1996, 19), personhood or *persona* is 'man clad in a condition'. Individuals become persons by wearing the 'matching paraphernalia' (Mauss

1996, 11) and are thus 'invested with the capacities of personhood specific to defined roles and statuses' (La Fontaine 1996, 132 citing Fortes 1978, 287). Considering the paraphernalia that matter from the second half of the third millennium BC onwards (Bell Beaker period; see Chapter 4), body ornaments acquired from distant locations – thus having a history of long-distance exchange – repeatedly figure in depositions. This recalls a central point in Platenkamp's (1988) ethnographic study of the Tobelo. He argues that personhood is constituted by things imbued with (inalienable) qualities. These are acquired through gift exchange and hence never the possession of an individual. They acquire meaning and moral value by being linked to previous 'owners' and reify important concepts or values. Such concepts or values, or even the thing itself, may be considered to ultimately belong to or reside in a broader, overarching realm of society which includes the ancestral, supernatural world. In a study of gift exchange in *Beowulf*, Bazelmans (1999, 168–188) shows that Beowulf's personhood can also be understood as being constructed through gift exchange. His 'image' or 'worth', for instance, is in an important part constituted by the weaponry he receives. In the poem it is said that he is 'by weapons made worthy' (ibid., 175). In a similar vein, surrendering the paraphernalia of personal identity to the landscape, then, may be seen as a form of 'dissolution' of such an identity,[6] in which objects return to entities where they might be considered to have ultimately come from (Hubert & Mauss 1964). This may be true for constituents of personal, as well as group identities. Returning or offering such items would be to make a statement of which objects are instrumental in the construction of identities, and therewith on 'anthropo'- or 'sociogenesis'.

Convention-breaking multiple valuable depositions like the Early Bronze Age Swedish Pile hoard (Chapter 2) contain a very broad range of both local and non-local items (Vandkilde 2017). Such assemblages evoke notions of *sociogenesis*. The assemblage objectifies how the local communities were connected to, spring from and yet are different from a supra-regional exchange network. *Mappa Mundi* hoards (Chapter 2), then, take this to an extreme, as they do not necessarily demonstrate the grip a local community had on broader exchange networks. Rather, they demonstrate its 'reach' to more exotic realms beyond it (Helms 1993; Needham 2000).

Depositions that include body ornaments and items relating to the 'condition into which man is clad', to paraphrase Mauss (1996, 19), rather relate to *anthropogenesis*. The surrendering of worn body ornaments suggests that the personal identities such objects signal are ultimately temporary, and ought to be returned to the land and the entities that supposedly live in it. Such acts may have been perceived as 'gifts' to such entities, but these can have been conceptualized in a concrete and clear way (as ancestors or gods having a specific appearance) as rather abstract forces or values thought to reside in that part of the land in which the things were laid to rest. If we are to call this 'religion', this is clearly not a separate social institution but rather something inextricably linked with the social and economic realm (Mauss 1993). It is about projecting and anchoring the social in the

Gifts to familiar gods? 123

landscape. This comes closest to a definition of religion given by Horton (1994, 31–32), who sees it as 'an extension of the field of people's social relationships beyond the confines of a purely human society' (cf. Bowie 2000, 23).

Other-worldly or 'transgressive'[7] objects

That fact that deposited things were sometimes physically transformed is one indication that the act of deposition was perceived as some sort of 'ultimate' version of a gift. Another is that Bronze Age communities sometimes selected items that already had some sort of primordial 'other-worldly' nature by their shape, design and materiality. Such objects mimic regular objects in appearance, but at the same time are set apart from them because they were fabricated using other – rarer – materials, in aggrandized forms and/or weights, or in shapes that are at best seen as an exaggeration of a regular form (cf. Chapter 3; Hansen 2001). The Ommerschans sword this book opened with is a case in point. It is not just an enlarged version of a regular dirk; it exceeds the human scale also in other aspects. In terms of craft, it

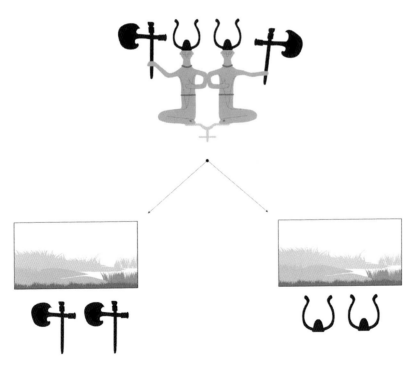

FIGURE 6.2 Objects that may have been part of the presentation of one supernatural entity and how these were separated in deposition. Based on the Grevensvaenge figurine and hoards of paired helmets (Viksø) and cult axes (Kaul 1998; Kristiansen & Larsson 2005, see text).
Source: Drawing by J. Porck, Faculty of Archaeology, University of Leiden.

exceeds the 'standard of the time'; it is virtuoso crafting (cf. Kuijpers 2018, 76, 264). There is a commitment to idealization in how decorative and practical elements that also appear on regular dirks are now applied with lines that are highly symmetrical and executed in set measurement units (cf. Butler & Sarfatij 1970/1971). It is also intriguing to see that for all the six swords of this kind, there never was a handle attached. A hilt links the dirk with a human being and makes it part of the extended human mind (Malafouris 2013). Together with its aggrandized shape and its outstanding crafted quality, the consistent lack of a hilt, then, might help to make this sword a supra-human object, that transgresses boundaries between the human and the supernatural world. Chapter 4 showed that such aggrandized objects already existed millennia before the Bronze Age. We are dealing with versions of normal objects that should be described using the adverb 'too' – they are 'too large', 'too heavy' or even 'too precious' to be used in a regular way (Figure 3.6). There is an element of transgression to it, which can also come to the fore in the fact that the skill required for making the object creates a distance and to some extent can make it 'other-worldly' (Helms 1993, 46–51). The elongated axe from Grembergen, Belgium is not so much an aggrandized axe; first and foremost it is an almost over the top transformation of regular axes (cf. Figure 3.4). We are thus dealing with things that refer to, but are also set apart from the mundane by their visuality and materiality – a reason why such objects tend to be interpreted as 'ceremonial' or 'religious' items by archaeologists.

Aggrandized versions of objects like swords are literally 'larger than life'. This material culture strategy of mimicking and aggrandizement is known all over the world. As the anthropologist Godelier (1999, 161–163) remarks, such objects can be used to embody key values. They are personified, and due their other-worldly character act as substitute for the divine (Chapter 3). Godelier calls them '*sacra*'. Because of their special appearance, they can be seen as transgressive objects which have to be treated in circumscribed ways only. As described in Chapter 4, more often than not this resulted in separate deposition. In the Bronze Age, the following kinds of transgressive objects can be identified.

'Objects citing objects'

Several examples of such objects have thus far been discussed in this book. For example: Early Bronze Age gold cups mimic ceramic vessels (Needham et al. 2006). In the later Bronze Age, there are giant and exquisite versions of dirks, swords, axes and spears (Butler & Bakker 1961; Hansen 2001). In the Nordic Bronze Age, there are woollen hats that are insignia of rank, but elsewhere in Europe (south Germany) elaborately decorated golden versions of such caps have been found – even gold hats that are elongated to impressive lengths (Gerloff 1995). The distinction between normal-sized chiefly caps and giant gold caps is particularly intriguing as Gerloff (1995) notes that a similar difference is known from Hittite iconography, where small caps are the dress items of kings, whilst long caps denote gods (also Kristiansen & Larsson 2005, 271). The Nordic realm also has a group of axes that is visually set apart, not only by the axes' exaggerated size and weight, but also by distinctive visual traits like decorations. These are the so-called cultic axes. (c. 1500–1100 BC; Jensen 2013, 435–440)

Objects without counterparts in the daily world

In the Nordic Bronze Age there are also rare examples of another group of objects designed to have other-worldly or transgressive qualities. These stand out due to their contrasting visual traits and crafting skill, and while remotely reminiscent of regular objects, they are embellished, distorted versions thereof and lack counterparts in other regions as well (Figure 6.2). They represent a class of their own (Chapter 2). Nevertheless, they still fit the crafting style of their region. Examples of this are the curved 'swords' (scimitars) of Rørby (Vandkilde 1996, 231–232) or the horned helmets found in a hoard at Viksø (c. 1100–700 BC; Kristiansen & Larsson 2005, 332–333).

Objects with prime cosmological referentials

Even though the horned helmets of Viksø have no clear counterpart in daily material culture, they still are some version of generic 'helmets' or 'hats'. There is a third group of objects that no longer refer to any regular thing. These are objects that directly refer to phenomena of cosmological significance (Levy 1982, 24). Needless to say, it is extremely difficult to identify such objects on archaeological grounds alone – there are many enigmatic objects known from Bronze Age Europe that we at present cannot identify and that perhaps also fall into the same category. The ones discussed here are those for which visuals and references in other media (rock art in particular) facilitate their identification. A case in point is the model of the solar disc in the Nordic Bronze Age. The gold disc that is carried by horses of the Bronze Age model found at Trundholm is generally identified as the sun disc, with its reverse silver side as representing the moon (Kaul 1998, 30–34). Very similar discs are known from burials such as that of the Egtved woman, where they were placed on the deceased's belt (Kristiansen & Larsson 2005, 298–302), indicating that depictions of the sun were important in their own right as well. Kristiansen and Larsson (2005, figure 137) argue that wheel-shaped discs had an equivalent role, based on the observation that similarly-sized versions were placed in the same bodily position in other graves. The sky disc of Nebra, showing stars, the Pleiades, a ship, and the moon on a large bronze disc, is another example of an object charged with cosmological meaning, though this so far seems to be a unique example (Figure 3.1; Meller 2013; Chapter 3).

Impersonating the supernatural?

With these transgressive objects we have returned to the classic discussion on Bronze Age religion in general and on the identification of gods in particular. In

126 Gifts to familiar gods?

FIGURE 6.3 Rock art figure depicted at Simris (Scania)
Source: Photograph by Fleming Kaul.

the Nordic Bronze Age, a striking feature of such objects is that they are sometimes depicted in rock art, or figure in bronze models. For example, on the rock-carving panel of Simris, Scania, two male figures are depicted presenting giant axes (Figure 6.3; Kaul 1998, Figure 6). Their shape deviates from regular axes and matches those of the cultic axes mentioned above, indicating that their excessive size is not merely a pictorial technique to emphasize a certain trait but represents sizeable axes that existed in real life as well. A bronze figurine that is now in the National Museum of Denmark, allegedly found at Grevensvaenge, has a helmet with two giant horns (c. 1100–700 BC; Kaul 1998, 19–21) (Figure 6.2). Documentation indicates that there were originally two such figurines with horned helmets found, and both carried a giant 'cultic axe' (Kaul 1998, 19–20, figures 4–5). These figurines were probably part of the model of a ship with other figurines (Glob 1962).

Following pictorial conventions from the Middle East (e.g. Hittite or Egyptian), Bronze Age rock carvings such as the one from Simris are often seen as depictions of gods, particularly because they are often much larger than other human figures on rock art scenes. But Kaul (1998, 56) notes that there is no pressing need to interpret them in such a way. Both horned helmets and cultic axes are real Bronze Age objects that were worn and used by people. Crucial for the present discussion is that such objects ended up be being deposited. The Trundholm model was deposited in a peat bog (ibid., 35–36). An almost identical version of the gold disc of the latter was found on the belt of the female buried at Egtved (Kristiansen & Larsson 2005, 298–302). All this implies that such rock carvings and scale models were probably not depictions of some divine world out there, but rather attempts to visualize how that world 'out there' was performed and made real 'down here' (cf. Kaul 1998, 11).

If the Nordic 'cultic' axes or horned helmets, or gold hats – to name an example from more southerly regions – really were attributes of the 'supernatural', then there were also occasions on which people used these to 'impersonate' or 'perform' the supernatural. Thus, in Bronze Age culture in northern Europe, the visualization, re-enactment and performance of cosmological stories seems to have been important in its own right (cf. Kristiansen & Larsson 2005, 352; Warmind 1994). The supernatural was not distant or abstract, but rather the 'gods' (if that term applies) were among Bronze Age people. Apparently, temporarily staging them in real life was important. People used special, transgressive attributes to present cosmological narratives, be it by impersonating cosmological beings or even gods by wearing and using certain objects, or by using scale models. The fact that we find such objects as depositions in the landscape or burials indicates that their use for such activities was preordained to come to an end as well (Kaul 1998, 36). The term 'transgressive objects' therefore seems more apt than 'other-worldly' (cf. Harrison 2006). Several of these special objects depicted on rocks, be they horned helmets, cultic axes, lurs (bronze trumpets) or cosmological scale models, were used in this world but survived in the archaeological record because they were ultimately taken out of the mundane world by being deposited in the landscape (cf. Kristiansen & Larsson 2005, figure 124). In Chapter 5, it was shown how the same happened with thousands of more common objects like trade stock. The fact that both common and transgressive objects underwent a similar fate suggests that this insertion of things in the land everywhere in Europe was part of a fundamental and widely shared world view during the Bronze Age.

An imagistic mode to convey religiosity

That such practices existed suggests that we are dealing with a 'religion' in which knowledge transmission through performance was key. According to Whitehouse (2004), there are basically two different modes in which religious knowledge is transmitted. The first is a doctrinal mode, where information is organized, often through semantics. The second is an episodic or imagistic mode, where ideas are conferred more non-verbally, through emotions, experiences and performances. The latter mode of religiosity is primarily aimed at small-scale audiences. One has to attend to get the experience and message (also Küchler 1997; Rowlands 1993; Wengrow 2011). The use of 'transgressive' objects in such ceremonies, then, implies that what happened in the Bronze Age best fits in with Whitehouse's 'imagistic mode of religiosity'. It leads to actions where the sought after effects are emotional in the first place: nothing remains but the memory of an act in which a powerful object was taken in by the landscape (Rowlands 1993). Almost by definition, such performances vary from place to place and time to time. Nevertheless, there are recurring elements in the selection of objects and execution of depositions across Europe. This means that memory derived from such performances had a 'connective' aspect (Assmann 2006, 88). Apparently, people strived to carry out things as they had been done before. As Assmann (2006, 81–100) puts it: it suggests such memory was a way to belong, to be part of a particular culture. Performances needed to be repeated time and again.

The variety indicates a lack of canonization in Bronze Age 'religious' practices. The point that all the items that featured in such ceremonies (horned helmets, cultic axes, but also lurs) makes sense if deposition was a performance in its own right (Rowlands 1993). Placing such objects in the landscape forever could have been envisioned as returning cosmologically-charged objects – of which humans were only the temporary possessors – to their true owners. There seem to have been at least three different ways in which such 'transgressive' items were removed from the daily realm.

1. Buried in a special place in the landscape, not directly associated with a human body (i.e. a grave), and accompanied by other items in such a way that *the deposition of the object itself is almost like a burial of a person*. This has, for example, been argued for the way in which the Nebra sky disc was deposited, the deposition of which evokes practices of burial of high status individuals (Meller 2004).
2. Buried in a special place in the landscape not directly associated with a human body, and in such a way that there is reason to argue *that only part of a whole was deposited*. It goes without saying that this is very difficult to prove, but sometimes there are cases where it at least seems likely. As the Grevensvaenge figurine both carries a cultic axe and a horned helmet, it may be assumed that they were part of one outfit (Kaul 1998, 18). Yet, as far as we known, horned helmets and cultic axes were never deposited together (Figure 6.2). The same applies to lurs and horned helmets. It might be ventured that we are dealing with cases here where outfits were taken apart, and meaningful elements deposited separately, in different places, evoking some kind of dismemberment of cosmological 'wholes' (cf. Derks 1998, 75; Oosten 1985, 1–2). Helmets, cultic axes and lurs were all deposited in pairs (Kaul 1998, 36) – suggesting that the fact of there being two of them was important.[8]
3. Buried on the body of a deceased, suggesting that *the transgressive item was an integral element of her/his portrayal as an ancestor*. The items are less often found separate from burials, implying that their value was closely tied to that of the human body and personhood, unlike the above categories, which are mainly found not in burials. Examples are sun discs and wheel crosses of the Nordic

Bronze Age that are sometimes found on the belts of female burials (Kristiansen & Larsson 2005, 298). The deceased are buried here in their capacity as a mediator between realms.

Conclusion: what archaeologists observe is deposition, not religion

This chapter discussed whether deposition could have been motivated by religion. Or: does it aid our understanding if we see metalwork deposition as religion (cf. Nongbi 2013, 156)? Like economy, religion is a modern category which was constituted in a specific, post-Enlightenment discourse (Nongbi 2013) in opposition to a concept of a rational economy. The way in which metalwork deposition is seen as evidencing gifts to gods was argued to project aspects of younger civilizations onto a deep past. It may be seen as a way to recognize familiarity into an otherwise unfamiliar 'Barbarian' past and to see an uncivilized Europe as forerunner of what are conventionally considered the founding civilizations of Europe. Above I argue that this is problematic on both theoretical and empirical grounds. Taken at face value, the evidence of deposition practices does not inform us on how Bronze Age people conceptualized the supernatural. When studying objects conventionally regarded as 'religious', it does make clear that special transgressive objects and social performance by real people were crucial for making the imagined conceivable and real (cf. Kaul 1998, 54; Warmind 1994). In a more general sense, depositional practices do share aspects of gift-giving, indicating that there is some ground for seeing it as an act of exchange (even though the nature of the perceived recipients remains unclear). The fact that what we see as 'economic' and 'religious' objects were part of such exchanges on equal terms, strongly implies that any concept of religion as a social institution does not make much sense when understanding Bronze Age behaviour. What we observe is deposition, *not* religion.[9] The evidence on Bronze Age metalwork deposition is resourceful in its own right. It consistently shows that objects, including 'religious' ones, ended their use-life by being distributed across and inserted into the landscape. If anything, the depositional evidence shows that religiosity was conveyed by human performance and inextricably linked to ideas about the constitution of a social whole that was anchored in the landscape (Brück forthcoming). As the key recipient of goods, it is to the study of the landscape that I will turn in the next chapter.

Notes

1 For the Neolithic and Bronze Age, Randsborg refers to more abstract terms like 'powers of the sky (.) responsible for, e.g. war', but his train of thought is comparable.
2 This reflects a more common belief in individuals as bounded entities. Mauss (1996) already argued that this is a modern concept. For non-modern society, concepts of personhood, including those of superhuman ones, are more fluid and relational. Thanks to Joanna Brück for suggesting this (see also Brück forthcoming).
3 Tacitus Germania (40). Translated by M. Hutton, revised by E.H. Warmington. Loeb Classical Library 35. Cambridge MA: Harvard University Press.

4 This title paraphrases Richard Dawkins' (2006) well-known polemic *The God Delusion*.
5 This find is still unpublished. Thanks are due to Tim Pestell (Norwich Museum), Neil Wilkin (British Museum) and Stuart Needham for sharing this information and for allowing Luc Amkreutz and myself to refer to it in Fontijn & Amkreutz 2018.
6 Cf. Bazelmans 1999, 168–188; Fontijn 2002, 231–232; Platenkamp 2016.
7 This term is taken from Harrison 2006, though my focus is more on objects transgressing boundaries between worlds than on taboos and ambiguities.
8 This has been taken to mean that these objects were deposited as attributes of 'twin gods' as known from Indo-European myths (Sprockhoff 1954, 84–89; Kristiansen & Larsson 2005). Paired deposition indeed is a pattern, which is likely to refer to social or cosmological ideas of the community in question. What such ideas were, however, is less clear. As argued earlier in this chapter, the entire notion of 'attributes of gods' is a problematic one, and so is the notion that a special role for twins is exclusively an Indo-European concept. Twins are imbued with special significance in other parts of the world as well (cf. Fortes 1973, 296).
9 Cf. Bloch's (2010) critique of evidence of 'religion' in early Neolithic Çatal Höyük (Turkey), which in his view is mainly evidence of 'houses', not so much of 'religion'.

Bibliography

Assmann, J., 2006. *Religion and cultural memory*. Stanford CA: Stanford University Press.
Bazelmans, J., 1999. *By weapons made worthy. Lords, retainers and their relationship in Beowulf* (Amsterdam Archaeological Studies 5). Amsterdam: Amsterdam University Press.
Bloch, M., 2010. Is there religion at Çatalhöyük ... or are there just houses? In: *Religion in the emergence of civilization. Çatalhöyük as a case study*, ed. I. Hodder. Cambridge: Cambridge University Press, 146–162.
Bowie, F., 2000. *The anthropology of religion*. Malden MA, Oxford, Melbourne and Berlin: Blackwell.
Bradley, R., 2000. *An archaeology of natural places*. London and New York: Routledge.
Brandherm, D., 2018. Fragmentation patterns revisited. Ritual and recycling in Bronze Age depositional practice, in: *Gifts, goods and money. Comparing currency and circulation systems in past societies*, eds D. Brandherm, E. Heymans and D. Hofmann. Oxford: Archaeopress, 45–65.
Brück, J., 2004. Material metaphors: the relational construction of identity in Early Bronze Age burials in Ireland and Britain, *Journal of Social Archaeology* 4, 7–33.
Brück, J., 2016. Hoards, fragmentation and exchange in the European Bronze Age, in: *Raum, Gabe und Errinerung. Weihgaben und Heiligtümer in prähistorischen und antiken Gesellschaften* (Berlin Studies of the Ancient World 38), eds S. Hansen, D. Neumann and T. Vachta. Berlin: Edition Topoi, 75–91.
Brück, J., forthcoming. *Personifying prehistory. Relational ontologies in Bronze Age Britain and Ireland*. Oxford: Oxford University Press.
Brück, J. and D.R. Fontijn, 2013. The myth of the Chief: prestige goods, power and personhood in the European Bronze Age, in: *The Oxford handbook of the European Bronze Age*, eds A. Harding and H. Fokkens. Oxford: Oxford University Press, 193–211.
Burkert, W., 1983. *Homo necans. The anthropology of Ancient Greek sacrificial ritual and myth*. Berkeley CA, Los Angeles CA and London: University of California Press.
Butler, J.J. and J.A. Bakker, 1961. A forgotten Middle Bronze Age hoard with a Sicilian razor from Ommerschans (Overijssel), *Helinium* I, 193–210.
Butler, J.J. and H. Sarfatij, 1970 / 1971. Another bronze ceremonial sword by the Plougrescant-Ommerschans smith, *Berichten van de Rijksdienst voor het Oudheidkundig Bodemonderzoek* 20–21, 301–309.

Dawkins, R., 2006. *The god delusion*. London: Transworld Publishers.
De Coppet, D., 1985. ...Land owns people, in: *Contexts and levels. Anthropological essays on hierarchy*, eds R.H. Barnes, D. de Coppet and R.J. Parkin, 78–90.
Derks, T., 1998. *Gods, temples and ritual practices. The transformation of religious ideas and values in Roman Gaul* (Amsterdam Archaeological Studies 2). Amsterdam: Amsterdam University Press.
Dietrich, O., 2014. Learning from 'scrap' about Late Bronze Age hoarding practices: a biographical approach to individual acts of dedication in large metal hoards of the Carpathian Basin, *European Journal of Archaeology* 17(3), 468–486.
Dumont, L., 1977. *From Mandeville to Marx. The genesis and triumph of economic ideology*. Chicago: University of Chicago Press.
Eliade, M., 2005. *The myth of the eternal return. Cosmos and history*. Princeton NJ and Oxford: Princeton University Press.
Fontijn, D.R., 2002. Sacrificial landscapes. Cultural biographies of persons, objects and 'natural' places in the Bronze Age of the southern Netherlands, c. 2300–2600 BC, *Analecta Praehistorica Leidensia* 33/34, 1–392.
Fontijn, D.R. and L. Amkreutz, 2018. Het verzonken zwaard van Ommerschans, in: *Wereldgeschiedenis van Nederland*, eds L. Heerma van Voss, M. 't Hart, K. Davids, K. Fatah-Black, L. Lucassen and J. Touwen. Amsterdam: Ambo/Anthos, 39–43.
Fontijn, D.R., L. Theunissen, B. van Os and L. Amkreutz, 2012. Decorated and 'killed'? The bronze sword of Werkhoven, *Analecta Praehistorica Leidensia* 43–44, 203–211.
Fortes, M., 1973. On the concept of the person among the Tallensi, in: *La notion de la personne en Afrique Noire*, ed. G. Dieterlen. Paris: Editions du Centre National de la Recherche Scientifique, 283–319.
Fortson, B.W.IV, 2010. *Indo-European language and culture. An Introduction*. 2nd edn. Malden MA and Oxford: Wiley-Blackwell.
Gerloff, S., 1995. Bronzezeitliche Goldblechkrone aus Westeuropa. Betrachtungen zur Funktion der Goldblechkegel vom Type Schifferstadt und der Atlantischen 'Goldblechschalen' der Form Devil's Bit und Atroxi, in: *Festschrift für Hermann Müller-Karpe zum 70. Geburtstag*, ed. A. Jockenhövel. Bonn: Habelt Verlag, 153–195.
Glob, P.V., 1962. Kultbåde fra Denmarks Bronzealder, *Kuml* 1961, 9–18.
Glob, P.V., 1970. *Højfolket: Bronzealderens Mennesker bevaret i 3000 År*. Denmark: Gyldendals Bogklub.
Godelier, M., 1999. *The enigma of the gift*. Cambridge and Oxford: Polity Press.
Guthrie, S., 1993. *Faces in the clouds: a new theory of religion*. Oxford: Oxford University Press.
Hänsel, A., 1997. Gaben an die Götter – Schätze der Bronzezeit Europas – eine Einführung, in: *Gaben an die Götter* (Seminar zur Ur- und Frühgeschichte der Freien Universität), eds A. Hänsel and B. Hänsel. Berlin: Museum für Vor- und Frühgeschichte, 11–22.
Hansen, S., 2001. 'Überaustattungen' in Gräbern und Horten der Frühbronzezeit, in: *Vom Endneolithikum zur Frühbronzezeit: Muster sozialen Wandels?* (Universitätsforschungen zur prähistorischen Archäologie, 90), ed. J. Müller. Bonn: Habelt Verlag, 151–174.
Hansen, S., 2013. Innovative metals: copper, gold and silver in the Black Sea region and the Carpathian Basin during the 5th and 4th millennium BC, in: *Metal matters. Innovative technologies and social change in prehistory and antiquity* (Menschen-Kulturen-Traditionen; Forschungscluster 2, Bd 12), eds S. Burmeister, S. Hansen, M. Kunst and N. Müller-Scheessel. Rahden: Leidorf Verlag, 137–167.
Hansen, S., 2016. A short history of fragments in hoards of the Bronze Age, in: *Materielle Kultur und Identität im Spannungsfeld zwischen Mediterraner Welt und Mitteleuropa* (Akten der Internationalen Tagung am Römisch-Germanischen Zentralmuseums Mainz, 22–24

Oktober 2014), ed. H. Baitinger. Mainz: Verlag des Römisch-Germanischen Zentralmuseums, 185–208.

Harris, O.J.T., K. Rebay-Salisbury, J. Robb and M.L.S. Sørensen, 2013. The body in its social context, in: *The body in history. Europe from the Palaeolithic to the future*, eds J. Robb and O.J.T. Harris. Cambridge: Cambridge University Press, 64–97.

Harrison, S., 2006. Skull trophies of the Pacific war: transgressive objects and remembrance, *Journal of the Royal Anthropological Institute*, N.S., 12, 817–836.

Helms, M.W., 1993. *Craft and the kingly ideal: art, trade, and power*. Austin: University of Texas Press.

Horton, R., 1994. *Patterns of thought in Africa and the West*. Cambridge: Cambridge University Press.

Hubert, H. and M. Mauss, 1964 [1898]. *Sacrifice. Its nature and functions*. Chicago: University of Chicago Press.

Innerhofer, F., 1997. Frühbronzezeitliche Barrenhortfunde – die Schätze aus dem Boden kehren zurück, in: *Gaben an die Götter* (Seminar zur Ur- und Frühgeschichte der Freien Universität), eds A. Hänsel and B. Hänsel. Berlin: Museum für Vor- und Frühgeschichte. 53–59.

Jensen, J., 2013. *The prehistory of Denmark. From the Stone Age to the Vikings*. Copenhagen: Gyldendal.

Kaul, F., 1998. *Ships on bronzes. A study in Bronze Age religion and iconography* (Studies in Archaeology and History vol. 3). Copenhagen: Publications from the National Museum.

Knight, M., 2018. The intentional destruction and deposition of Bronze Age metalwork in South West England. Unpublished Ph.D. thesis, Exeter University.

Kristiansen, K. and T.B. Larsson, 2005. *The rise of Bronze Age society. Travels, transmissions and transformations*. Cambridge: Cambridge University Press.

Küchler, S., 1997. Sacrificial economy and its objects, *Journal of Material Culture* 2, 39–60.

Kuijpers, M.H.G., 2018. *An archaeology of skill. Metalworking skill and material specialization in Early Bronze Age Central Europe*. London and New York: Routledge.

La Fontaine, J.S., 1996. Person and individual: some anthropological reflections, in: *The category of the person. Anthropology, philosophy and history*, eds M. Carrithers, S. Collins and S. Lukes. Cambridge: Cambridge University Press, 123–140.

Lambek, M., 2008. Value and virtue, *Anthropological Theory* 8(2), 133–157.

Levy, J.E., 1982. *Social and religious organization in Bronze Age Denmark* (British Archaeological Reports International Series 124), Oxford: Archaeopress.

Lincoln, B., 1986. *Myth, cosmos and society. Indo-European themes of creation and destruction*. Cambridge MA and London: Harvard University Press.

Malafouris, L., 2013. *How things shape minds. Theory of material engagement*. Cambridge MA and London: MIT Press.

Manker, E. 1957. *Lapparnas heliga ställen*. Stockholm: Nordiska Museet.

Mauss, M., 1993 [1923/1924]. *The gift. The form and reason for exchange in archaic societies*. London: Routledge.

Mauss, M., 1996 [1938]. A category of the human mind: the notion of the person; the notion of self, in: *The category of the person. Anthropology, philosophy and history*, eds M. Carrithers, S. Collins and S. Lukes. Cambridge: Cambridge University Press, 1–25.

Meller, H., 2004. Der Körper des Königs, in: *Der geschmiedete Himmel. Die weite Welt im Herzen Europas vor 3600 Jahren*, ed. H. Meller. Stuttgart: Konrad Theiss Verlag, 94–97.

Meller, H., 2013. The Sky Disc of Nebra, in: *Handbook of the European Bronze Age*, eds H. Fokkens and A. Harding. Oxford: Oxford University Press, 266–269.

Menke, M., 1978/1979. Studien zu den frühbronzezeitlichen Metalldepots Bayerns, *Jahresbericht des Bayerischen Bodendenkmalpflege* 19/20, 1–305.

Mulk, I.-M., 1997. Sacrificial places and their meaning in Saami society, in: *Sacred sites, sacred places* (One World Archaeology 23), eds D.L. Carmichael, J. Hubert, B. Reeves and A. Schanche. London and New York: Routledge, 121–131.

Nebelsick, L., 2000. Rent asunder: ritual violence in Late Bronze Age hoards, in: *Metals make the world go round. The supply and circulation of metals in Bronze Age Europe. Proceedings of a conference held at the University of Birmingham in June 1997*, ed. C.F.E. Pare. Oxford: Oxbow Books, 160–175.

Needham, S., 2000. Power pulses across a cultural divide: cosmologically driven acquisition between Armorica and Wessex, *Proceedings of the Prehistoric Society* 66, 151–207.

Needham, S., K. Parfitt and G. Varndell (eds), 2006. *The Ringlemere Cup. Precious cups and the beginning of the Channel Bronze Age.* London: British Museum Press.

Nongbi, B., 2013. *Before religion. A history of a modern concept.* New Haven CT: Yale University Press.

Oosten, J.G., 1985. *The war of the gods. The social code in Indo-European mythology.* London: Routledge & Kegan Paul.

Orlandini, P., 1965–1967. Gela-depositi votive di bronzo premonetale nel Santuario die Demetra Thesmophoros a Bitaleni, *Annali del Instituto Italiano di Numismatica* 12–14, 1–20.

Ovsyannikov, O.V. and N.M. Terebikhin, 1997. Sacred space in the culture of the Arctic regions, in: *Sacred sites, sacred places* (One World Archaeology 23), eds D.L. Carmichael, J. Hubert, B. Reeves and A. Schanche. London and New York: Routledge, 44–81.

Pals, D.L., 2006. *Eight theories of religion.* Oxford: Oxford University Press.

Platenkamp, J.D.M., 1988. Tobelo. Ideas and values of a North Moluccan society. Ph.D thesis, University of Leiden.

Platenkamp, J.D.M., 2016. Money alive and money dead, in: *The archaeology of money. Proceedings of the workshop 'Archaeology of Money', University of Tübingen, October 2013* (Leicester Archaeology Monographs), eds C. Haselgrove and S. Krmnicek. Leicester: University of Leicester, 161–181.

Randsborg, K., 1995. *Hjortspring. Warfare and sacrifice in early Europe.* Aarhus: Aarhus University Press.

Rowlands, M.J., 1993. The role of memory in the transmission of culture, *World Archaeology* 25, 141–151.

Sahlins, M., 1996. The sadness of sweetness. The native anthropology of Western cosmology, *Current Anthropology* 37(3), 395–428.

Sprockhoff, E., 1954. Nordische Bronzezeit und frühes Griechentum, *Jahrbuch des Römisch-Germanischen Zentralmuseums zu Mainz* 12, 28–109.

Vachta, T., 2016. Thesaurierungsprozesse bronzezeitlicher Hortfunde anhand ihrer Kompositionselemente, in: *Raum, Gabe und Errinerung. Weihgaben und Heiligtümer in prähistorischen und antiken Gesellschaften* (Berlin Studies of the Ancient World 38), eds S. Hansen, D. Neumann and T. Vachta. Berlin: Edition Topoi, 93–117.

Van der Vaart-Verschoof, S., 2017. *Fragmenting the chieftain. A practice-based study of Early Iron Age Hallstatt C elite burials in the Low Countries* (PALMA 15). Leiden: Sidestone Press.

Vandkilde, H., 1996. *From stone to bronze: the metalwork of the Late Neolithic and earliest Bronze Age in Denmark* (Jutland Archaeological Society Publications XXXII). Aarhus: Aarhus University Press.

Vandkilde, H., 2017. *The metal hoard from Pile in Scania, Sweden. Place, things, time, metals, and worlds around 2000 BC.* Aarhus: Aarhus University Press.

Warmenbol, E., 1992. Le matériel de l'âge du bronze: le seau de la drague et le casque du héros, in: *La collection Edouard Bernays. Néolithique et âge du bronze, époque gallo-romaine et médievale*, eds E. Warmenbol, Y. Cabuy, V. Hurt and N. Cauwe. Brussels: Musées Royaux d'Art et d'Histoire, 67–122.

Warmind, M., 1994. Aspects of Bronze Age religion from the point of view of a historian of religion. *Adoranten* 1984, 5–9. Årsskrift för Scandinavian Society for Prehistoric Art.

Weiner, A.B., 1992. *Inalienable possessions: the paradox of keeping-while-giving*, Berkeley CA, Los Angeles CA and Oxford: University of California Press.

Wengrow, D., 2011. 'Archival' and 'sacrificial' economies in Bronze Age Eurasia: an interactionist approach to the hoarding of metal, in: *Interweaving worlds. Systemic interactions in Eurasia, 7th to the 1st Millennia BC*, eds T.C. Wilkinson, S. Sherratt and J. Bennet. Oxford: Oxbow Books, 135–144.

Whitehouse, H., 2004. Toward a comparative anthropology of religion, in: *Ritual and memory. Towards a comparative anthropology of religion*, eds H. Whitehouse and J. Laidlaw. Lanham MD and Oxford: Altamira Press, 187–204.

Wiseman, R., 2017. Random accumulation and breaking: the formation of Bronze Age scrap hoards in England and Wales, *Journal of Archaeological Science* 90, 39–49.

7

THE RECEIVING LANDSCAPE

This chapter argues that landscape was more than just the scenery in which depositional actions were conducted; it was an integral part of it and is considered the most concrete main player that can be empirically investigated by archaeological means. To some extent, metalwork can be seen to have been 'shared' with the landscape. The categories currently used in analysis of depositions, like 'wet' or 'dry' are problematic, as is the notion of exclusive, historically defined cult places. I argue that deposition places should be understood as relational, and that the ambiguous and zonal nature of deposition landscapes make sense from an experiential 'dwelling' perspective (sensu Ingold 2000). The profound deep history of some depositional landscapes should not be explained from collective memory per se. What was transferred through time was not the memory of unique historical places where ancestral depositions once happened. Rather, it was an 'imagined' reality (sensu Bloch 2012, 115) – beliefs about relations between place templates – that were transmitted over generations. It is argued that such a system may be unfamiliar to us, but is empirically researchable with the evidence and techniques available.

Landscapes instead of places

The previous chapter argued that Bronze Age metalwork depositions share features with objects circulating as gifts between humans. It also demonstrated that it is very difficult to grasp how Bronze Age people perceived the supposed recipients of such 'gifts'. What the selective nature of such depositions does make clear, however, is that the recipients were seen to manifest themselves *as* or *at* locations in the landscape. However it may have been perceived, the landscape itself is a researchable, concrete key to the ideas that shaped Bronze Age depositional practices. Nevertheless, it is precisely for depositional landscapes of the Neolithic and Bronze Age that we run into considerable interpretive problems.

To elucidate these, I will start with an example of Late Iron Age depositional practices. Figure 7.1 shows the river Meuse in the Netherlands and Belgium, close to the German border. As research by Van Hoof (2007) makes clear, a considerable number of finds have been dredged from the river or found in its back swamps (including iron swords and bronze ornaments, but also ceramic vessels). Figure 7.1 shows these finds are clustered in a few locations. The most important find spot is near Roermond at the confluence of the rivers Roer (Ruhr) and Meuse. In the Roman period, a temple dedicated to the native goddess Rura was probably built at this spot (Roymans 1990, 89). The generally accepted interpretation is that a Late Iron Age cult place situated on a prominent location in the landscape became the site for one situated in a building in the Roman period.

Figure 7.1 also shows the same landscape, but around 1,000 years earlier. The location of Late Bronze Age metalwork finds like swords, spearheads, axes and ornaments is shown (based on Fontijn 2002, figure 14.1 and data in chapters 6–8). In all likelihood, the depicted finds represent objects that were deliberately deposited in the landscape. This raises a number of questions. If we accept that the Late Iron Age Roermond site was one cult place, does the Late Bronze Age figure depict dozens of 'cult places' located everywhere in the Meuse valley? Once a temple was constructed, the Roman period cult site was physically demarcated. Something comparable is much harder to detect in Bronze Age evidence. Bronzes were deposited within the river, along the edges of the valley or in the hinterland. In some cases there are concentrations of finds, but it is unclear if this results from selective preservation or research factors. If the Late Iron Age map evokes the notion of demarcated sacred space or at least a ritual focus (Derks 1998, 133) in a landscape (Van Hoof 2007), it would follow that the Bronze Age map implies that a vast part of the landscape would be 'sacred'. I used this distribution map in a previous publication to make the point that it is better to speak of deposition zones rather than places for the Bronze Age (Fontijn 2002, 262–263). In retrospect, this raises more questions than answers, such as: what constitutes a 'zone'? How can something that is so vaguely defined relate to conscious acts of selectively placing metal in the landscape? Which social behaviour created such depositional patterns? A Late Iron Age and Roman cult place at least resonates with concepts known today, like churches, mosques or synagogues. Yet, the very phenomenon of a selective deposition of metalwork shows Bronze Age and Neolithic depositional landscapes were far from unstructured (cf. Bradley 2000; Fontijn 2002; Rundkvist 2015). The central question of this chapter therefore is: what made a location the 'right place' for a deposition in the Bronze Age?

A depositional location as a place *category*

Through time, archaeologists studying Bronze Age metalwork depositions have been trying to make sense of them by categorizing depositional locations. Throughout this book, we have seen many examples. Distinctions are made

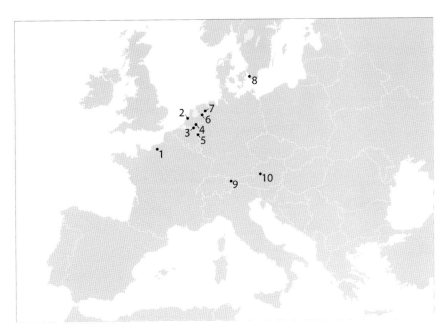

FIGURE 7.0 Sites mentioned in this chapter: 1. Cap Hornu; 2. Voorhout; 3. Hoogeloon; 4. Haelense Beek; 5. Roermond; 6. Ommerschans; 7. Bourtanger Moor (also Bargeroosterveld and Angelslo-Emmerhout); 8. Pile; 9. Mooschbruckschrofen (Piller); 10. Rabenwand (Kainischtal).
Source: J. Porck, Faculty of Archaeology, University of Leiden.

between objects that were placed in hoards or in graves, within or outside settlements, or in wet vs. dry locations.

It is easy to criticize such an approach. For example, there is no consistent criterion behind such categorizations: a 'dry' location can represent many kinds of locations (including a settlement or grave). Using a category like a 'dry' context usually underscores that we often fail to grasp its environmental specifics. For example, one characteristic of many hoard finds in western Europe is that they tend to be situated outside settlements and cultivated landscapes. They tend to be more prominent in what we would call 'natural' (i.e. unaltered) places, not marked by human-made structures (Bradley 2000; Hansen 2013). The term 'natural', however, is problematic, as the observation that precious metalwork was deliberately placed in all sorts of 'unaltered' places clearly implies such places were regarded as imbued with cultural meanings, defying any kind of nature–culture divide (Brück forthcoming; Fontijn 2002).

Nevertheless, detailed regional studies have shown that confluences of rivers, springs and fords in stream valleys repeatedly played host to depositional practices (Ballmer 2012; Bradley 2000; Fontijn 2002; Neumann 2015; Vachta 2016). The same is true for mountain tops and passes through hills and caves (Soroceanu 2012). Such recurrent associations between metalwork and particular kinds of places in the landscape suggests deposition was governed by a widely-shared and long-lived

138 The receiving landscape

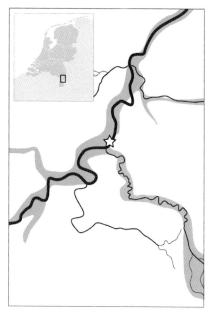

FIGURE 7.1 Metalwork depositions in the Meuse valley of the southern Netherlands/ northern Belgium. Left: metalwork deposition sites dating to the Late Bronze Age (1100–800 BC); right: metalwork deposition dating to the Late Iron Age, showing a cluster around the confluence of the rivers Meuse and Roer near present-day Roermond. Information from Fontijn 2002, figure 14.1.
Source: Drawing by J. Porck, Faculty of Archaeology, University of Leiden.

desire to link particular valuables to particular kinds of places. It may be assumed that the same applies to the cultural notions that went with these objects (Fontijn 2002). By deposition, cultural values and aspects of personal identity became 'anchored' in the landscape (Brück forthcoming). This primarily reflects the interaction between local communities and the environment they knew intimately. This means that depositional sites in, for example, southern England (Yates & Bradley 2010) were of a different nature than those in the landscape of the Swiss Alps (Ballmer 2012). Detailed studies sometimes reveal that there were subtle differences between different kinds of places. Numerous depositions have been recognized in the Belgian-Dutch valley of the Meuse, many of which are in wet places. Focusing on those placed in the swamps in the hinterland vs. those in the river Meuse itself, it is interesting to see that the latter appears to have been the preferred receptacle for swords during a period of hundreds of years (Fontijn 2002, figure 14.1). The river clearly was seen as a 'sword place' in contrast to the swamps in the hinterland used for depositing other kinds of objects. I suggested previously that the major river may have been more of a social boundary between groups and a context for martial, perhaps elite depositional ceremonies, whereas the hinterland swamps rather seem to have functioned as deposition area within local communities (also Mullin 2012).

Thus, it can be argued that people's preference to deposit metalwork at particular kinds of places (neglecting others) indicates that to a certain extent a notion of 'place categories' steered depositional practices. We should bear in mind, then, that it is possible that terms used here so far, like 'tops of mountains' or 'stream valleys' probably do not do justice to the undoubtedly more subtle understandings held by the Bronze Age people who deposited the metal there. It may well have been specific features within such zones that people really focused on. One of the few well-documented hoard finds in a stream valley serves as an example.

When I studied the Bronze Age metalwork finds of the southern Netherlands and northern Belgium, I established that throughout the Bronze Age, many bronzes were deposited in the small, numerous stream valleys that dissect the sandy Pleistocene landscape between the rivers Meuse, Demer and Scheldt (Fontijn 2002, figure 10.1). In only a few cases, something more specific could be said regarding such locations. At Rijsbergen-Bakkebrug, a Middle Bronze Age bronze high-flanged axe was found near to where there was a bridge in historical times (Fontijn 2002, app. 2.4). This bridge was built at a location that was originally a ford.[1] This suggested it was not a random location in the stream that was selected, but that perhaps there was a preference for a particular kind of location in it. Jan Roymans had a similar idea. In a number of archaeological field projects in stream valleys of the southern Netherlands, he particularly focused on what should have been fords by nature (zones where the high borders of the valley approach each other; Roymans & Sprengers 2012). In some of them, Bronze Age metalwork finds were made (ibid.). At Hoogeloon-Kleine Beerze, Roymans and his team found the remnants of a Roman bridge (dam) location, which necessitated an excavation (ibid.). They discovered a Middle Bronze Age palstave hoard next to the Roman dam (this hoard was mentioned in Chapter 5). Surprisingly, it became clear that this hoard was not deposited in the stream or its back swamps itself. Roymans discovered that the bronzes were thrown in a location where fresh water wells up – a kind of location rather well known to farmers in the area as this is a source of fresh water for cattle that never freezes in winter (ibid., and Fontijn & Roymans forthcoming). Cattle imprints from a higher layer on this spot suggest it was also used as such, at least in younger prehistoric periods (Iron Age; Roymans & Sprengers 2012, 42–43). The excavators also discovered that there was probably a Bronze Age barrow situated near the riverbank. In all, this made clear that the bronzes were not just deposited in 'a ford', a stream, or the marshy back swamps of it, but rather in a very specific part of it – a place of relevance for cattle herders, situated along a route, and perhaps a local meeting place (Fontijn & Roymans forthcoming; Roymans & Sprengers 2012). The broad categorization 'stream valley' thus conceals that we are in many cases probably dealing with instances where bronzes were deposited in highly specific parts of such landscapes, locations of significance in local social geography.

Why a concept of place category does not make sense

At the same time, however, the notion of 'place categories' is unhelpful for understanding the depositional landscape. If 'river' would be a meaningful category for Bronze Age people who wanted to deposited metalwork, what then was actually considered to be part of a river? Is it the flowing water that people came to for placing valuables in? The gravel islands in between the currents, or the peaty back swamps beyond? And how to tackle river dynamics: the fact that what is dry ground in summer can be permanently flooded in winter? To be sure, the low resolution of our data usually hampers detailed observations. Even if there is detailed information, it can be confusing. At Haelense Beek (NL), a bronze high-flanged axe was buried in a small pit at the flanks of a stream (Verhoeven 2003). It was obviously dry when buried, but given its position in the valley it may have been flooded at another point in time. Is this to be qualified as a dry or a wet location? One could argue that the ambiguity, or 'in-between character' fits in with the liminal and transitional qualities of such places and may therefore in its ambiguity be the essence of what the 'river' or 'stream category' entailed (cf. Derks 1998, 12–15). But there are also cases where the concept of 'place category' no longer applies and where we should look for alternative ways to make sense of place selection.

Bourtanger Moor (Netherlands and Germany)

This becomes clear when considering zones in the landscape that have a long history of depositional practices. A case in point is the Bourtanger Moor, located on

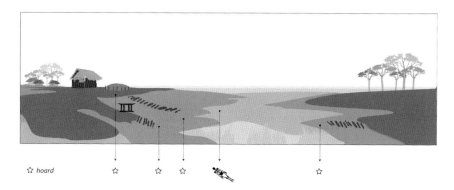

FIGURE 7.2 Artist's impression showing locations of Middle- and Late Bronze Age deposition sites projected on a transsect from Angelslo-Emmerhout settlement to Bourtanger Moor. Hoards are to be found both on dry land (probably heath with barrows) and at various locations in peat bogs (in which there were several trackways and a ceremonial building). One of the depositions is a human body. Based on more exact information in Butler 1961 and 1990; Casparie 1972; Fontijn 2012; Van der Sanden 1996.

Source: Drawing by J. Porck, Faculty of Archaeology, University of Leiden.

both sides of the German–Dutch border. It once was one of the largest peat bogs in Europe, before it was almost entirely reclaimed in the nineteenth and twentieth century (Van der Sanden 1996, 30). The bog is famous for the large numbers of special finds it yielded. Hundreds of items were discovered during its reclamation, ranging from Neolithic cattle horns and hoards of polished axes to numerous instances of Bronze Age metalwork, as well as pottery and domestic objects from the Iron Age and medieval periods (ibid.). In particular, the bog is well-known for a number of human bodies found in it, including a Bronze Age one (Van der Sanden 1996). There are several trackways leading into and across the moor, dating from the Neolithic, Bronze Age and Iron Age (Casparie 2005). The bog is also known for a (c. 1700–1400 BC) Bronze Age wooden ceremonial building the remains of which were found here: the so-called temple of Bargeroosterveld (Van der Sanden 2000; Waterbolk & van Zeist 1961).[2] Recalling the point made above, one would expect that either the bog, or perhaps even the ceremonial building in it, were foci for depositional activities (Bradley 1990, 133; Butler 1961, 106–108; Fontijn 2012, 54–61). However, mapping the metalwork finds in this peat bog shows that they were all found in all parts of the bog – close to its edge, but also deep in its centre (cf. also Van Beek 2015, 22–23). Intriguingly, there are also concentrations of finds discernable. Although shaped by chance discoveries and research intensity, they at least suggest that objects were not deposited haphazardly and that even inside the bog, there may have been particular features that were focal points for Bronze Age depositions. For some actions, people apparently went deep into the bog, whereas for others they only entered the transition zone of dry to peat land (ibid.). This indicates that just placing bronzes in a bog in itself was not enough. Apparently, there were zones in this huge bog that were worth travelling to for depositing such an object.

Bogs are not one monotonous landscape, but have relief and patches of deviating vegetation (like alderbrook or birchwood trees lining the periphery; Casparie 1972; Van Beek 2015). In the heart of the Bourtanger Moor, there also was open water (Casparie 1972). Though it remains difficult to see at this moment what it was in the bog landscape that pulled people towards certain zones within it, there must have been specific visible environmental features like deviating vegetation or lakes that attracted and focused people's attention during consecutive visits.[3]

In the case of the Bourtanger Moor, however, there was more than varieties in vegetation and hydro-geography. Butler (1961) has already remarked that there was a remarkable concentration of Late Bronze Age hoards in the vicinity of what is now the hamlet of Bargeroosterveld (where the building was found). Although the precise location of most hoards remains unclear, it is certain that some were not located in the bog at all (Butler 1961; Fontijn 2012, table 1). Rather, they are found alongside its boundaries in a zone, probably a heath, dotted with burial mounds (Butler 1961). Apparently, it was not only 'wet' landscapes where metal was deposited, but there must have been something else that attracted people to certain places (in a similar vein: Van Beek 2015, 22–23). The presence of trackways leading into the bog indicates that this part of the land was an area where the bog was accessed by people. Some 1.5 km to the west, lay the Bronze Age settlement of Angelso-Emmerhout, and Butler (1990, 49–50) seems to suggest that there was a route from there to the bog. This would first lead through a zone with barrows before entering the peat. Thus, the hoards of Bargeroosterveld may not have been linked to the bog in itself, but rather have been situated along the route leading to (or from) the bog. Here we see that when it came to deposition, there must have been more than just a single 'place category' like 'bog', however broadly defined, that mattered. Rather, it was an entire area that included *both the dry landscapes with barrows and the peat bogs with trackways* (Fontijn 2012). The question we are faced with must be: why was such a landscape preferred?

Rabenwand (Austria)

It is then helpful to realize that what we see at the flat and watery Bourtanger area is true for deposition landscapes in very different environments as well. A spectacular 'dry' example is the Late Bronze Age deposition landscape of the Rabenwand in Austria (Figure 7.3; Windholz-Konrad 2012). Here, the valley of the Traun creates an impressive passageway through the Alps to the Hallstatt lake. No less than 45 metalwork hoards were discovered and hundreds of single finds. As many were discovered during recent fieldwork, detailed information is known on the depositional location. Windholz-Konrad (2012, 117) states that hoards are situated close to settlements and among what must have been roads through the Alp

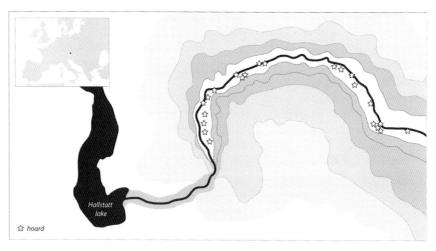

FIGURE 7.3 Metalwork deposition zone in the Rabenwand area, along the river Traun. Indicated are locations of hoards in the valley which cuts through the mountains. Schematized and with simplified contour lines. After information in Windholz-Konrad 2012, figure 3.

Source: Drawing by J. Porck, Faculty of Archaeology, University of Leiden.

passage. She argues hoards were located close to erratic rock formations (*Felswanden*) often with partly reddish coloured rocks (ibid., 134), and/or were placed in cavities along local hubs in infrastructure. As her distribution maps show, hoards were positioned everywhere in the valley, *as long as the location met the above mentioned criteria*. Thus, depositions were apparently repeated time and again, but there was apparently no desire to focus on one particular place in the valley, but *rather on places with similar landscape characteristics*. The latter likely should be read as relating to movement through the landscape – to social geography – as the valley is a crucial route through the Alps (Neumann 2015, 223).

Depositional landscapes as relational

What are the implications of the above examples for grasping what constituted an appropriate depositional location in the Bronze Age? In both areas, repeated depositions were not focused on one single location in the landscape through time. A 'cult place' – to use a phrase from historical periods – obviously was not a unique 'historical' place to be visited time and again. On the other hand, it was also not the case that a new metalwork deposition could be carried out just anywhere as long as the location was perceived as falling under a specific category like 'wet' or 'top of the mountain'. Instead of a single-feature category logic, the preferred location seems to have been selected on the basis of multiple characteristics. To judge from the cases described above, what seems to be relevant is that a deposition was carried out at a location the characteristics of which met certain conventions (in the Austrian case, near a special kind of rock formation at an intersection in the Alp passage (Windholz-Konrad 2012)). Perhaps there even was a desire to avoid locations that were previously used, although this is hard to prove. A depositional location thus was positioned in relational space, as experienced by how people moved around in the landscape. In the Bourtanger case, it may have been the passage to and from the huge peat bog that made this particular zone stand out as a preferred deposition location. In the Austrian Alps case, we must be dealing with a crucial and probably impressive corridor linking spatially segregated communities and therefore a pivotal passage in the broader social landscape (cf. Windholz-Konrad 2012; Neumann 2015). Following Ingold's (2000, 192) theory of the primacy of a dwelling perspective, meanings are not so much 'attached to the world' – as would be the case if the single-feature perspective held true – but rather 'gathered from it' by people interacting and actively living, travelling and dwelling in the landscape (also: Vachta 2016, 184). If the location choice for deposits in zones is linked to a narrative of – for example – accessing or leaving the bog via the barrow landscape, or travelling through the mountain pass rather than a concern with one particular place or environmental category, it is easier to understand the zonal nature of metalwork deposits and their fuzzy boundaries. After all, from an experiential perspective the limits of a river valley or the top/slope of a hill are also hard to pin down and rather something one experiences (Ingold 2000, 203). As Ingold (2000, 192) puts it, a boundary is not an inherent characteristic of something in the physical environment, but rather something that is experienced as such by people moving around. The deposition landscape thus is primarily relational. It is not, however, tied up with purely individual experiences, as we have seen in the examples; the locations selected in the Austrian Alps case, for example, clearly follow similar – yet multiple – conventions, which makes depositional place selections essentially something that can be GIS modelled and tested by means of scaffolding modelling techniques (for the GIS techniques: Llobera 2012; for an archaeological example from Sweden: Rundkvist 2015).

What constituted a deposition place?

If it was a dwelling perspective through which places gathered significance, then why were particular kinds of locations chosen for depositions? What was it in people's engagement with their environment that led them to bury valuables at these specific locations? The best way to study this is to work with data from situations where we have evidence of repeated depositional activities in the same environment over time, so-called Multiple Deposition Zones (Fontijn 2002, 260).

Historically speaking, once archaeologists started to accept that hoarding was a deliberate practice, often intended to be permanent, a new problem presented itself. How was it possible that there were certain zones that were visited for burying special items time and time again? Sometimes, we are dealing with landscapes with depositional histories stretching across thousands of years, from the Early Neolithic up until the Iron Age, or even historical times (e.g. Koch 1998, 161–164; Fontijn 2007). This is all the more remarkable if it is realized that we are dealing with non-monumental landscapes – i.e. landscapes without human-made lasting markers. That landscapes like the Bourtanger Moor could have such impressive long-term histories is therefore often seen as evidence of deep cultural memories. Knowledge of where forebears deposited valuables would have been preserved and transmitted across generations, representing an astonishing accomplishment for non-literate societies. Although I myself also held this opinion before, I came to different insight later on (Fontijn 2007).

Ingold (2000, 189) argued that perceiving one's environment is itself 'an act of remembrance', though he is careful to note that this is not the same as recalling something that is 'stored in the mind'. Rather he sees it as 'engaging perceptually with an environment that is itself pregnant of the past' (ibid.). If a Bronze Age inhabitant were to wander through a landscape marked by barrows and other visible monuments, it is conceivable that she would be made aware there was a human past that went back long before she lived. After all, round mounds have been built ever since the third millennium BC, and they were a ubiquitous landmark almost everywhere in Europe. Even if she might not know the intimate details of the person buried in one, she would have recognized such mounds as the work of former inhabitants and as funerary locations (cf. Fontijn 2007). But what was there in the Alp passage or Bourtanger Moor that made people aware that it was a landscape 'pregnant' with the depositions of a (deep) past? Apart from specific environmental scenery, as far as we know there was nothing but rocks or vegetation that marked previous deposition places. This is all the more intriguing for those cases, evidenced in Denmark or the Netherlands, where there seem to have been huge time gaps between Early Neolithic and Bronze Age depositions (cf. Fontijn 2007, figure 4; Koch 1998, table 1). Did people deliberately seek out locations where depositions had taken place long before? Did Bronze Age people know what *we* know: that they were re-using a depositional zone from the Neolithic? And if they did, as is usually assumed, how is it possible that such precise locational knowledge was transmitted over generations?

Episodic and semantic memory

Do the long-term histories of some deposition landscapes result from collective memory? The answer to this question is nuanced and should start by commenting on what memory actually is. Memory is usually seen as equivalent to what is called 'episodic memory', the recalling of events (e.g. Assmann 2006, 1). But there is also 'semantic memory', which has to do with encoding what the eyes see by filtering information and looking for patterns that the brain recognizes (Fernyhough 2012, 89–90; 156–157). Encoding is a process learnt through life and entails ways to deal with information that allow communication. As Halbwachs (1975) famously argues, such learnt patterns are primarily social, which is why he speaks of collective memory. As pattern recognition by the brain is behaviour learnt in interaction with others, memories of an individual are by definition social as well (Assmann 2006, 3). As Assmann (2006, 4) puts it, memory is a socio-genetic force; knowing where and how something happened can mark oneself as member of a group. In our case, knowing where and how depositions ought to be done could have been elemental in defining membership of groups. Following studies on group sociology (Cohen 1985; cf. Gerritsen 2003, 111–113), I previously suggested that having such intimate knowledge of depositional procedures (knowing the right place and the right ways) may have defined membership of depositional or sacrificial communities (Fontijn 2002, 271). I now see, however, that this was only part of the story (cf. also Fontijn 2012; Rundkvist 2015, 22). It may be that communities living close to Bourtanger Moor or the Alp passage had detailed knowledge of their environment and where their predecessors usually inserted metalwork into the landscape. It is less likely, however, that Late Bronze sacrificial communities of Bourtanger Moor, for example, knew that Neolithic communities from the fourth millennium BC also visited these same boggy areas to deposit valuables. That is why I argue that there is more going on than social memory. Remembrance also draws on cultural images, myths or axioms regarding the values associated with certain kinds of landscape that are part of culture in a much broader sense. The memory invoked during expeditions to Bourtanger Moor is cultural just as much as it is social. Assmann's (2006) notion of 'cultural memory' therefore seems to be appropriate here as well. Certain basic images and notions learnt from childhood on, and a dwelling place in the local landscapes, may have given structure and narrative coherence to what one was seeing and remembering. Following Ingold's (2000, 192) train of thought, cultural memory is not abstract but embodied, coming about through dwelling in one's local environment.[4] Paraphrasing Malafouris (2013), one could say the landscape, in a way, 'shapes the mind', by a reciprocal process of socialized cultural notions learnt from childhood that were continuously confronted with what lies out there.

That bogs were recognized as appropriate deposition areas in so many parts of Europe is only possible if there was some sort of simplification and stereotyping behind the way people viewed landscape. Deposition zones were probably traditional so-called 'place images' (Shields 1991, 47) in Bronze Age culture (cf. Chapman 1998, 111; Fontijn 2002, 260; 2007, 77–80). This implies that when Bronze Age communities used the same bog for depositions as did Early Neolithic communities long before them, this need not necessarily have been steered by the idea that people were returning to a depositional place of their Neolithic forebears. Rather, it implies that the features of what constituted an appropriate location for a deposition in both periods overlapped. As Rundkvist (2015, 22) aptly puts it, the idea 'might not be "This is a known place where the Lady of the Lake has been contacted before"', but '"This is the *kind* of place where She may be contacted"' (italics as in the original).

Fernyhough (2012, 79–90) argues that memory is not really an act of accessing internally stored experiences. Rather, [socially and culturally, DF] encoded semantic information can create or construct a sense of familiarity with an environment, regardless of whether one has actually visited it before. Drawing on theories of cognition (Gregory 1998; 2009), Wells (2013, 20) makes the point that 'seeing' entails a process by which the brain selects what it deems significant. Culturally, a location along the Alp passage may have been recognized as appropriate for a deposition. Perhaps this process was steered by a narrative that a mythical deposition was once done on a site with such and such features, and that this now was repeated (as in socio- or anthropogenetic origin myths, cf. Chapter 6; Lincoln 1986). Whether the location selected really was the site of a previous deposition may have been more a concern of modern science (looking for exclusive historical truths; cf. Barrett 1994, 77–81). In the Bronze Age, what 'is' and what 'ought to be' may be the same (Bazelmans 1998, 66; also Dumont 1977). But since the depositional behaviour that flows from it is patterned, as modern scientists we do have means to more or less predict where such depositional actions took place (Yates & Bradley 2010; Fontijn 2002, 282–283; Kok 2008; Rundkvist 2015).

Landscape as an imagined reality

Understanding depositional landscapes as a relational network made up by culturally recognized 'place images' (Shields 1991, 47) or templates has the following implication. It suggests that places in the landscape were not only visited for depositions because of their physical qualities, but also because they were part of what Searle (1995, 66) calls an imagined 'institutional reality', or, as Bloch calls it, an 'imaginary system' (2012, 115). With this term, a system is meant 'which consists of norms, institutions, roles etc.' (ibid.). Such a system constitutes, as Searle (1995, 66–71) puts it, an 'institutional' and 'non-empirical' reality. In a long-term deposition landscape, what was transferred over such long time periods probably were not the deeds of true ancestors and forebears, but rather *the basic outline of a system of rules on which kind of places* were the 'appropriate' receptacles for broad categories of valuables. This fits much better with the kind of evidence that we have from Bronze Age landscapes. After all, what the record of multiple deposition zones mainly evidences is that there was a preference for a certain 'category' of place, defined in relation to other elements in the landscape. It is the relational setting – a system if you like – that is repeated, not necessarily the emphasis on specific physical places themselves (as Figure 7.1 shows).

One may compare this to a statement made about the French, mentioned by Bloch (2012, 113). Bloch writes that to say that 'the French' have existed since the sixth century AD is understood to denote that the French existed as an 'imagined community' (cf. Anderson 2006). That is, a community made up of conventions, roles and structures.

Thus, if we regard it as an institutional imagined system, 'cultural memory' *sensu* Assmann (2006, chapter 1) can create a sense of familiarity and belonging, regardless of whether it is based on actual historical facts at all (cf. also Fernyhough 2012, 90).

Depositional landscapes as 'other places'[5]

How would we conceptualize the Bronze Age if we were to leave out depositional landscapes altogether and base ourselves only on evidence from settlements and graves? For many regions in western Europe, like Great Britain, northern and western Germany or Scandinavia, the evidence of settlements gives us a picture of self-sufficient, local communities, as finds of imported goods like metalwork are largely absent in such contexts. For Middle Bronze Age Britain, France or the Low Countries, the burial evidence would also not alter this picture radically, as the regional burial record does not display striking differences in social status; imported items and special metalwork tend to be lacking there as well (Fontijn 2002, 277–278; Roymans & Kortlang 1999). As settlements rarely show indications of defensive structures and weaponry is also rare, one might easily make the error of seeing these societies as relatively peaceful ones.

The picture of society, however, alters radically if we include hoards and single finds, which usually do consist of precious items from far-away places. They demonstrate that these communities were anything but local, and were integrated in long-distance networks. The many weapons among them demonstrate the significance warfare held, making painfully clear how flawed a picture of a society can be that is based on just one kind of context (cf. Fontijn 2005). At the same time, such contextual comparisons show that depositional landscapes must have been special areas to the people using them. They are receptacles for valuables that emphasize ideas that contrast with images of self-identity that are played out in the context of daily agricultural life, and sometimes also in the ancestral realm as portrayed in graves. This is why Hansen (2012, 40) sees depositional zones as 'other places' or 'heterotopia', borrowing a term coined by Foucault (1984). Whether this term really fits what Foucault originally intended for it is something that should not bother us here. What is clear, is that depositional zones are often the locations where valuables were being left that contrast markedly with notions and values prevalent in other contexts of daily life. Think for example of items showing-off the links between the local community and societies living far away, as seen in the Swedish Pile hoard (Chapter 2; Vandkilde 2017). Or one could think of objects that present notions that are ambiguous and potentially threatening, like rare ceremonial items, or weaponry (cf. Fontijn 2005).

One aspect which fits the heterotopia concept, is that metalwork depositions may be linked to different moments in time (Foucault 1984, principle 4). As Hansen (2012, 40) remarks, a recurrent feature of Bronze Age depositions is that they can be collections of objects that were gathered over the course of many generations, sometimes even 200 years. Tomedi (2012) showed that this is, for example, the case for the Moosbruckschrofer hoard from the Middle Bronze Age (Austria; cf. Vachta 2012 for examples from the Czech Republic).

A final point is that the objects inserted into the landscape often contrast so markedly to the broader social landscape. Metalwork depositions often consist of collections of foreign, ceremonial or rare objects and materials that are lacking in other contexts in the vicinity. A case in point is the Ommerschans hoard (Chapter 1) from the northeastern Netherlands – a *Mappa Mundi* hoard (Chapter 2) demonstrating the far reach of communities that appear to be profoundly locally oriented in other respects. As seen before, hoards consisting of foreign objects may be one-offs in their immediate surroundings, but have a similar content to depositions made in other regions (Chapter 5: the French Cap Hornu hoard with rib convertibles, or the French and British palstave hoards of Hoogeloon and Voorhout in the Low Countries). So, some deposition places indeed contrast to what happened beyond: they are places where imported things were associated with local/regional things, transgressive things, and there may be a concern with things and actions from the past. As such, they indeed are 'other places' (Hansen 2012).

All over Europe, a recurring characteristic of depositional landscapes is that they are zones lacking lasting human-made traces. As Hansen (2013) puts it, we are dealing with 'votive offerings without temples' (translation mine). As unaltered landscapes, lacking any kind of monumental human-made structure, depositional landscapes are beacons of stability in a world that was visibly changing and increasingly bore the signs of human manipulation. Was it because of their unchanged, permanent, and their all-that-surrounds-us features that 'natural' locations were so widely seen as suited to make the long-term order of society manifest (cf. Bradley 2000)? Was it for such reasons that the unaltered landscape was the receptacle of anything that is ambiguous, potentially conflicting or presencing worlds other than the local one? These are questions more easily posed than answered. Given the longevity and permanence of unaltered depositional landscapes, it is at least clear that we should not ask ourselves why such landscapes lack temples for dedications to the supernatural, but rather why people at some stage deemed it necessary to concentrate such activities in human-built, confined spaces. I will come back to this in Chapter 8.

Conclusion: an unfamiliar but predictable logic?

This chapter has shown that the logic behind the selection of places in the landscape deemed suitable for metalwork deposition is an unfamiliar one. There does not seem to have been a concern with one unique location that was revisited for historical reasons. Nor can deposition sites be tied to one particular landscape category. What best seems to fit the available evidence is to consider the choices of depositional landscapes as relational ones – 'the right place to deposit' (cf. Chapter 2) seems to have been determined from an experiential perspective (Llobera 2012). It was a combination of environmental characteristics that seem to have determined what was a preferred location. In the examples discussed here, it was particularly specific routes through the landscape that seem to have mattered. The 'right' depositional location, for example, might have been 'at the end of the route from the settlement towards the bog, along the barrows' (the Bourtanger Moor case). Given the availability of good data, such models are testable using GIS techniques. Using GIS-scaffolding models, hypotheses can be tested as to which combination of environmental elements best matches the presence of metalwork depositions in a small area (cf. Llobera 2012, 503–505). Through repeated hypothesis testing, a combination of factors can be found that best predicts the location of different depositions. If this is successful, then one may have identified something of the system that guided long-term use – the 'institutional reality' (Searle 1995, 66) or system behind it. This chapter argued that it is such a system, instead of episodic, historical memory itself, that was transferred from generation to generation, and created the remarkable, unfocused deposition zones that are so characteristic of the Neolithic and Bronze Age. Although this research has so far not been brought to completion,[6] the fact that several scholars independently have thus far managed to broadly identify key factors explaining depositional practices, is promising (Fontijn & Roymans forthcoming; Kok 2008; Rundkvist 2015; Yates & Bradley 2010). Although far from proving the workings of such a system to have been unravelled, it is inspiring to see that in some cases the search for depositional locations in contract archaeology has been successful (Roymans & Sprengers 2012).

To conclude: the practice of burying metalwork in the landscape may have been much less familiar than the cult-place focused offerings of civilizations like the Romans. On the other hand, Bronze Age depositional landscapes seem to have been structured and are therefore, to some extent, predictable.

Notes

1 Information provided by J. Verhagen (Tilburg, NL) in letter to the author.
2 The function of this small building remains unclear, but there is no indication that it functioned as a focal point for metalwork depositions (Fontijn 2012; Van der Sanden 2000).

3 This is currently under investigation by M. Doorenbosch (Faculty of Archaeology, Leiden University).
4 Fernyhough (2012, 130) points out that a well-known mnemotechnique is to organize information spatially, by fixing it to a set route through space.
5 Foucault 1984; Hansen 2012.
6 This is currently being researched by C. Popa (Faculty of Archaeology, Leiden University).

Bibliography

Anderson, B., 2006. *Imagined communities. Reflections on the origin and spread of nationalism.* London and New York: Verso.
Assmann, J., 2006. *Religion and cultural memory.* Stanford CA: Stanford University Press.
Ballmer, A., 2012. Topografie bronzezeitlicher Deponierungen. Fallstudie Alpenrheintal. Ph. D. thesis, University of Zürich.
Barrett, J.C., 1994. *Fragments from antiquity. An archaeology of social life in Britain, 2900–1200 BC.* Cambridge MA and Oxford: Blackwell.
Bazelmans, J., 1998. Geschenken en waren in premodern Europa: enkele gedachten over de waarde van kostbaarheden uit schatvondsten, *LEIDschrift* 13(3), 59–78.
Bloch, M., 2012. *Anthropology and the cognitive challenge.* Cambridge: Cambridge University Press.
Bradley, R., 1990. *The passage of arms. An archaeological analysis of prehistoric hoards and votive deposits.* Cambridge: Cambridge University Press.
Bradley, R., 2000. *An archaeology of natural places,* London and New York: Routledge.
Brück, J., forthcoming. *Personifying prehistory. Relational ontologies in Bronze Age Britain and Ireland.* Oxford: Oxford University Press.
Butler, J.J., 1961. A Bronze Age concentration at Bargeroosterveld, *Palaeohistoria* VIII, 101–126.
Butler, J.J., 1990. Bronze Age metal and amber in the Netherlands (I), *Palaeohistoria* 32, 47–110.
Casparie, W.A., 1972. Bog development in southeastern Drenthe (the Netherlands). Ph.D. thesis, University of Groningen.
Casparie, W., 2005. Het hoogveen ontsloten. Houten wegen en paden in de Drentse venen, in: *Nederland in de prehistorie,* eds L. Louwe Kooijmans, P. Van den Broeke, H. Fokkens and A. Van Gijn. Amsterdam: Bert Bakker, 401–406.
Chapman, J., 1998. Objectification, embodiment and the value of places and things, in: *The archaeology of value. Essays on prestige and the process of valuation* (British Archaeological Reports International Series 730), eds D. Bailey and S. Mills. Oxford: Archaeopress, 106–130.
Cohen, A.P., 1985. *The symbolic construction of community.* London and New York: Routledge.
Derks, T., 1998. *Gods, temples and ritual practices. The transformation of religious ideas and values in Roman Gaul* (Amsterdam Archaeological Studies 2). Amsterdam: Amsterdam University Press.
Dumont, L., 1977. *From Mandeville to Marx. The genesis and triumph of economic ideology.* Chicago: University of Chicago Press.
Fernyhough, Ch., 2012. *Pieces of light.* New York: Harper Perennial.
Fontijn, D.R., 2002. Sacrificial landscapes. Cultural biographies of persons, objects and 'natural' places in the Bronze Age of the southern Netherlands, c. 2300–2600 BC, *Analecta Praehistorica Leidensia* 33/34, 1–392.
Fontijn, D.R., 2005. Giving up weapons, in: *Warfare, violence and slavery* (British Archaeological Reports International Series 1374), eds M. Parker Pearson and I.J. Thorpe. Oxford: Archaeopress, 145–154.

Fontijn, D.R., 2007. The significance of 'invisible' places, *World Archaeology* 39(1), 70–83.
Fontijn, D.R., 2012. Landscapes without boundaries? Some thoughts on Bronze Age deposition areas in North-West Europe, in: *Hort und Raum – aktuelle Forschungen zu bronzezeitlichen Deponierungen in Mitteleuropa* (Berlin Studies of the Ancient World 10), eds S. Hansen, D. Neumann and T. Vachta. Berlin: De Gruyter, 49–68.
Fontijn, D.R. and J. Roymans, forthcoming. Branded axes, thrown into a pool? The Hoogeloon hoard and the shape-based bronze economy of the Northwest European Bronze Age, *Oxford Journal of Archaeology*.
Foucault, M., 1984 [1967]. Of other spaces: utopias and heterotopias, *Architecture/Mouvement/Continuité* no. 5, October, 1–9.
Gerritsen, F., 2003. *Local identities. Landscape and community in the late prehistoric Meuse-Demer-Scheldt region* (Amsterdam Archaeological Studies 9). Amsterdam: Amsterdam University Press.
Gregory, R.L., 1998. *Eye and brain: the psychology of seeing*. Oxford: Oxford University Press.
Gregory, R.L., 2009. *Seeing through illusions*. Oxford: Oxford University Press.
Halbwachs, M., 1975 [1925]. *Les cadres sociaux de la mémoire*. New York: Arno Press.
Hansen, S., 2012. Bronzezeitliche Horte: Zeitliche und räumliche Rekontextualisierungen, in: *Hort und Raum – aktuelle Forschungen zu bronzezeitlichen Deponierungen in Mitteleuropa* (Berlin Studies of the Ancient World 10), eds S. Hansen, D. Neumann and T. Vachta. Berlin: De Gruyter, 23–48.
Hansen, S., 2013. Bronzezeitliche Deponierungen in Europa. Weihgaben ohne Tempel, in: *Sanktuar und Ritual. Heilige Plätze in archäologischen Befund*, eds I. Gerlach and D. Raue. Rahden: Marie Leidorf Verlag, 371–387.
Ingold, T., 2000. *The perception of the environment. Essays in livelihood, dwelling and skill*. London and New York: Routledge.
Koch, E., 1998. *Neolithic bog pots from Zealand, Møn, Lolland and Falster* (Nordiske Fortidsminder Serie B vol. 16). Copenhagen: Nordiske Fortidsminder.
Kok, M.S.M., 2008. The homecoming of religious practice. An analysis of offering sites in the wet low-lying parts of the landscape in the Oer-IJ area (2500 BC–AD 450). Unpublished Ph.D. thesis, University of Amsterdam.
Lincoln, B., 1986. *Myth, cosmos and society. Indo-European themes of creation and destruction*. Cambridge MA and London: Harvard University Press.
Llobera, M., 2012. Life on a pixel: challenges in the development of digital methods within an 'interpretive' landscape archaeology framework, *Journal of Archaeological Methods and Theory* 19(4), 495–509.
Malafouris, L., 2013. *How things shape minds. Theory of material engagement*. Cambridge MA and London: MIT Press.
Mullin, D., 2012. The river has never divided us. Bronze Age metalwork deposition in Western Britain, *Oxford Journal of Archaeology* 31(1), 47–57.
Neumann, D., 2015. *Landschaften der Ritualisierung. Die Fundplätze Kupfer- und Bronzezeitlicher Metalldeponierungen zwischen Donau und Po* (Topoi – Berlin Studies of the Ancient World 26). Berlin and Boston: De Gruyter.
Roymans, N., 1990. *Tribal societies in Northern Gaul. An anthropological perspective* (Cingula 12). Amsterdam: Amsterdam University Press.
Roymans, N. and F. Kortlang, 1999. Urnfield symbolism, ancestors, and the land in the Lower Rhine region, in: *Land and ancestors. Cultural dynamics in the Urnfield period and the Middle Ages in the southern Netherlands* (Amsterdam Archaeological Studies 4), eds F. Theuws and N. Roymans. Amsterdam: Amsterdam University Press, 33–61.
Roymans, J. and N. Sprengers, 2012. Tien Bronzen bijlen bij een Romeinse dam. Herinrichting beekdal Kleine Beerze, deeltraject Hoogeloon-Vessem, gemeenten Bladel en Eersel. Resultaten archeologische begeleiding en opgraving, *RAAP Rapport* no. 2537.

Rundkvist, M., 2015. *In the landscape and between worlds. Bronze Age deposition sites around lakes Mälaren and Hjälmaren in Sweden* (Archaeology and Environment 29). Umeå: Department of Historical, Philosophical and Religious Studies, Umeå University.

Searle, J.R., 1995. *The construction of social reality.* New York: The Free Press.

Shields, R., 1991. *Places on the margin. Alternative geographies of modernity.* London: Routledge.

Soroceanu, T., 2012. Die Fundplätze der bronzezeitlichen Horte im heutigen Rumänien, in: *Hort und Raum − aktuelle Forschungen zu bronzezeitlichen Deponierungen in Mitteleuropa* (Berlin Studies of the Ancient World 10), eds S. Hansen, D. Neumann and T. Vachta. Berlin: De Gruyter, 227–254.

Tomedi, G., 2012. Der mittelbronzezeitliche Schatzfund vom Piller. Eine kulturhistorische Lokalisierung, in: *Hort und Raum − aktuelle Forschungen zu bronzezeitlichen Deponierungen in Mitteleuropa* (Berlin Studies of the Ancient World 10), eds S. Hansen, D. Neumann and T. Vachta. Berlin: De Gruyter, 151–168.

Vachta, T., 2012. Multidepotfundstellen in Böhmen, in: *Hort und Raum − aktuelle Forschungen zu bronzezeitlichen Deponierungen in Mitteleuropa* (Berlin Studies of the Ancient World 10), eds S. Hansen, D. Neumann and T. Vachta. Berlin: De Gruyter, 179–197.

Vachta, T., 2016. *Bronzezeitliche Hortfunde und ihre Fundörte in Böhmen* (Berlin Studies of the Ancient World 33). Berlin: Edition Topoi.

Van Beek, R., 2015. An interdisciplinary approach to the long-term history of raised bogs: a case study at Vriezenveen (the Netherlands), *Journal of Wetland Archaeology* 15(1), 1–33.

Van der Sanden, W.A.B., 1996. *Vereeuwigd in het veen: de verhalen van de Noordwest-Europese veenlijken.* Amsterdam: De Bataafsche Leeuw.

Van der Sanden, W.A.B., 2000. Het tempeltje van Barger-Oosterveld, *Nieuwe Drentse Volksalmanak* 117, 135–143.

Van Hoof, L., 2007. Daily rituals: depositions in the Dutch river Meuse Basin, in: *L'âge du fer dans l'arc jurrassien et ses marges. Dépôts, lieux sacrés et territorialité à l'âge du fer* (Actes du XXIXe colloque internationale de L'AFEAF Bienne (canton de Berne, Suisse), 5–8 octobre 2005), eds P. Barrai, A. Daubigney, C. Dunning, G. Kaenel and M.-J. Roulière-Lambert. Presses Universitaires de Franche-Comté, 433–438.

Vandkilde, H., 2017. *The metal hoard from Pile in Scania, Sweden. Place, things, time, metals, and worlds around 2000 BC.* Aarhus: Aarhus University Press.

Verhoeven, M.P.F., 2003. Ruilverkavelingsgebied Land van Thorn. Een archeologische begeleiding, *RAAP-Rapport* 917.

Waterbolk, H.T. and W. van Zeist, 1961. A Bronze Age sanctuary in the raised bog at Bargeroosterveld (Dr.), *Helinium* 1, 5–19.

Wells, P., 2013. *How ancient Europeans saw the world: Vision, patterns, and the shaping of the mind in Prehistoric times.* Princeton NJ: Princeton University Press.

Windholz-Konrad, M., 2012. Das Deponierungsareal bei der Rabenwand im steirischen Kainischtal in Österreich. Zum ausgeprägten Hortphänomen entlang der Traun im Alpendurchgang zwischen Zinkenkogel und hohem Sarstein, in: *Hort und Raum − aktuelle Forschungen zu bronzezeitlichen Deponierungen in Mitteleuropa* (Berlin Studies of the Ancient World 10), eds S. Hansen, D. Neumann and T. Vachta. Berlin: De Gruyter, 117–150.

Yates, D. and R. Bradley, 2010. The siting of metalwork hoards in the Bronze Age of Southeast England, *Antiquaries Journal* 90, 41–72.

8

ECONOMIES OF DESTRUCTION

'Keeping-while-destroying'?

This final chapter brings the conclusions of the previous chapters together and interprets what Bronze Age people were trying to accomplish when they were selectively depositing metalwork in the landscape. I argue that the destruction of things may, paradoxically, lead to a form of keeping. Using Graeber's and Lambek's theories, I suggest that by depositing valuables, some other form of value was created and that such practices had consequences for the social fabric of Bronze Age Europe. The evidence of Bronze Age depositions is one way in which political and moral economies intertwine. This chapter brings nuance to theories that see the Bronze Age as a clear start of a familiar, rational-economic Europe. Rather, I argue that it helps us to broaden our view on what economies really are, and that in order to achieve something, a society has to give things up.

Introduction

In this book, I have tried to establish what Bronze Age people wished to accomplish when they systematically destroyed valuable things and materials. Lurking in the background, there is an equally relevant question: why does the massive deposition of metalwork during the Bronze Age actually pose such an interpretive challenge to us? In Chapter 1, I argued that this is because we have been using short-term principles such as accumulation or scarcity ('value as price'), to explain what are actually long-term ideas on '*cultural* values' (cf. Lambek 2008). What looks like destruction from a short-term perspective, may be 'singularization' from a long-term one (cf. Kopytoff 1986). The problem is that archaeology has been looking for answers either exclusively in the field of short-term 'rational economy', or in long-term 'religious ideas'. Both tend to be seen as each other's opposite, are rooted in the same post-Enlightenment way of thinking (Brück 1999), and are so-called redescriptive concepts (Nongbi 2013, 15, 21–24) – they refer to concepts that need not represent a categorical reality for the prehistoric people involved. In order to escape the limitations that our concepts of economy and religion set, I went back to empirical evidence that is usually seen as closely linked to either 'economic' or 'religious' actions.

It was demonstrated that what we tend to see as straightforward economic material was systematically involved in what we consider to be un-economic depositional practices – the systematic deposition of recyclable, and often scarce, metalwork (Chapter 5). I concluded that the evidence shows that deposition was a way to link short- to long-term practices. More specifically: as this happened in a selective manner, it must have been a key concern of Bronze Age people to keep convertibles from different spheres of exchange strictly separate in depositions.

As argued in Chapter 6, it is very difficult to prove that many supposed 'religious offerings' really were the 'gifts to gods' archaeologists usually suppose them to be. Rather, I argue that 'religious' objects deposited actually inform us on how people made other-worldly concepts conceivable to themselves and linked them to human society. The archaeological evidence shows how such objects were also carefully and selectively buried in the landscape. So what we archaeologically see of 'religion' is in part selective deposition of things that were used to make cosmological ideas conceivable (cf. Kaul 1998).

FIGURE 8.0 Sites mentioned in this chapter: 1. Marchésieux; 2. Agneaux; 3. Voorhout; 4. Hoogeloon; 5. Ommerschans.

Source: J. Porck, Faculty of Archaeology, University of Leiden.

The findings of the previous chapters were brought to their logical conclusion in Chapter 7. We only get to know about both 'economic' and 'religious' objects because they were both part of one system of selective deposition. This implies that it was not just objects that made values conceivable to people, but also how they were inserted in the landscape. I argue that the way things were placed in the land does not relate to some historical unicity of the places in it, but rather because people living in it regarded specific areas as the culturally appropriate recipients for specific kinds of objects.

Thus, what unites the archaeological evidence of 'economy' and 'religion' is that both 'come about' through people engaging with specific objects of which we – as archaeologists – only come to learn *because prehistoric people systematically deposited them in the landscape in a particular way*. This means that both objects and landscape constituted people's thoughts during the act of a deposition. It also means that the thoughts and ideas that motivate such a practice are not either 'value as price' or 'value as culture'. Rather – and this is key – *the meaning of the act is in the process of deposition* (cf. Becker 2013; Lambek 2008). Selective deposition should be understood as the transformation of one kind of value into another (Lambek 2008, 149). In 'giving up' valuables, 'value' is created (cf. ibid.). This implies that the eternal question 'why were Bronze Age people doing this?' is actually hard to answer in a satisfactory way. This is not only because the kind of selective deposition discussed in this book clearly was 'average behaviour' – a phenomenon resulting from thousands of individual local actions that probably were all steered by an equivalent number of ideas and motivations (Chapter 2; Ball 2004). It is also because the 'why' may be in the 'how' (cf. Lambek 2008).

How bronze things make abstract concepts of value conceivable

Throughout this book, I gave examples of how abstract, mental concepts of value were made concrete through things. Early Bronze Age *Ösenringe* may represent a system of standardized weight units of commensurable commodity value. Yet, nothing indicates that there was an overall metrological system beyond *Ösenringe* which governed the conversion of bronze in general (Chapter 5; Lenerz-de Wilde 1995; Pare 2013). Bronze Age people apparently needed such rings in order to make the more abstract concept of *Ösenring* standard weight conceivable. Likewise, Bronze Age people made aggrandized versions of common things, like the Ommerschans sword. This implies that people needed extra-ordinary versions of common things to conceive of a hierarchical order of things, with superhuman entities transgressing on top (Godelier's 1999 'sacred things'). Regardless whether it is about value as price or cultural values, value is constituted and made thinkable by valuables (Renfrew 2001, 99).

For a system of value that is importantly shape-based, it makes a difference if metal is just one of the materials from which valuables are made (as it was in the Neolithic TRB culture; Chapter 4), or whether valuables constituting different spheres of value are all made out of the same metal, as we have it in the Bronze

FIGURE 8.1 Zones in Europe where there are many Bronze Age/Early Iron Age metalwork hoards (hatched). Information after Reinhold 2005 and Hänsel & Hänsel 1997 but shown here in simplified form.
Source: Drawing by J. Porck, Faculty of Archaeology, University of Leiden.

Age (I called this a 'metallized' system of value in Chapter 4). This is because value is inherently comparative and referential (Graeber 2005, 451). A metallized system has different affordances and potential in both the sphere of value comparison and value conversion. I argued that the affordance for a bronze object to communicate cultural information lies primarily with its shape and general appearance. Unlike other important materials such as stone, these almost exclusively have to do with the agency of the person who creates them – the smith (Chapter 4; Fontijn 2009; Kuijpers 2018; Sørensen 1987). Also, the ever-present possibility of re-melting makes it much easier to blur distinctions between valuables, as one high-order valuable can be re-shaped into a lower-order one (or *vice versa*) without leaving any visible trace (cf. Simmel 2011, 163). It thereby presents a new tension and potential ambiguity to the management of value classes that is less prominent for other materials from which valuables were made, like stone or amber. It also may create a greater necessity to find ways to nevertheless keep spheres of valuables separate.

'Keeping-while-destroying'?

Things may make concepts of value thinkable, but how can the deposition and even destruction of things relate to value? In what follows, I will argue that, counter-intuitively, there is a way in which 'destruction' amounts to a sense of 'keeping'. A system of selective deposition affords social potential for action, may produce ideas of truth and yet allow for change at the same time.

Many deposition practices discussed in the book were steered by an intentional concern with irreversibility. Objects were physically transformed, or located in places from where it is practically impossible to retrieve them, like rivers or lakes (in which case material resources were being destroyed). The fact that so much metalwork was found in the ground in modern times in itself indicates that at least a large part must have been deliberately left there in the Bronze Age with the intention to leave it in perpetuity. From a human perspective, it is an ultimate form of alienation that differs from commodity exchange because there is no human receiver – as such, it equals destruction (Chapter 3).

However, the archaeological evidence discussed also demonstrates that more was at stake than just destroying or hiding things from view by burial. This book gave many examples of how depositional practices followed strict conventions concerning association and dissociation of things, and how specific things were buried in specific parts of the landscape only. Such conventions, a system of selective deposition, imply that there was a recurrent and widely-shared concern with doing this in a particular way (Chapter 2). This indicates that the very act of deposition itself was a way to linking things deposited with human actors *by the quality of the performance itself* (cf. Lambek 2008). We have seen examples where objects were dismantled (used axes deposited without shafts; Chapter 5), physically transformed (Chapter 6), placed in a special order (e.g. axes placed in circles; Chapters 4 and 5), laid on platforms in bogs (Ommerschans; Chapter 1) or being placed in a vertical position (the Stoboru swords; Chapter 1). There also is a recurrent concern with depositing certain kinds of objects in specific kinds of places (e.g. Late Bronze Age swords in western Europe in rivers; Early Bronze Age halberds and *lunulae* not being placed in graves; Chapters 1 and 2). Although the specifics may vary from region to region, deposition was steered by a commitment to 'the right way of doing things', implying the details of its performance mattered greatly to people and were ways to make them singular (cf. Kopytoff 1986).

In some cases, the very act of depositing things may have been an impressive act in itself. Letting a gold-glimmering object like the large ceremonial sword of Ommerschans sink down into a dark peat bog may have had a dramatic effect on the onlookers considering the extraordinary nature of such an object in their community (cf. Fontijn 2002, 276). The burial of 59 Armorican axes during the Early Iron Age in Agneaux, northwest France (Chapter 5; Marcigny & Verney 2005) itself may not immediately have been a spectacular act. Yet, the burial of useable convertibles was carefully done and must have been something out of the ordinary. After all, commodities are made to circulate. There is also evidence that the location was chosen with care: close to an ancestral burial landscape (ibid.). As the find of another such pit nearby indicates, it was considered to be an act important enough to repeat (Marcigny & Verney 2005).

If experiencing valuables has the cognitive effect of making value as a more abstract concept thinkable (see above), then the act of removing those valuables from view may also have a mental effect on onlookers and participants. Placing valuables in the landscape, following specific conventions and then hiding them from view, may itself have worked to 'anchor' visual information in people's memory of the act (cf. Hutchins 2005). As several anthropologists have argued, evocative acts in which things are shown and then hidden may be an important strategy of non-literate societies to imprint the significance of certain items – and the concepts with which they are associated – on onlookers (Küchler 1997; Rowlands 1993). Whitehouse (2004) calls such acts 'imagistic' practices in which meaning is created through performance (Chapter 6). This can result in their disappearance or destruction, by which they 'become a memory in their absence' (Rowlands 1993, 146). Displaying a combination of things before they disappear from view forever may be a powerful way to emphasize – or 'objectify' – their association (Thomas 1996, 169), or even to give it some autonomy (Hodder 2012, 32). It may lead to an act of reification, where objects 'created by humans can become so separate that they are perceived as having an external reality' (ibid.). As Rowlands (1993, 146) puts it, they 'become the essence of what has to be remembered'. Thus, removing things from society in a public performance affects the relation between humans and things in life, and can even lead to transforming things into more abstract notions that they are thought to stand for. So, giving up or destroying valuable *things* may create *value as an abstract concept or socio-cultural quality* (cf. Lambek 2008). Thus, giving things up, in a way, amounts to preserving or 'keeping' important social concepts. In her seminal work, Weiner (1992) argued that gift-giving is actually 'keeping-while-giving'. Borrowing her terminology, there is a way in which we may call deposition 'keeping-while-destroying'.

What is reified in selective deposition is a certain *order* of things (Chapter 5). It is about a consistent association and dissociation of things and places (even though the objects themselves and the kinds of landscapes may vary from region to region and from period to period; Chapter 2). It is a way to acknowledge that certain kinds of things have a different value than other kinds of things. This need not go back to clearly defined referential meaning. It is rather the kind of non-discursive meaning that we only become aware of when we observe non-normative practices (Kopytoff 1986, 67). For example, it is only when we find a mayoral chain of office (Chapter 2) being placed around the neck of a deceased individual who once was mayor that we come to realize that this is not how such valuables ought to be treated. Or, to give a prehistoric example: in the Early Iron Age of the Meuse-Lower Rhine region, both Wesseling axes and Geistingen token axes were common exchange items circulating in the same society. Yet, in depositions they were never associated, which suggests that associations of both simply did not make sense to the communities involved. I take this to imply that as valuables, they 'did' different things and functioned in different kinds of transactions (Chapter 5). Thus, selective deposition is a system founded on principles of separation between different spheres of value (Chapters 2 and 5).

Although the deposited thing itself is often practically alienated after a deposition (it is no longer in reach), the idea behind it may acquire an added relevance and thus may become more anchored in the minds of people involved – as an idea or notion that may become inalienable to group identity (Küchler 1997). This is all the more so if the deposition is perceived as some kind of gift to the supernatural itself; as argued in Chapter 3, this would mean to give the supernatural something that belonged to it anyway, enhancing a permanent 'keeping'. With deposition, paradoxically, alienation thus breeds inalienability (also: Küchler 1997, 42).

Deposition practices thus may have been the means by which the object's social role was shielded from alienation and made 'singular' (Kopytoff 1986, 69–70). Ultimately, such notions are always linked to cultural values, and thereby to a lasting, overarching long-term sphere that defines what is worthwhile in human life (Bloch & Parry 1989, 23–28; Graeber 2005, 443). As the emphasis is very much on keeping things in check, on separation and on repeating actions (like the widespread tradition of placing weapons in rivers and keeping them out of burials), we are perhaps not so much dealing with things that were 'given up', but rather with cultural notions of value that were perceived as being *kept* (Godelier 1999).

Political vs. moral economies: how deposition links short-term to long-term transactions

Selective deposition of metalwork may reflect human concerns which are cultural in nature. Yet, the objects in it more often than not must have been acquired through short-term transactions. It is undeniable that Bronze Age Europe knew an extensive supra-regional metal trade (Ling et al. 2014). Bronze was crucial in political economies that were marked by unbalanced and ever-shifting power

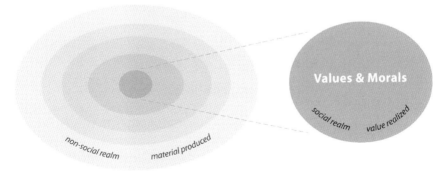

FIGURE 8.2 Political versus moral economies as spatial model, displaying zones where value is produced and where it is realized, after information in Bloch & Parry 1989; Graeber 2005; and Platenkamp 2016.

Source: Drawing by J. Porck, Faculty of Archaeology, University of Leiden.

relations in which calculation and (individual) gain were key (Earle et al. 2015). Using the insights of Bloch and Parry (1989) and Kopytoff (1986), I argued in Chapters 1 and 3 that in every society short- and long-term transactions exist together and must be connected and balanced. Throughout this book, I have argued that in Bronze Age Europe, the deposition of metalwork in the landscape was a pivotal way of maintaining that balance.

In Chapter 5, we saw that trade stock which entered a local community, from time to time was placed in the landscape following certain conventions. Imported valuables from afar, such as the set of Welsh and French Middle Bronze Age palstaves that ended up on the Dutch coast at Voorhout (Chapter 5; Fontijn 2008), were buried as a package in a small pit. The package was inserted in a peat bog in the coastal dunes and never taken out again until it was found in the twentieth century AD. We saw that the same happened with the rare set of French and British palstaves at Hoogeloon that were thrown into a pool in a stream valley (Fontijn & Roymans forthcoming). By being made part of the local landscape, the actors may forcefully have made the point that material from a 'distant' beyond (on which they practically were dependent since they lacked their own metal sources), was integrated into what must have been the most lasting and meaningful element of their community: the local landscape in which their community had been living and thriving for so long (Fontijn 2008; Fontijn and Roymans forthcoming; cf. Becker 2013, 255; Sørensen 1987).

That such actions were relatively rare implies that the cases where material was inserted and left in perpetuity were *pars pro toto* actions that may have had the effect of making general trade transactions with outsiders morally acceptable (Bloch & Parry 1989; Fontijn 2008; Needham 2001). A small part was inserted into the long term through a deposition (to become linked with the landscape and perhaps supernatural entities or ancestors considered to live in it), making mundane trade transactions acceptable (cf. Bloch & Parry 1989). As Shennan (1993) was one of the first to put it: *the short-term cycle may have 'fed' the long-term cycle.*

In Chapter 6, I showed that the same strategy of inserting valuable things in the landscape also applies to what are usually seen as 'religious' or 'high-order' valuables, like those that are called special, 'transgressive' (Harrison 2006) objects or paraphernalia used to stage or impersonate transgressive beings. Chapter 6 shows that such items were also buried in the land. This implies that a concern with placing things inside the landscape was much broader than just commodities or items from afar. If we realize that this is not just true for large parts of Europe during the Bronze Age, but also for the preceding Neolithic (Chapter 4) and succeeding Iron Age (Kok 2008), locating things in the land seems to have been a transcultural way of dealing with items that were imbued with a certain ambiguity. In late prehistoric Europe, placing things in the land – deposition – must have been a crucial way of dealing with material culture, to transmit information and to imprint and communicate essential knowledge and 'truths' about values and their ordering (Fontijn 2002, 274–275).

Wrapping up, a seemingly un-economic act like metalwork deposition in the end becomes meaningful and *yields* something when perceived from the perspective of a more encompassing socio-cultural whole. As material that is implemental in economy in the narrow (short-term) sense, contributes to the upholding of a broader social and moral totality, this means our Bronze Age evidence suggests that the commonly used notion of economy should be drastically expanded. A political economy was inextricably linked to what has been called a 'moral economy' in some anthropological and historical circles (Fontaine 2014; Gregory 2015, xxxvii–xxxviii; Thompson 1971). *To acquire something for oneself in short-term exchanges, means to yield something of it to society as a whole.* As Gregory (2015, xxxvii) puts it: if political economy is about value as price, 'a moral economy is the theory of the *just* price'. Self-interest in one field, ultimately should be coupled to a sense of solidarity or justice in another field. Translated to the Bronze Age, accumulating prestigious metalwork in trade or violent encounters like perhaps raiding (Earle et al. 2015), apparently ought to find a pendant in acts by which some of this material is again 'given up' and made part of a broader social whole overarching the agency and motivations of individuals.

Social potential: how concealing valuables may create a 'capacity to act'

One reason why 'imagistic' performances can have great social effect is because they play with 'the tension between display and potency of concealment' (Lambek 2008, 147). Things, and the order of valuables they evoke, are shown to onlookers in the same act that hides them from view (Küchler 1997). Another reason lies in the fact that hiding valuables and rendering them invisible socially is an ambiguous enterprise. As Graeber (2001, chapter 4) argues: visuality and materiality of valuables has the effect of making abstract values real, specific and concrete. This means that once hidden from view, they lose specificity, become prone to imagination and get more ambiguous. The fact that valuables are no longer used implies they no longer can be used in perpetuating society. In the early medieval *Beowulf* poem, the dragon Grendel who steals wealth from the people and keeps it from circulating is clearly seen as an anti-social force (Bazelmans 1999, 115). The sword Excalibur from the late medieval Arthurian legend on the other hand, that waits for the right person to take it out of its rock, shows that a 'kept', non-circulating valuable may also create a potential for acting in the future (Wengrow 2010, 100). Graeber (2001, 98), citing Hobbes, remarks that what is unknown or uncertain could be anything and therefore 'it could do anything as well'. Hiding valuables in the ground therefore is not necessarily an anti-social action that is tantamount to the dissolution of social bonds, as Platenkamp (2016, 179) argues. Rather, depositions owe much of their non-social evocations not due to the fact that they are anti-social in themselves, but *because they are socially elusive and ambiguous*. Invisible valuables of which people know they are 'somewhere out there', escape social processes and regulations that are central in exchange transactions (cf. Graeber 2001, 103). For example, there may be a moment when the hidden material will turn up and start to circulate again, thus creating a potential for acting in the future for those who buried it. The significance of hoarding as social action was already

162 Economies of destruction

recognized by Marx, and as Graeber (2001, 101) is keen to emphasize, Marx did not see this as something unique to capitalist society, nor did he see it as entirely linked to short-term transactions. Marx (quoted in Graeber 2001, 101) mentions the case of non-Muslim merchants in Delhi who hoard money deep in the ground, expecting it may be of use for their life in the hereafter. Viking communities had a rather similar belief while hoarding valuables (the so-called Law of Odin; Bradley 2000, 50).

Was deposited material also 'kept' in a more practical way?

The above discussion brings us to a crucial question: was deposition also a practical way to 'keep' material, in that it was taken out at some later stage? As mentioned

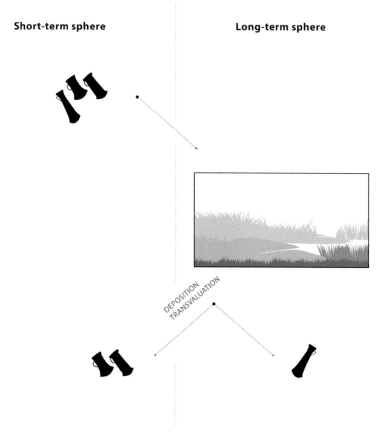

FIGURE 8.3 Model showing how material acquired in short-term transactions may have been transformed and transferred to the long-term sphere through deposition. A large part of deposited material, then, was taken out after some time to be inserted in short-term transactions. Based on a theory in Needham 2001.
Source: Drawing by J. Porck, Faculty of Archaeology, University of Leiden.

in the opening chapter of this book, interpreting metalwork as material that was temporarily stored in the landscape has been the easiest way to make seemingly uneconomic action, economic again. It is also one of the most unconvincing explanations, as it has to use individual anecdotes such as people forgetting the location of their hoards to explain a long-lived, persistent pattern of permanent deposition (cf. Bradley 1990, chapter 1; Fontijn 2002, 14–15). I do, however, think there is at least some circumstantial evidence that much material deposited in the ground was taken out again, and that permanent and temporary deposition are two sides of the same coin.

Basing himself on what he calls 'scrap hoards' from the last phase of the Late Bronze Age in England and Wales, a seminal model recently published by Wiseman (2017) suggests a recycling rate of 85–95 per cent. This means only 15–5 per cent of the metalwork was deposited in the landscape and remained there. He argues that the scrap hoards he studied are characteristic of how pools of metal for re-melting take shape (consisting of broken bronzes showing no selection at all).[1] Using a different model, for the Late Bronze Age in the southern Netherlands I once estimated a comparable 16 per cent of the metal a local community had was deposited permanently, provided deposition took place just once within 25 years. If it should happen on a yearly basis, the rate of permanent deposition must even be below 1 per cent (Fontijn 2002, 215). Likewise, Needham (2007, 283) also showed that permanent deposition must have been limited. In a thought experiment, he argues that if the metal stock was not replenished within c. 50 years, and 2 per cent of the metal was to be permanently placed in the landscape, the entire stock would have been gone within 50 years. If the deposition rate were 10 per cent, this would already happen within ten years. Particularly in non-metalliferous regions where replenishment of stock depends on long-distance trade contacts, these models all suggest that communities must have created their own pools of material for recycling.

Wiseman (2017) argues that scrap hoards are good examples of the kind of metal pools one would expect to be collected for recycling purposes. However, Wiseman builds his views on hoards that were obviously not temporary at all: they remained in the landscape until found in modern times. This brings me to a crucial point: are ('profane') temporary storage and permanent ('ritual') deposition of metalwork really entirely different practices?

The evidence from Chapter 5 suggests that this is not the case. Case studies of so-called trade hoards from different regions and different periods showed time and again that hoards in retrievable ('profane') and those in irretrievable ('ritual') positions in the land were not really different in composition or general treatment of the objects. Hoards that were usually interpreted as profane stores of material often showed the same commitment to treatment and ordering as those traditionally regarded as ritual. They are also strictly selective, as there is a clear tendency to deposit like with like (Wesseling axes are not associated with Geistingen axes, see above). This is also true for the scrap hoards Wiseman describes. They are one particular kind of deposition (namely, of completely fragmented bronze) among contemporary others: swords in rivers, specific objects in graves, axes of the same kind in hoards on dry land, etc. This implies something that has already been suggested long before by Needham (2001), namely that temporary 'ritualization' or 'singularization' need not conflict with a possible later re-entry of the same material into society (cf. also Becker 2008; 2013). Although this remains so far hypothetical (we currently are unable to match material in circulation with that what was deposited), the necessity of recycling makes this something one may expect. The examples given by Graeber (2001) mentioned in the previous section ensure that temporary hiding may have been a powerful social strategy. So, next to a concern with permanently consigning a (small) part of the material in circulation to the landscape, there may have existed another concern to take a considerable part of that material out of the landscape again and allow its re-entry into the social system (Needham 2001). This means the 'keeping' in 'keeping-while-destroying' was not just metaphorical, but may sometimes have been practised literally as well (Figure 8.3).

The potential of depositional acts to produce 'truths' and still allow for change

If objects did stay in the landscape, depositional acts are practices that leave no other traces than memory in the minds of the onlookers (cf. Rowlands 1993). With the remnants of the act hidden from view, and even the location where it took place characteristically unmarked (Chapter 7), this makes it the kind of act that may be quite effective to produce criteria of truth for non-literary societies lacking any other ways of 'external symbolic storage' apart from material culture and their environment (Boyer 1990; Renfrew 2001, 95). This is particularly so for objects that themselves already carry a certain social ambiguity, like items coming from afar or 'transgressive' objects do (Harrison 2006). It may not be a coincidence that such objects in the Bronze Age were deposited in parts of the landscape that have a similar ambiguity in social terms. These landscapes are typically unaltered by human hand, and lack clear boundaries themselves (Chapter 7; Fontijn 2012).

Solely relying on the memory of an act to account for what actually was deposited means that the memory and the account may eventually fade and become fuzzy. These are situations where the division between what 'ought to be' and what 'is' may become easily blurred. According to Dumont (1977), the (Cartesian) distinction between 'ought to be' and 'being' may be much less significant to non-modern societies than it is to us (also: Bazelmans 1998, 66). Chapter 7 showed how this for example becomes apparent in the attitude of Bronze Age communities towards landscape when it came to deciding where a depositional practice had to take place. The fact that depositions leave a non-visible, non-concrete result not only makes them eminently suitable for dealing with items that themselves have a certain ambiguity (objects coming from afar, items reifying social inequality, transgressive objects; Fontijn 2002, 278–279). It also makes it a practice that holds a potential for expressing social change, precisely because it is carried out in a setting that seems to be profoundly traditional. What is reified in depositional actions is not so much the significance of certain things – rather it is a particular order of things: spheres of valuables that can and those which cannot be associated. This book barely touched upon historical developments in depositional practices, but it might be worthwhile to briefly discuss one example to elucidate how social and ideological changes may first be expressed in depositional practices.

A pervasive trait of the Middle and Late Bronze Age in the southern Netherlands is that weaponry is strictly kept out of graves (Fontijn 2002, chapter 11). Swords and spears were deposited in watery places, usually in complete state. It has been argued that this means that there was a widespread 'taboo' on weapon deposition in burials (Fontijn 2002, 110–112, 149, 188–189; Roymans & Kortlang 1999, 56). Yet, with the beginning of the Early Iron Age, for the first time a new group of sword graves became manifest in burial ritual: the often astonishingly lavish Hallstatt C chieftains' graves (Van der Vaart-Verschoof 2017). Intriguingly, the first swords to appear in graves are broken and follow local deposition norms, as if the notion of a taboo still prevailed (Fontijn & Fokkens 2007). At the same time, complete versions of bronze swords kept on being deposited in watery locations, like they always were. It seems as if the initial insertion of swords in a manner carefully adapted to local burial norms (in broken and incomplete state) mentally paved the way for the convention-breaking depositions of Hallstatt C chieftains' equipment, including intact weaponry, that followed (Fontijn & Fokkens 2007; Van der Vaart-Verschoof 2017, 83–84). People may well have believed they were doing things as they had always done, a belief that may have been fostered by the fact that concrete evidence of depositions in these cases remains hidden. Overseeing developments over the course of few generations, however, to an archaeological eye it is clear that notions expressed in depositions were gradually changing.

'Sacrificial' vs. 'archival economies'

As Bloch and Parry (1989) make clear, the tendency to give up something acquired in short-term transactions and use it to sustain the long term is a fundamental trait of any human economy. I have argued that what happened in Bronze Age Europe – inserting specific things into specific parts of the landscape – was the Bronze Age version. As the examples in Chapter 4 showed, it was also an important practice for thousands of years in the European Mesolithic and Neolithic. I also mentioned examples from North America and India where similar things happened (Chapter 1). Using a term once coined by Küchler (1997) for a somewhat different kind of process, this has been called a 'sacrificial economy'[2] (Chapter 5; Fontijn 2002, 275; Wengrow 2011).

Yet, if we broaden our scope, it is also clear that not every ancient society systematically placed valuables in the landscape, i.e. had such a sacrificial economy (Figure 8.4). Charting this practice, it becomes clear that it is rare in contemporary Bronze Age Early State organizations where bronze was a crucial valuable, as it was

166 Economies of destruction

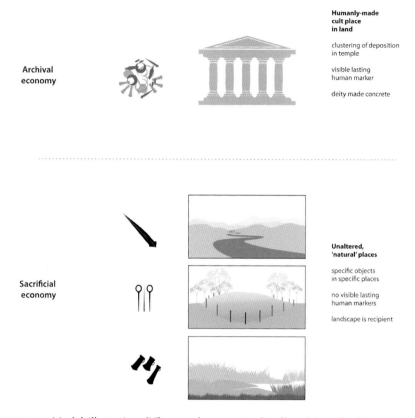

FIGURE 8.4 Model illustrating differences between 'archival' and 'sacrificial' economies, based on a theory discussed in Wengrow 2011 and further points raised in the text of this chapter. Objects in the temple deviate from what was really offered and only serve for comparison of practices.
Source: Drawing by J. Porck, Faculty of Archaeology, University of Leiden.

in Minoan and Mycenaean Greece (Figure 8.1; Hänsel & Hänsel 1997). It is also lacking in large parts of the Bronze Age Middle East and in the Indian Harrapan civilization (Wengrow 2011, figure 11.1). Reinhold (2005) makes an intriguing observation on this. While charting evidence for selective deposition of metalwork, she argues it extends from Europe all the way east until halfway to the Caucasus. However, in the other part of it, metal hoards are lacking: instead there are temples. A system using the institution of temples seems to exclude a practice of selective deposition of metalwork in the landscape. This strongly suggests that the practice that has been central to this book – the systematic giving-up of valuables by placing them in the landscape – was something characteristic of loosely organized, semi-egalitarian, non-literate societies as we have them in most parts of Europe during the Bronze Age.

Why would that be so? An intriguing answer to this question can be found in the work of Wengrow (2010; 2011), who relates this to the different ways in which value was managed. According to him, there are essentially two ways in which this can be done.

1. In what he calls 'archival economies', value is managed and classified 'through constant circulation' (Wengrow 2011, 137). It is based on measurement systems and archival procedures such as sealings and record keeping, which are religiously authenticated by regular, centralized public institutions such temples or palaces (Figure 8.5; Wengrow 2011, 137). Written record-keeping serves as 'external symbolic storage' (cf. Renfrew 2001, 95).
2. In sacrificial economies, upholding ranked spheres of valuables is crucial, and value on such orderings is created, maintained and authenticated by what Whitehouse (2004) calls 'imagistic' performances (cf. Chapter 6). These are naturally aimed at small, local audiences, and the outcome of these typically retains a certain ambiguity as it lacks a visible, lasting material manifestation (in contrast to a temple). In sacrificial economies, it is the objects and the landscape which function as 'external symbolic storage' (cf. Renfrew 2001, 95–99).

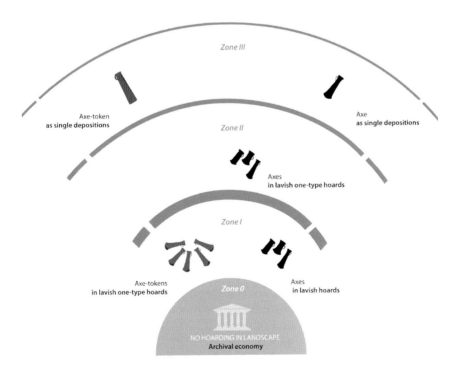

FIGURE 8.5 The three-zone model discussed in Chapter 5, now extended with the hypothetical 'Zone 0' (Wengrow's (2011) 'archival economies') in which the value of metal was managed by circulation and hardly any selective deposition took place.

Source: Drawing by J. Porck, Faculty of Archaeology, University of Leiden.

In sacrificial economies, 'authentication' implies that participants must know the 'right way of doing things' (to judge which objects ought to be deposited together, how to treat them and where to deposit them, see above and Küchler 1997). This involves cultural and social knowledge. But as a performance, the effect of the practice is aimed at those who are present, so this knowledge is primarily local in nature. As argued in Chapter 7, the deposition locations themselves evidence this. Visible, lasting cult buildings for depositions are consistently lacking (cf. Hansen's (2013) 'votive offerings without temples'; Chapter 7). One would have to have an insider's cultural knowledge to recognize them (although there is a system behind it; Chapter 7). A depositional act targets those who are present. There is no concrete, lasting result visible to others. This makes it suitable for keeping knowledge restricted, local, and ambiguous, and harder to bring under centralized control (cf. Rowlands 1993).

A sacrificial economy is well-suited for re-contextualizing ambiguous things from afar. Things from outside are displayed, brought in line with local norms and values, in the same act that removes or even destroys them by consigning them to the most eternal element of a local community's life: their landscape (Chapters 5 and 7). It allows people to connect to a non-local world, but also to shield themselves from it and to retain what is considered important in the community itself (Wengrow 2011, 141). Sherratt (1994) argued that such actions may have been one way in which local groups could retain a sense of independence in an early globalizing world (cf. Wengrow 2011, 141). By systematically placing valuable things in the ground, Bronze Age people sought to reconcile their growing dependence on an outside world with key concerns of local society (Sørensen 1987; Wengrow 2011; cf. Bloch & Parry 1989). They managed, shielded and ordered value according to their world view, by allocating specific things to specific places in the landscape, making sure that what was meaningful was 'kept' *and* contained in that part of the land where it belonged.

One may wonder if sacrificial economies also prevented certain social developments from taking place. In retrospect, its effects are impossible to detect as many more processes influence social evolution. However, as deposition practices target local audiences and have an outcome that is non-visible and non-material, they are not typically the kind of social contexts that lend themselves to centralized control. Systematically giving up valuables also prevents decisive concentration of resources on which enduring influence and therewith power is built. Power may certainly be derived from impressive social performances but these are situational and hard to transmit to successive generations (cf. Borgerhoff Mulder et al. 2009). If it is important to repeatedly stop material from circulating, this may have been important locally, but it potentially makes the building of alliances through exchange on a broader spatial level harder. This is particularly problematic in political economies in which influence and power for an important part derive from the contingencies of alliance-making, as was the case in most of Bronze Age Europe (Earle 2002, 17; Friedman & Rowlands 1977, 228).

Back to Ommerschans – when Bronze Age things return, do values become 'price' again?

This book started with the theory that people's engagement with the new material bronze in many ways heralded the start of a new Europe that is the first to have some familiarity for us. But the evidence of metalwork depositions sits in the way – or does it?

In Chapter 1, I argued that such ideas are dangerously close to a self-serving, euro-centric grand narrative on the birth of rational economies and ultimately of capitalism. It is precisely because of such ideas that the ubiquitous and extremely long-lived tradition of the destruction of that same metalwork in the Bronze Age has posed such an interpretive challenge. This book showed metalwork deposition as practised in the Bronze Age has profoundly unfamiliar characteristics. It indeed does not conform to norms of rational-economics that are familiar to a capitalist system. However, it also cannot be understood solely as a system governed by religious ideas. The evidence we have primarily tells us about how people used objects to conceive of a world beyond daily reality, and how the landscape was essential to this. If we wish to call this religion, it proves hard to see it as an emulation of the familiar religious ideas of civilizations that modern society tends to see as fundamental to 'European civilization,' like those of the Graeco-Roman or Viking ages. I argue that Bronze Age deposition practices are neither economy, nor religion. Rather, they are one of the most ubiquitous and long-lived practices in the deep history of Europe. They are practices in which the outcome of *familiar*, rational economics was brought to bear on and contributed to the cultural identity and morals of local communities which are largely *unfamiliar* to us.

Having started this book from one particular conception of economy, and using evidence that seems at odds with it, a final conclusion could be that what we see in the Bronze Age is what economies really are: contexts of action where self-interest and power steer behaviours that are ultimately linked to and enfolded by over-arching moral and socio-cultural concerns (Dumont 1977). The very fact that in our own time, social debates are about 'the moral limits of markets' (Sandel 2012), shows that this is even true for our own society, just as much as it signals a concern.

I started this book with the find of the magnificent Ommerschans hoard in the late nineteenth century (Chapter 1), and used it to illustrate the problems we – people living in a capitalist society – have in trying to make sense of the ostentatious destruction of such a valuable object. At the end of this book, such an 'odd' act may now fall into place. Locating such an object in a bog may have been a way in which an important cultural valuable achieved an ultimate inalienability and may have been considered as a way of 'keeping'. What to us is an enigmatic association of an unused, transgressive object of top quality, with intensively used things of daily life, like chisels, may now be seen as one way in which a local community reconciled the daily reality of life to that of an overarching order of places and lands imagined that goes far beyond that. The presence of a simple bronze spiral – metal stored for re-melting? – may likewise evoke their access to fundamental material resources (like pools of metal for recycling). I suggested before that locating such items on the sword makes it like a map of the broader world (*Mappa Mundi*) and what matters in it, constituted and made tangible by the objects.

However, for more than 120 years after it was discovered, the Ommerschans hoard remained in a private collection, and for all that time, hardly anything was known of its precise whereabouts. Several generations of archaeologists based theories on there being an object that once must have held great value to Bronze Age people, without ever having been able to see the object for themselves (Butler & Bakker 1961; Butler & Sarfatij 1970/1971; Fontijn 2001). Furthermore, in the region where it was originally found, amateur archaeologists, local historians and the family of the finder kept alive the memory of what was once found but was now gone (Amkreutz & Fontijn 2018). By remaining hidden and invisible all that time, one could say the Ommerschans hoard also in modern times retained its ambiguity and therewith its 'capacity to act' (Graeber 2001, chapter 4), as I suggested buried valuables in the Bronze Age did.

We owe it to the efforts of Luc Amkreutz and his colleagues at the National Museum of Antiquities in Leiden, and the generous financial contributions of several institutions,[3] that the elusive hoard finally returned. Amkreutz was the first for decades to locate the owners of the hoard and finally to see what had been hidden from archaeology for such a long time. Attempts to purchase the hoard for the National Museum of Antiquities initially failed. When the object was brought to public view for the first time, it was at an auction. In a reversal of long- to short-term transactions, scholarly publications on its scientific and cultural value were used to substantiate the minimum price for which it should be sold. When it finally was sold – as the most expensive archaeological object ever purchased in the Netherlands, the price itself stirred some debate – illustrating how long-term value (a 'priceless' cultural assemblage) and short-term concerns (market value) have an uneasy, but inextricable, relation in a modern economy.[4]

Fortunately for the broader public, the hoard finally could be purchased, and it is now on permanent display, as an iconic object of the European Bronze Age in general and of Dutch prehistory in particular, at the National Museum of Antiquities in Leiden. But by being made visible to all, one may also wonder if this showing of a set of objects that Bronze Age people intended to hide from view forever, would actually be in line with *their* notions of 'the right way' to treat valuables ...[5]

The Ommerschans sword as an object ended its history in the Bronze Age in an act that played with the tension between showing and concealing (cf. Lambek 2008, 147). By some whim of fate, with its unearthing thousands of years later, a new cycle of hiding and displaying began to enhancing it with new value in the modern age.

Bronze Age deposition and us

This book discussed how Bronze Age people gave up valuable things and placed them in the landscape. I find it likely that on many occasions they took them out again and re-used the material, but the hundreds of thousands of metal objects that remained in the landscape at least demonstrate that they also intentionally gave up valuable material. It should be realized that this was a practice with an uncertain outcome – to whom or what it was perceived to be given may have been vague and open to human manipulation, as nothing remained of the act besides memory (see above; Chapter 3; cf. Rowlands 1993). The same is true regarding the benefits of such a giving-up – did good things indeed happen because Bronze Age people did this? This was equally ambiguous and could have been explained by the actors in any way they wished. But (anonymously) giving up something for an uncertain outcome, as a moral act, is also something we do in our own economy. Think of donating to charity, or buying organic food to protect the environment (cf. Godelier 1999, 14; Mauss 1993, 17–18, 65). The very fact that multinationals hesitate to give up something of their wealth to help protect the very environment they destroy with their businesses, may even be seen as economically *irrational*. After all, in the long-term, their extra efforts may help sustain the very world in which their business thrives.

Bronze Age depositions demonstrate the complexities any economy has – how receiving, accumulating and giving-up are intertwined.[6] If economy is 'the study of incentives' (Levitt & Dubner 2005, 16), then these 'incentives' are social and moral as well (ibid., 17). That the classic view of rational economies guided by self-interest is too narrow, has been recognized by economists for a long time (e.g. Chang 2014; Hann & Hart 2011). Still, debates on the nature of economy in what are considered to be non-modern or non-Western societies are among the most heated ones in the history of anthropology (Hann & Hart 2011, chapters 4–5). The pervasiveness of a one-sided emphasis on a particular kind of political economy (with rational-economic or even capitalist undertones) in the Bronze Age is also surprising, given the general nuancing and refinement of such views in anthropology in more recent times (e.g. Robotham 2005). All this may reflect that what concerns scholars discussing economy is not always what people themselves were really doing, but also a specific economic ideology (Dumont 1977).

Having argued how a political economy in the Bronze Age is part of a broader concern with culture, identity and morality, an easy solution could be to state that depositional practices are rational as well. Like Hann and Hart (2011, 173), I think this is ultimately unhelpful.[7] What happened in depositions is finally about the quality of action and performance (cf. Lambek 2008). As such, it may indeed be 'irrational' from a political-economic point of view, but it follows strict conventions regarding association and dissociation of things and places. To borrow a useful phrase from Ariely (2010) in a book on behavioural economics, it may be 'irrational' from that point of view, but it is still 'predictable'. The social power of selective deposition emerges precisely *because there is a tension between short-term political economies and the morality involved in giving things up and placing them in the landscape*.

The European Bronze Age does not lend itself to a celebration of the early emergence of a kind of economy modern people feel familiarity with. Neither is it suited to sustain a conceptualization of the deep past as its opposite – a society indulging in irrational, destructive religious acts that upheld social equality and social sharing. The archaeological evidence of the Bronze Age shows prehistoric economies had both familiar and unfamiliar traits – they were preoccupied with power and conflict, but also with forging social bonds and reducing tensions resulting from the participation of small communities in a pan-European metalwork exchange system. They were rational and irrational at the same time, just like modern economies are. With an obvious debt to the seminal work of Graeber (2001), Mauss (1993) and Lambek (2008), I wish to conclude by stating that, if anything, the evidence of Bronze Age depositions shows something very human. To achieve something in society, something else must be given up. Value, in a way, is created by giving up that which is valuable.

Notes

1 See Knight 2018 for arguments that broken material in such hoards does show selection.
2 Independently of one another, both Wengrow (2011) and myself use this term to imply that material circulating in 'economies', was repeatedly 'sacrificed'. Küchler (1997), however, focuses on elaborate ceremonial wood carvings, the Malanggan, which were made in New Ireland for ceremonies and left to decay in the forest afterwards. She sees 'economy' as referring to the Western trade which these statues became part of after their disposal.
3 Such as the 'Vereniging Rembrandt', the 'Mondriaan Stichting, 'Aankoopfonds RMO', and 'vriendenvereniging RMO'.
4 On this uneasy relationship: Hart 2005 and Sandel 2012.
5 Küchler (1997) sees the presence of 'destroyed' wood carvings from New Ireland in modern Western museums as representing a similar uneasiness.
6 Previous studies to make a comparable point are e.g. Innerhofer 1997 and Menke 1978/ 1979. However, these see the giving-up primarily as a 'gift to god', whilst this book argues that this may be problematic and instead sees giving-up as a social and moral act that may have had a broader reach and more ambiguous scope.
7 Cf. Sykes 2009, 163.

Bibliography

Amkreutz, L. and D.R. Fontijn, 2018. Bringing it all back home, *Past. Newsletter of the Prehistoric Society*, Spring, 1–3.
Ariely, D., 2010. *Predictably irrational. The hidden forces that shape our decisions*. New York: HarperCollins.
Ball, Ph., 2004. *Critical mass. How one thing leads to another*. London: Arrow Books.
Bazelmans, J., 1998. Geschenken en waren in premodern Europa: enkele gedachten over de waarde van kostbaarheden uit schatvondsten, *LEIDschrift* 13(3), 59–78.
Bazelmans, J., 1999. *By weapons made worthy. Lords, retainers and their relationship in Beowulf* (Amsterdam Archaeological Studies 5). Amsterdam: Amsterdam University Press.
Becker, K., 2008. Left but not lost, *Archaeology Ireland* 22(1), 12–14.
Becker, K., 2013. Transforming identities: new approaches to Bronze Age deposition in Ireland, *Proceedings of the Prehistoric Society* 79, 225–263.
Bloch, M. and J. Parry, 1989. Introduction: money and the morality of exchange, in: *Money and the morality of exchange*, eds J. Parry and M. Bloch. Cambridge: Cambridge University Press, 1–31.

Borgerhoff Mulder, M., S. Bowles, T. Hertz, A. Bell, J. Beise, G. Clark, I. Fazzio, M. Gurven, K. Hill, P.L. Hooper, W. Irons, H. Kaplan, D. Leonetti, B. Low, F. Marlowe, R. McElreath, S. Naidu, D. Nolin, P. Piraino, R. Quinlan, E. Schniter, R. Sear, M. Shenk, E. Alden Smith, Ch. von Rueden and P. Wiessner, 2009. Intergenerational wealth transmission and the dynamics of inequality in small-scale societies, *Science* 326, 682–688.

Boyer, P., 1990. *Tradition as truth and communication. A cognitive description of traditional discourse* (Cambridge Studies in Social Anthropology). Cambridge: Cambridge University Press.

Bradley, R., 1990. *The passage of arms. An archaeological analysis of prehistoric hoards and votive deposits.* Cambridge: Cambridge University Press.

Bradley, R., 2000. *An archaeology of natural places*, London and New York: Routledge.

Brück, J., 1999. Ritual and rationality: some problems of interpretation in European archaeology, *European journal of Archaeology* 2, 313–344.

Butler, J.J. and J.A. Bakker, 1961. A forgotten Middle Bronze Age hoard with a Sicilian razor from Ommerschans (Overijssel), *Helinium* I, 193–210.

Butler, J.J. and H. Sarfatij, 1970 / 1971. Another bronze ceremonial sword by the Plougrescant-Ommerschans smith, *Berichten van de Rijksdienst voor het Oudheidkundig Bodemonderzoek* 20–21, 301–309.

Chang, H.-J., 2014. *Economics: the user's guide.* New York: Penguin Books.

Dumont, L., 1977. *From Mandeville to Marx. The genesis and triumph of economic ideology.* Chicago: University of Chicago Press.

Earle, T., 2002. *Bronze Age economies: the beginnings of political economies.* Boulder CO: Westview Press.

Earle, T., J. Ling, C. Uhnér, Z. Stos-Gale and L. Melheim, 2015. The political economy and metal trade in Bronze Age Europe: understanding regional variability in terms of comparative advantages and articulations, *European Journal of Archaeology* 18(4), 633–657.

Fontaine, L., 2014. *The moral economy. Poverty, credit and trust in Early Modern Europe.* Cambridge: Cambridge University Press.

Fontijn, D.R., 2001. Rethinking ceremonial dirks of the Plougrescant-Ommerschans type. Some thoughts on the structure of metalwork exchange, in: *Patina. Essays presented to Jay Jordan Butler on the occasion of his 80th birthday*, eds W.H. Metz, B.L. van Beek and H. Steegstra. Groningen and Amsterdam: Privately published by Metz, Van Beek & Steegstra, 263–280.

Fontijn, D.R., 2002. Sacrificial landscapes. Cultural biographies of persons, objects and 'natural' places in the Bronze Age of the southern Netherlands, c. 2300–2600 BC, *Analecta Praehistorica Leidensia* 33/34, 1–392.

Fontijn, D.R., 2008. 'Traders' hoards': reviewing the relationship between trade and permanent deposition: the case of the Dutch Voorhout hoard, in: *Hoards from the Neolithic to the Metal Ages in Europe: technical and codified practices* (British Archaeological Reports International Series 1758), eds C. Hamon and B. Quillec. Oxford: Archaeopress, 5–17.

Fontijn, D.R., 2009. Land at the other end of the sea? Metalwork circulation, geographical knowledge and the significance of British/Irish imports in the Bronze Age of the Low Countries, in: *Bronze Age connections. Cultural contact in prehistoric Europe*, ed. P. Clark. Oxford: Oxbow Books, 129–148.

Fontijn, D.R., 2012. Landscapes without boundaries? Some thoughts on Bronze Age deposition areas in North-West Europe, in: *Hort und Raum – aktuelle Forschungen zu bronzezeitlichen Deponierungen in Mitteleuropa*, eds S. Hansen, D. Neumann and T. Vachta. Berlin: De Gruyter. 49–68.

Fontijn, D.R. and H. Fokkens, 2007. The emergence of Early Iron Age 'chieftains" graves in the Southern Netherlands, in: *The Early Iron Age in North-Western Europe*, eds C. Haselgrove and R. Pope. Oxford: Oxbow books, 354–373.

Fontijn, D.R. and J. Roymans, forthcoming. Branded axes, thrown into a pool? The Hoogeloon hoard and the shape-based bronze economy of the Northwest European Bronze Age, *Oxford Journal of Archaeology*.
Friedman, J. and M. Rowlands, 1977. Notes towards an epigenetic model of the evolution of 'civilisation', in: *The evolution of social systems*, eds J. Friedman and M. Rowlands. London: Duckworth, 201–278.
Godelier, M., 1999. *The enigma of the gift*. Cambridge and Oxford: Polity Press.
Graeber, D., 2001. *Toward an anthropological theory of value: the false coin of our own dreams*. New York: Palgrave.
Graeber, D., 2005. Value: anthropological theory of value, in: *A handbook of economic anthropology*, ed. J.G. Carrier. Northampton MA and Cheltenham: Edward Elgar, 439–454.
Gregory, C.A., 2015 [1982]. *Gifts and commodities*. Chicago: Hau Books.
Hann, Ch. and K. Hart, 2011. *Economic anthropology. History, ethnography, critique*. Malden MA and Cambridge: Polity Press.
Hänsel, A. and B. Hänsel (eds), 1997. *Gaben an die Götter* (Seminar zur Ur- und Frühgeschichte der Freien Universität). Berlin: Museum für Vor- und Frühgeschichte.
Hansen, S., 2013. Bronzezeitliche Deponierungen in Europa. Weihgaben ohne Tempel, in: *Sanktuar und Ritual. Heilige Plätze in archäologischen Befund*, eds I. Gerlach and D. Raue. Rahden: Marie Leidorf Verlag, 371–387.
Harrison, S., 2006. Skull trophies of the Pacific war: transgressive objects and remembrance, *Journal of the Royal Anthropological Institute*, N.S., 12, 817–836.
Hart, K., 2005. Money: one anthropologist's view, in: *A handbook of economic anthropology*, ed. J.G. Carrier. Northampton MA and Cheltenham: Edward Elgar, 160–175.
Hobbes, Th., 1968 [1651]. *Leviathan*. Harmondsworth: Penguin.
Hodder, I., 2012. *Entangled. An archaeology of the relationships between humans and things*. Chichester: Wiley-Blackwell.
Hutchins, E. 2005. Material anchors for conceptual blends, *Journal of Pragmatics* 37, 1555–1577.
Innerhofer, F., 1997. Frühbronzezeitliche Barrenhortfunde – die Schätze aus dem Boden kehren zurück, in: *Gaben an die Götter* (Seminar zur Ur- und Frühgeschichte der Freien Universität), eds A. Hänsel and B. Hänsel. Berlin: Museum für Vor- und Frühgeschichte, 53–59.
Kaul, F., 1998. *Ships on bronzes. A study in Bronze Age religion and iconography* (Studies in Archaeology and History vol. 3). Copenhagen: Publications from the National Museum.
Knight, M., 2018. The intentional destruction and deposition of Bronze Age metalwork in South West England. Unpublished Ph.D. thesis, Exeter University.
Kok, M.S.M., 2008. The homecoming of religious practice. An analysis of offering sites in the wet low-lying parts of the landscape in the Oer-IJ area (2500 BC–AD 450). Unpublished Ph.D. thesis, University of Amsterdam.
Kopytoff, I., 1986. The cultural biography of things: commoditisation as process, in: *The social life of things*, ed. A. Appadurai. Cambridge: Cambridge University Press, 64–91.
Küchler, S., 1997. Sacrificial economy and its objects, *Journal of Material Culture* 2, 39–60.
Kuijpers, M.H.G., 2018. *An archaeology of skill. Metalworking skill and material specialization in Early Bronze Age Central Europe*. London and New York: Routledge.
Lambek, M., 2008. Value and virtue, *Anthropological Theory* 8(2), 133–157.
Lenerz-de Wilde, M., 1995. Prämonetäre Zahlungsmittel in der Kupfer- und Bronzezeit Mitteleuropas, *Fundberichte aus Baden-Württemberg* 20, 229–327.
Levitt, S.D. and S.J. Dubner, 2005. *Freakonomics*. London: Penguin.
Ling, J., Z. Stos-Gale, L. Grandin, A. Billström, E. Hjärthner-Holdar and P.O. Persson, 2014. Moving metals II: provenancing Scandinavian Bronze Age artefacts by lead-isotope and elemental analyses, *Journal of Archaeological Science* 41, 106–132.

Marcigny, C. and A. Verney, 2005. La nécropole d'Agneaux (Manche) et ses dépôts, in: *La Normandie à l'aube de l'histoire, les découvertes archéologiques de l'âge du Bronze 2300–800 av. JC.*, eds C. Marcigny, C. Colonna, E. Ghesquière and G. Verron. Paris: Somogy Éditions d'Art, 120–121.

Marx, K., 1967. *Capital* (3 vols). New York: New World Paperbacks.

Mauss, M., 1993 [1923/1924]. *The gift. The form and reason for exchange in archaic societies*. London: Routledge.

Menke, M., 1978/1979. Studien zu den frühbronzezeitlichen Metalldepots Bayerns, *Jahresbericht des Bayerischen Bodendenkmalpflege* 19/20, 1–305.

Needham, S., 2001. When expediency broaches ritual intention: the flow of metal between systemic and buried domains, *Journal of the Royal Anthropological Institute incorporating Man* 7, 275–298.

Needham, S., 2007. Bronze makes a Bronze Age? Considering the systemics of Bronze Age metal use and the implications of the selective depositions, in: *Beyond Stonehenge: essays on the Bronze Age in honour of Colin Burgess*, eds C. Burgess, P. Topping and F. Lynch. Oxford: Oxbow Books, 278–287.

Nongbi, B., 2013. *Before religion. A history of a modern concept*. New Haven CT: Yale University Press.

Pare, C., 2013. Weighing commodification and money, in: *The Oxford handbook of the European Bronze Age*, eds H. Fokkens and H. Harding. Oxford: Oxford University Press, 508–527.

Platenkamp, J.D.M., 2016. Money alive and money dead, in: *The archaeology of money. Proceedings of the workshop 'Archaeology of Money', University of Tübingen, October 2013* (Leicester Archaeology Monographs), eds C. Haselgrove and S. Krmnicek. Leicester: University of Leicester, 161–181.

Reinhold, S., 2005. Vom Ende Europas? Zu den Depotfunden im Kaukasus, in: *Interpretationsraum Bronzezeit. Bernhard Hänsel von seinen Schülern gewidmet* (Universitätsforschungen zur prähistorischen Archäologie 121), eds B. Horejs, R. Junge, E. Kaiser and B. Teržan. Bonn: Habelt Verlag, 345–373.

Renfrew, C., 2001. Commodification and institution in group-oriented and individualizing societies, in: *The origin of human social institutions* (Proceedings of the British Academy), ed. W.G. Runciman. Oxford: Oxford University Press, 93–117.

Robotham, D., 2005. Political economies, in: *A handbook of economic anthropology*, ed. J.G. Carrier. Cheltenham: Edward Elgar, 41–58.

Rowlands, M.J., 1993. The role of memory in the transmission of culture, *World Archaeology* 25, 141–151.

Roymans, N. and F. Kortlang, 1999. Urnfield symbolism, ancestors, and the land in the Lower Rhine region, in: *Land and ancestors. Cultural dynamics in the Urnfield period and the Middle Ages in the southern Netherlands* (Amsterdam Archaeological Studies 4), eds F. Theuws and N. Roymans. Amsterdam: Amsterdam University Press, 33–61.

Sandel, M.J., 2012. *What money can't buy. The moral limits of markets*. New York: Farrar, Straus and Giroux.

Searle, J.R., 1995. *The construction of social reality*. New York: The Free Press.

Shennan, S., 1993. Commodities, transactions and growth in the Central European Early Bronze Age, *Journal of European Archaeology* 1(2), 59–72.

Sherratt, A.G., 1994. Core, periphery and margin: perspectives on the Bronze Age, in: *Development and decline in the Mediterranean Bronze Age* (Sheffield Archaeological Monographs 8), eds S. Stoddart and C. Mathew. Sheffield: J.R. Collis, 335–346.

Simmel, G., 2011 [1900]. *The philosophy of money*. London: Routledge.

Sørensen, M.L.S., 1987. Material order and cultural classification: the role of bronze objects in the transition from Bronze Age to Iron Age in Scandinavia, in: *The archaeology of contextual meanings* (New Directions in Archaeology), ed. I. Hodder. Cambridge: Cambridge University Press, 90–101.

Sykes, K., 2009. *Arguing with anthropology. An introduction to critical theories of the gift.* London and New York: Routledge.

Thomas, J., 1996. *Time, culture and identity. An interpretive archaeology.* London and New York: Routledge.

Thompson, E.P., 1971. The moral economy of the English crowd in the eighteenth century, *Past and Present* 50, 76–136.

Van der Vaart-Verschoof, S., 2017. *Fragmenting the chieftain. A practice-based study of Early Iron Age Hallstatt C elite burials in the Low Countries* (PALMA 15). Leiden: Sidestone Press.

Weiner, A.B., 1992. *Inalienable possessions: the paradox of keeping-while-giving,* Berkeley CA, Los Angeles CA and Oxford: University of California Press.

Wengrow, D., 2010. *What makes civilization? The ancient Near East and the future of the West.* Oxford: Oxford University Press.

Wengrow, D., 2011. 'Archival' and 'sacrificial' economies in Bronze Age Eurasia: an interactionist approach to the hoarding of metal, in: *Interweaving worlds. Systemic interactions in Eurasia, 7th to the 1st millennia BC,* eds T.C. Wilkinson, S. Sherratt and J. Bennet. Oxford: Oxbow Books, 135–144.

Whitehouse, H., 2004. Toward a comparative anthropology of religion, in: *Ritual and memory. Towards a comparative anthropology of religion,* eds H. Whitehouse and J. Laidlaw. Walnut Creek CA and Oxford: Altamira Press, 187–204.

Wiseman, R., 2017. Random accumulation and breaking: the formation of Bronze Age scrap hoards in England and Wales, *Journal of Archaeological Science* 90, 39–49.

Yule, P., 1985. *Metalwork of the Bronze Age in India* (Prähistorische Bronzefunde XX-8). Munich: C.H. Beck.

INDEX

Page references in *italics* refer to figures. Page references in **bold** refer to tables.

Abelheira *96*, 98
abstract 47, 49, 52, 146; concept of supernatural 59, 122, 127, 129n1; concept of value 155, 158, 161; form 57; *see also* system
abstraction 69, 90
action: act of sacrifice *see* sacrifice; capacity to act 105, 161, 170; destructive 120; individual act 25, 34, 39, 117; local 155; moral act 11, 59, 171, 172n6; political 59; ritual 4–5, 25, 105, 121; (un-) economic act 11, 13, 87, 160, 163
aDNA 7, 77–8
adze 65–9, 71–2; amphibolite 65; stone 64, 66–8, 72; LBK 66, 69
aes formatum 89, 91, 93, 95, *97*, 98, 103–4; *see also* convertible
agency 28, 115, 156; individual *see* individual
aggrandized/aggrandizement/exaggerated 1, 6, 14, 27, 54–7, 60, 65, 68–9, 72–6, 80, 123–5, 155; axe *see* axe; sword *see* sword
Agneaux 99, *100*, 101–2, 105, *154*, 157
alienable 51–2, 87, 104–5; alienable-inalienable dichotomy 47–9, 52–4, *53*, 58–60, 105, 118, 159; alienation 13–4, 16, 48, 51, 157
alienation *see* alienable
alignment *see* position
alliance 11, 168
amber 75, 156; hoard *see* hoard

ambiguity: of concept 46, 167; of place 140; of things 160, 164, 170; of value management 157; social 164
Amesbury Archer 78
ancestor 9, **13**, 59, 115, 121–2, 128, 147, 160; ancestral realm *see* realm; ancestral societies 122
Angelslo-Emmerhout *137*, *140*, 142
Appadurai, A. 51, 87–8
appearance: differentiation in 53, 72, 98–9; identical 105; foreign *see* foreign; 'right' *see* 'right'; standardized *see* standardized; similarity in 53, 58, 88, 90–1, 98 *see also* mimic; unique 38–9
archaeological record 3, 22–4, 27, 39, 91, 127
archival economy *see* economy
Aschering 86–7, *92*
Assmann, J. 128, 145, 147
association 27, 34–5; between humans and things 50; between things 28, 35, *38*, 38, 45, 48, 74, 157–8, 170; between things and gods 116; between things and places 23, 39, 137, 158, 171; *see also* dissociation; double exclusive logic of 29, 31–3; selective 28
average: behaviour *see* behaviour; depositional practices *see* deposition
axe 12, 23, 28, 35–8, *38*, 47, 50–1, 54, 65, 88–101, *94*, *97*, *102*, 104, 106n3, 107n5, 107n9, 114–9, 124–6, 136, 157, 164;

aggrandized 55, 57, 69, 73–5, 124; Amelsbüren 100–2, *100*; Amorican 31, 100–3, *100*, 157; axe-adze 72; axe blade 86, 92–8, 103; bronze 2–3, 8, 23, 36, 54–7, *79*; battle 77; copper 6, *69*, 71–5, 79, *79*; cultic *123*, 125–8; flanged 44, 107n6, 139–40; flat 35, 74; flint 74–6; Geistingen 31, 99–100, *100*, 102, 158, 163; hoard *see* hoard; jade(ite) 7, 68–70, *69*, 74–5; jade axe head 68–70, 73–5, 80n1; miniature 89, 100–1; nick-flanged 36; Normand 95; polished 141; Portland *100*, 101; Salez 45, 91; shafthole 6, 71–2; Sompting 101; stone 36, 66–8, 73, 77; token 6, 98–104, *99*, *100*, *102*; Wesseling 99, 158, 163

barrow 35–6, 77, 139, *140*, 142, 144, 149; landscape 101, 105, 143
bead 70–1, 75
behaviour: average 22, 24–7, 29, 33, 39, 107n6; depositional 6, 25, 35, 49, 136, 146; destructive 3, 6, 9; economic *see* economy; ritual *see* ritual
Bell Beaker culture (BB) 78–9, *79*, 122
biography: cultural 26
Birchington 96, *96*, 97
Bloch, M. 130n9, 146–7; and J. Parry 51, 60, *159*, 165
Bloody Pool *114*, 119
Bluff *see* locations
body adornment *see* ornament
bog *see* locations; mixed bog deposits *see* deposition; *see also* trackway
boundary 27, 139, 143
Boutanger Moor *140*, 140–5, 149
Breitkeile 66, 68, 75
Bronzization *see* globalization
bulk 86–7; metal 87; trade *see* trade
burial mound *see* barrow
Bygholm *69*, 74

Cap Hornu *92*, 93, 106, 137, 148
capitalism 9–10, 169
Cǎrbuna *69*, 72
Çatal Höyük 130n9
cenotaph 71
Childe, V.G. 9
chisel 1, 44, 86, 169
circulation *see* exchange
Cobidalto *96*, 98
Čoka *69*, 71
collectivity **13**, 26
commodity 8, 44, 51–6, 86–8, 103–6, 117–8, 120, 155; *see also* alienable;

see also currency; exchange *see* exchange; *see also* Ösenringe
competition 8–13, **13**
concealment *see* hiding
convention 49, 60, 88, 104, 126, 147; as consensus in archaeological discipline 103, 106n1, 112, 129; convention-breaking 22, 35–6, 39, 122, 165; depositional 1, 6, 11, 15, 22, 27, 34–6, 51, 65–6, 72, 79, 91, 143–4, 157–8, 160, 165, 171; *see also* 'right'; transcultural 68, 73, 79
convertible 52, 80, 86, 88–93, 95, 98–9, 103–5, 118, 148, 154, 157; ornament 89; token 89, 95, 118; tool 89, 90–91
copper 3, 7–8, *8*, 64, *69*, 70–6, 80n2; alloy 2, 8, 36, 89–90; axe *see* axe; dagger *see* dagger; Europe *see* Europe; hoard *see* hoard; potlatch *see* potlatch; ring *see* ring
copying 27
Corded Ware Culture (CWC) 77–8; hoards *see* hoard
cosmology 54, 128; cosmological acquisition 37; cosmological ideas/notions/narratives 48, 54, 112, 127, 130n8, 154; cosmological objects 56, 125, 127–8
cultural: biography 26; memory *see* memory; trans- *see* transculture; value *see* value
currency 44–6, 54, 60, 86–7, 117; *see also* monetary system; *see also* money; *see also* ring, ring-money

dagger 35, *38*; copper 71, 79, *79*; gold 48, 69; flint 107n7
deposition: convention-breaking deposition *see* convention; depositional behaviour *see* behaviour; depositional context 24, 32, 39, 72, 74; depositional conventions *see* convention; depositional histories 26, 144; depositional location 31, 136, 142–3, 149; depositional pattern 25–31, 39, 98, 136; depositional practice 33–9, 40n3; early Neolithic 31, 64–8, 116, 144–6; *Mappa Mundi* depositions *see Mappa Mundi*; (multiple) deposition zone *see* zone; mixed bog deposits 74; permanent 9, 87, 106, 163; (self-organized) system of 34, 64, 75; selective 3, 6, 12, 14, 16–7, 22–43, 63–85, *94*, *97*, 100–2, *102*, 112–4, 117, 136, 154–9, 166, *167*, 171; temporary 87, 97, 106, 163–4
destruction: act of *see* action
Dieskau II 92, *92*
dirk *see* sword

Index

disc 71, 127; sky *see* Nebra; solar 116, 125, 128
dissociation: of things 34, 157; of things and places 22, 34, 157–8, 171
divine twins *see* gods
do ut des 113
double exclusive logic of association *see* association
Drouwen *23*, 36–7
dry *see* locations
Durankulak *69*, 71
Durkheim, E. 25, 48
dwelling perspective 135, 143, 144–6

Earle, T. 8, 10
Early State 165
(East-)Rudham *114*, 119
economy: archival 111, 134, 165–7, *167*, 176; Bronze Age economies 7–10, 86; circular 8; destructive 1–21; economic action *see* action; economic behaviour 3–6, 17n6, 171; economic hoard *see* hoard; economic rationality *see* rational economy; economic same *see* same; economicity 9, 45, 49, 87; market 5–6, 13; moral 13, **13**, 153, 159–61, *159*, 173; political 8, 10–3, **13**, 59, 153, 159, *159*, 161, 171; rational 1, 5, 9, 87, 112, 129, 153, 169, 171; sacrificial 104–6, 109, 111, 132, 165–8, 175–6
effect: cognitive/emotional/mental 105, 128, 157–8; small-world 22, 36–7, 93, 96; social 52, 161
egalitarianism 26
Egtved *113*, 125, 127; woman 125
elite 8, 11, 139; burial *see* grave; Hallstatt *see* Hallstatt; warrior 11
embodied connectivity 78
enchainment 24
Europe; concept of/'first familiar' 1, 7, 9, 153; Copper *69*, 70–2; European civilization 129, 169; Jade 68–70, *69*, 72
exchange: ceremonial 70; convertible *see* convertible; exchangeable *see* alienable; gift 15, 59, 122; item 23, 27, 45, 54, *57*, 88, 158; as network *see* network; long-term (spheres of) *see* long-term; (circulation) of things/commodity 10, 23, 26, 44, 53, 57, 65–70, 72–4, 87, 94, 103–4, 106n1, 118, 157; short-term (spheres of) *see* short-term; sphere of 14, 51, 58–9, 76, 86, 103–5, 154; system (of) 72–3, 92, 172; token *see* token; as transaction 48, 57, 92, 104–6, 120–1, 129, 161, 168; value *see* value

familiar 1, 45, 87, 112–34, 146–7, 153; Europe *see* Europe; familiar-unfamiliar dichotomy 16, 135, 149, 169, 171–2
Ferguson, N. 9
foreign: local-foreign contrast *see* origin; material 36, 65, 68, 71, 74, 148; object/item/thing 36, 39, 75, 80, 118, 148
Foucault, M. 148
fragmentation 31; fragmented (metal)/fragments (of things) 22, 26, 28, 51, 54, 90, 101–3, 107n6, 117–9, *120*, 163; *see also* hoard, scrap
Funnel Beaker culture (TRB) 64, 73–8, 80, 155

Gatteville *95*, 97
Geistingen 31, 99, 100, *100*, 102, 158, 164
Gela *113*, 117
gender 7, 77; female 125, 127, 129; male 7, 9, 65, 71, 126
gift: exchange *see* exchange; to gods *see* gods; to supernatural entities *see* supernatural
Gingleta-Ganfei *96*, 98, 105
globalization 7, 34; early globalizing world 168
gods 34, 59–60, 116; anthropomorphic 115; attributes of 114, 117, 124–5, 127, 130n8; depictions of 126; as divine twins/twin gods 4, 7, 130n8; gifts to/sacrificed to 4, 24–5, 59, 87, 112–4, 117, 129; Germanic/Viking Age 114–6; God (Christianity) 53, 114, 130n4, 154, 172n6; Graeco-Roman (pantheon) 114–5, 117; Indo-European (pantheon) 115–6, 130n8
gold 2, 6, 28, 31, 38, 45, 48, 63–4, 70–3, 78–9, 124–5, 127; dagger *see* dagger; golden ring *see* ring; hat 124, 127; *lunula see* lunula
Graeber, D. 3, 17n6, 44, 46–7, 51, 55–8, 60n1, 63, 153, 161–2, 164, 172
grave 3, 6, 11, 24–8, 31–3, 37–9, *38*, 44, 54, 65–7, 70–80, *79*, 89–90, 103, 125, 128, 137, 147, 157, 164–5; chieftain/Hallstatt 28, 50, 53, 103, 165; cremation 101; megalith(ic) (tombs) 73, 80n1, 101; elite (burial) 24, 31; ritual *see* ritual; urnfield (burial/cemetery) 12, 25; warrior 36
Grembergen *45*, 54, *55*, 57, 124
Grevensvaenge *113*, *123*, 126, 128
Gröbers-Bennewitz 2, *2*, 92, *92*
Guesman *100*, 101

Haag-an-der-Amper *92*, 93
Haelense Beek *137*, 140

Halberd 28, 31, 35, 38, *38*, 63, 79, *79*, 92, 157
Hallstatt: graves *see* grave; lake 142; objects 24, 165
Hänsel, B. 34, 116–7
Hansen, S. 48, 57, 71–2, 147–8, 168
helmet 125, 128; horned *123*, 125, 126–8
heterotopia *see* other places
hiding 157–8, 161, 164, 170
hoard: amber 75; (bronze) axe 86, 91–103, *94*, *97*, *99*, *100*, *102*; connector 35; copper/Copper Age 71–4; CWC 77–8; flint axe 74; hoarding 105, 144, 161–2; locations *see* locations; *Mappa Mundi see Mappa Mundi*; merchant's *see* trade hoard; metalwork 4, 24, 117, 142, *156*; one-type 91, *97*, 98, 107n7; *Ösenringe*/ring 44–5, 52, 58, 86, 90–3; palstave 86, 94–8, *95*, *96*, 139, 148; ritual/religious 16, 46; scrap 26, 28, 117–9, 163, 172n1; settlement 6, 93–4; stone adze/axe 65–8, 72, 141; trade/economic 16, 46, 86–8, 103–5, 119, 163
Hoogeloon *96*, 96–7, 106, 137, 154, 160; Hoogeloon-Kleine Beerze 139, 148
Hvilshøj 75

identity 12, 51–3, 120–2, 147, 159, 169, 171; personal *see* personhood; relational 119, 129n2
inalienable 12, 15–6, *15*, 49–50, 104, 118, 122, 169; alienable-inalienable dichotomy *see* alienable
individual: act *see* action; itinerary; as object/deposition 24–6, 95, 103; *see also* parity; as person 5, 9, 11–4, **13**, 16, 25, 49–50, 71, 77–8, 119, 121–2, 128, 129n2, 145, 158, 161; power *see* power
Indo-European *see* (proto-)Indo-European
Ingold, T. 135, 143–4, 146
ingot 91, 99, 106n2, 117; clasp-ingot *see Rippenbarren*; ring ingot *see Ösenringe*
inflation 11
innovation 9
Inowrocław *45*, 48
insignia 8, 44, 51, 54–5, 71, 125
institutional: fact 47; reality 51, 146–7, 149
iron: sword *see* sword
irrational *see* rational
irreversibility 119, 157

jade 7, 68–74, 80n1; arm ring *see* ring; axe *see* axe; Europe *see* Europe; hoard *see* hoard

keeping-while-destroying 156, 158, 164
keeping-while-giving 117–8, 158

Kopytoff, I. 26, 51, 58, 104, 160
Kristiansen, K. 10; and Larsson 54
Kwakiutl *see* potlatch

La-Chapelle-du-Bois-des-Faulx *96*, 97
Lambek, M. 16, 58, 120, 153, 172
landscape: barrow *see* barrow; characteristics 143; local 29, 106, 138–9, 143, 145–6, 148, 160; movement through 143 *see also* route
Langdon Bay 103
Langton Matravers *100*, 101, 104
Lenerz-de Wilde, M. 89, 90–1, 94, 107n5
Lengyel Culture 71
life: as daily life 29, 65, 72–3, 75, 118, 147–8, 158, 168–9; larger than life 124, 126 *see also* aggrandized; of objects 3, 16, 23–4, 26, 28, 59, 70, 72, 74, 80, 88, 105, 115, *120*, 129; of people 25–6, 30, 50, 113, 121, 127, 145, 159, 162
Lille Ajstrup 75
Linear Pottery or *Bandkeramik* culture (LBK) 64–72, 76
local 36; action 155; landscape *see* landscape; local-foreign contrast 22, 36–9, 73–6; norms 165, 168; object/item/thing 37, 39, 73, 75, 122; perception/thought/ideas 26, 34–5, 80
locations: bog 1–3, 16, 29–34, 66, 74–6, 87, 93, 97, 100, 105, 127, *140*, 141–6, 149, 157, 160, 169; bluff 93–4, 105; depositional location *see* deposition; dry 135, 137, *140*, 140–2, 164; natural 137, 148; river *see* river; semi-wet 12; stream (valley) 3, 25, 28, 137–40, 160; swamp 101–2, 105, 136, 138–40; uncultivated 29, 73; wet 6, 67–8, 70, 77, 93–4, 98, 118–9, 137–8, 140–1, 143; wetlands 35, 66–7
logic: double exclusive logic of association *see* association; long-term *see* long-term; relational 22, 34, 39; short-term *see* short-term
long-term (exchange/spheres/transactions) *15*, 26, 59, 88, 117, 144–9; long-term – short-term dichotomy 12–6, **13**, 46, 49, 55, 59, 105–6, 153–4, 159–62, *162*, 165, 170–1
Lundby 66
lunula 6, 31, 33–4, 38, 63, 78, *79*, 157
lur 127–8

Mappa Mundi 37, 118, 122, 148, 170
Marchésieux 101–2, 104–5, *154*
martiality *see* warriorhood

Marx, K. 105, 162; Marxism 10
material: foreign *see* foreign; materiality 27, 48, 69, 123–4, 161; recyclable *see* recycling; strategy *see* strategy; token *see* token
Maure-de-Bretagne 3, 100, *100*, 104
Mauss M., 59, 121–2, 129n2
memory 105, 128, 135, 145–6, 158, 164, 170–1; collective 145; cultural 145–7; episodic 145, 149; semantic 145; social 145
Menez-Ru *100*, 101
metal: fragment metal *see* fragmentation; metallization *see* metallization; metalwork hoard *see* hoard; Ösenring metal *see* Ösenringe; scrap 1, 35, 103–4 *see also* scrap hoard; trade *see* trade
metallization 63, 71, 72; metallized 63, 75, 80, 156
mimic 27, 53–6, 99, 102, 123–4; *see also* appearance; *see also* object citation
Moigrad *69*, 72–3
Mollerup *69*, 75
money 45, 51–3, 105, 117, 162; early *see* primitive; primitive 45, 86; ring-money *see* ring
Monte Viso 68, *69*
Mooschbruckschrofen *137*, 148
moral 1, 12–3, 15, 26, 49, 59, 104–6, 113, 122, 160, 169; act *see* action; moral economy *see* economy; morality 12–4, **13**, 171
München-Luitpoldpark *45*, *47*

natural *see* locations, uncultivated
Nebra 44–56, *45*, *46*, *113*, 125, 128
network: affiliation 35, 38, *38*; exchange/ trade/circulation 7–9, 11, 35–7, 70, 78, 122, 147, 163; network science 35, 37; networked strategies 11; relational 146

Obereching *92*, 93
object citation 27, 48, 76
Olympia *114*, 119
Ommerschans 1–4, *2*, *5*, *23*, 34, 37, *45*, *113*, *137*, 148, *154*, 157, 169–70; sword/ dirk *see* sword
order: specific ordering *see* 'right'
ornament: *see also* bead; body ornament (ation)/adornment 57, 70–1, 75, 78, 89, 121–2; convertible *see* convertible; *see also* hat; *see also* lunula; as object 6, 12, 28, 54, 57, *57*, 72–5, 78, 88, 92, 136; *see also* Ösenringe; *see also* ring
Ösenringe/looped neck ring 23, 27, 45, *47*, 48, 52–7, *57*, 58, 87, 89–94, *90*, *94*, 107n5–6, 155; *Ösenring* metal 90, 106n3; hoard *see* hoard; *see also Rippenbarren*
Oss 24
Ostheim *69*, 70
other; (economic) same-(cultural) other dichotomy *see* same; other place *see* place; other-worldly 27, 56, 60, 68–70, 73, 76, 120, 123–7, 154
'ought-to-be'-'is' dichotomy 146, 164
Oxborough *23*, 34–5

palstave 86, 94–5, *95*, *96*, 96–8, *97*, 139, 148, 160; Acton Park 95–6
Pantheon *see* gods
Pare, Ch. 89
parity 78
pars pro toto 106, 119, 160
performance 49, 58, 104–5, 127–9, 157–8, 161, 167–8, 171
person-thing dichotomy *see* thing
persona see personhood
personhood 76, 78, 80, 120–2, 128, 129n2; *persona* 78, 121; personal identity 75, 121–2, 138; person-thing dichotomy *see* thing; restricted 78
Pfedelbach *92*, 93–4
Pile *23*, 35, 93, 122, *137*, 148
pit alignment *see* position
place: cult 31, 117, 135–6, 143, 149; particular *see* particular; right *see* right; unaltered 137; category 136–2; image 146; other places/heterotopia 147–8
position: circle 3, 12, 28, 70, 99, 101, 104, 157; pit alignment 102, 104–5; triangle 101, 104; vertical 3, 70, 157
post-Enlightenment (way of) thinking/ philosophy 5, 9, 129, 153
potlatch 7, 53, 57
power 1, 8, 15, 26, 120, 169, 171–2; acquisitive 51–2, 88; creation of 10–1, 168; individual 11, 13, **13**, 159–60; powerful object 51, 128; supernatural *see* supernatural
practice: depositional *see* deposition; social 29, 63, 72, 80
prestige goods 10–11
profane: profane-ritual dichotomy *see* ritual
proper way of acting *see* right way of acting
(proto-)Indo-European: culture 114; gods/ pantheon *see* gods; language 77, 116; legacy 7; myths 130

Rabenwand 137, 142, *142*
Ragelsdorf *92*, 93, 107n6
rational: economic rationality/rational economy *see* economy; irrational 1, 17n6;

rational-irrational dichotomy 6, 9, 16, 171–2
razor 1, 36, *38*; Pantalica 37
reality: categorical 154; daily 169; imagined 135, 146; institutional *see* institutional
realm: ancestral 122, 147; human 16, 74, 122, 124, 129; supernatural 121–2
recasting *see* recycling
recycling 3, 8, 23, 64, 106, 118, 163–4, 170
regional: *see also* exchange; *see also* local; *see also* network; object 35–6, 73, 75, 148; scale/perspective **13**, 36–7; studies 3, 137
relational 24, 26, 35; identities *see* identity; landscape 135, 143–4, 147, 149; logic *see* logic; network *see* network
religion 34, 45, 49, 54, 112, 121, 123, 126–7, 129, 130n9, 154–5, 169; imagistic (mode of) religiosity 127–8, 158, 161, 167; religiosity 9, 16, 46, 49, 112, 127–9; religious hoard *see* hoard; religious idea 153, 169; religious knowledge 127; religious offerings 154 *see also* sacrifice
Renfrew, C. 47
rib *see* Rippenbarren
Riedl 92, 107n6
'right': appearance 27, 39, 52, 54, 88, 91; ending 67, 70, 78; location/place 28, 30–1, 136, 145, 149; ordering 28, 105; receptacle/recipient 75; selection 28; treatment 12, 16, 28, 31–2, *33*, 49–52, 70, 124, 158, 168, 170; way of acting/doing things 12, **13**, 23, 25–6, 29, 36, 39, 50–1, 66, 145, 157, 168, 170
Rijsbergen-Bakkebrug 139
ring 35, 117; (jade) arm- 68; copper 70; golden (hair-/ear-) 36, 78, 79; ring-money 90; (looped) neck-rings *see* Ösenringe
Rippenbarren *89*, *90*, 90, 91–3, 104, 106, 107n5, 148; *see also* Ösenringe
ritual 7, 9, 11, 16, 35, 70, 73, 117, 136; grave/burial 78, 165; meaning/significance 10, 46, 54, 116; profane-ritual dichotomy (distinction, boundary) 4–5, 9, 16, 17n9, 27, 87, 93–4, 163; ritual action *see* action; ritual consumption 11; ritualization 104–6, 164
river 3, 12, 25, 29–31, 40n3, 59, 63, 68, 70, 77, 93, 95, 98, 101, 105, 115, 118–9, 140, 143, 157, 159, 164; Bug 73; Demer 139; Main 68; Meuse 6, 65, 99, *100*, 102–3, 136, 138–9, *138*, 158; Rhine 6, 99, *100*, 102–3, 158; Roer (Ruhr) 136, *138*; Scheldt 54, *55*, 57, 139; Somme 93; Traun 142, *142*

road 142
rock art 125, *126*
Roermond 136, *137*, *138*
Rørby 24, 39, *113*, 125
Rössen culture 66
route 98, 142–3, 149, 150n4; *see also* trackway

sacra 52, 57, 69, 76, 124; *see also* inalienable; *see also* thing, sacred
sacrifice 59, 74, 87, 114–5, 120, 172n2; least-sacrifice(-maximum-gain) 5, 13; to gods 24; sacrificial economy *see* economy
sacrificial economy *see* economy
Saint-Thois *96*, 97
Salcombe 103
salt 8
same: (economic) same-(cultural) other dichotomy 10–3; sameness 56–8
San Sosti *113*, 115
Schkopau 2, 3, 12, *23*, 28, *92*, 93
scimitar *see* sword
Searle, J.R. 47, 51, 146–7
selection: selective association *see* association; selective deposition *see* deposition
semi-wet *see* locations
settlement 3, 6, 24–7, 29, 31, 35, 39, 65–7, 70–4, 101, 137, *141*, 142, 143, 147, 149; hoard *see* hoard
short-term (economy/exchange/spheres/transactions) *14*, 58, 87–9; long-term – short-term dichotomy *see* long-term
silver 2, 64, 70, 101, 125
Simris *113*, *126*, 126
singularization 15, 29, 51, 153, 164; singular thing *see* thing
Skeldal 93
space 149, 150n4; ideological 16; relational 143; sacred 136
sphere: of exchange 14, 58–9, 76, 86, 103–5, 154; long-term *see* long-term; short-term *see* short-term; of value 105–6, 155–6, 158, 165, 167
Staffordshire *23*, 24, 26, *113*
standardized 51; appearance 101; form 89; standardization 91, 95, 107n5; shape 95; size 54, 57; weight 54, 57, 89, 90
status: change in, transformation of 88, 119–20; *see also* insignia; personal *see* personhood; religious, sacred 44, 53; (high) social 8, 44–5, 55, *57*, 65, 128, 147
Stein-Berg aan de Maas 65–8
Stoboru 2, 3, 28, 157
storage 3; external symbolic 164, 167; temporary 94, 105–6, 163

Index **183**

strategy: material (culture) 27, 124
stream valley *see* locations
supernatural 116, 121–2, 124–5, 127, 129, 148, 159; as abstract *see* abstract; beings **13**, 114, 120, 123, 160; gifts to supernatural entities 59, 112, 118, 120, 159; impersonating 125, 127; powers/forces 112–5, 119, 129n1; recipients 118, 120; relations with 119; things 112; realm *see* realm
supra-human object *see* transgressive
supra-regional: comparison 103; *see also* exchange; *see also* network; *see also* foreign; *see also* transculture; scale/perspective **13**, 15, 36–7, 63, 107n4; style 12, 78
swamp *see* locations
sword 3, 6, 24, 28–30, 44, 48–50, 56–7, 63, 118, 136–8, 157, 161, 164–5, 170; aggrandized 69, 124 *see also* Ommerschans sword/dirk; curved/scimitar 125; iron 136; Ommerschans (-Plougrescant)/dirk 1–6, *4*, *5*, 12–6, 27–8, 34, 37, 53, 56, *56*, 119, 123, 155–7, 171; Sögel 36
system: abstract system of thought 54; (abstract) system of measurement/metrological 54, 88–9, 91, 155, 167; (abstract) system of weight 54, 88–9, 106n4 *see also* standardized; belief 121; of exchange *see* exchange; imaginary/imagined 52, 146–7; of meaning 52, 54–5, 60; monetary 106n1 *see also* money; of quantification **13**, 54; (self-organised) system of deposition/systematic deposition *see* deposition; shape-based 91 *see also aes formatum*; of value (conversion) 63–4, 73, 103

temple 106, 115, 136, 141, 148, *166*, 166–8, *167*; of Bargeroosterveld *140*, 141–2
them: us-them dichotomy *see* same
thing: alienable *see* alienable; common 44, 52, 58, 60; exchange of *see* exchange; inalienable *see* inalienable; linked to persons 48–52; person-thing dichotomy 48; personified 49, 53; sacred 52, 155; singular 51
tin 3, 8, *8*, 64, 98, 101; alloy/tin-bronze *see* copper, alloy
token: material 48; token axe *see* axe; token convertibles *see* convertibles
tools 1, 3, 5, 8–9, 24, 27, 35, 37, 54, 65–6, 69, 71, 73, 88–9, 104, 115
trackway *140*, 141–2

trade 4, 8–9, 13, 16, 35, 45, 86, 88, 103–4, 106n1, 159–61, 172n1; bulk 87; hoard *see* hoard; metal; network *see* network; stock 27, 52, 86–7, 93–4, 97, 105–6, 127, 160
transaction 13, **13**, *14*, 48, 52, 88, 91–2, 103–4, 106, 114, 118, 158, 160, *162*; long-term *see* long-term; short-term *see* short-term; social 92, 99, 104, 106
transculture: transcultural 33, 63, 68, 70, 160; transcultural convention *see* convention; transcultural object 38, 66, 68
transformation: genetic 7; of items/things 28, 118, 124; physical 12, 28, 31, 119, 121; of value 27, 155
transgressive: culture- 63, 80; object 112, 123–5, 127–9, 148, 161, 164; time- 63, 76, 103
TRB *see* Funnel Beaker culture
treatment: special *see* 'right'
Trundholm 2, 3, *113*, 125, 127

uncultivated *see* locations
Únětice culture/group/import 11, 35, 92
unfamiliar *see* familiar
us: us-them dichotomy *see* same

Vâlcele 69, *69*
valuable: *see also* convertible; definition of *see* value, definition of; *see also sacra*; stone valuable 64; non-metal valuable 64; metal valuable 64, 72–3; as ranked 51; and value 47–8
value: classes 58, 60, 104, 156; cultural 10, 13, **13**, 16, 26, 44, 54–6, 60, 88, 104–5, 138, 153, 155, 159, 170; definition of 55–8; exchange 45–6, 88; as practice 55–8; as price **13**, 16, 44, 60, 153, 155, 161; sphere of *see* sphere; social 26, 48; socio-religious 44, 46
Vandkilde, H. 7, 33, 35, 66, 91, 96, 98, 107n7
Varna *69*, 71–2; II 71
Veldhoven *23*, 25
Vendeuil *69*, 70
Viksø *113*, *123*, 124
visual: visual properties/traits 28, 125; visual referencing 47, 51, 69, 72; visuality 48, 124, 161; visualization 35, 38, 127, 158
Voorhout 86–7, *96*, 96–8, *137*, 148, 160
votive (offerings) *see* gifts to gods

Wageningen *23*, 35
warriorhood/martiality 7, 14, 29, 48, 50, 139; elite *see* elite; grave *see* grave
Weiner, A.B. 52, 158

Wessex culture 11
wet *see* locations
wetlands *see* locations
Wolliner 66
world view *see* cosmology
Worsaae, J.J.A. 4, 6, 11

zone: deposition 139–40, *142*, 143, 145–8, 150; metalliferous *8*; multiple deposition 144, 147; non-metalliferous *8*; three-zone model 91–4, *92*, *94*, 95–6, *97*, 98, *102*, 103, *168*; transition 141–2